D1509192

Conversations with Green Gurus

Conversations with Green Gurus

The Collective Wisdom of Environmental Movers and Shakers

Laura Mazur and Louella Miles

A John Wiley & Sons, Ltd., Publication

To Maz, Mike, Ollie, Louis and Georgia – in the hope of a sustainable future

Contents

Foreword

This book has come along at exactly the right time. As economic problems dominate the headlines, it might be easy to forget the importance of
sustainability to the future success of business and the planet. As the
stories in this book show, far from being a financial burden on businesses,
building a green economy is good for the bottom line.

At Business in the Community we work with businesses across the UK,
helping them to develop and showcase their corporate responsibility
approaches. Our current environment campaign, the Prince's May Day
Network (www.maydaynetwork.com) was founded by perhaps the leading
'green guru', HRH The Prince of Wales. It is helping over 1350 businesses
and organisations of all sectors and sizes to embrace the benefits and tackle
the challenges of the necessary move to a low-carbon economy.

Through this campaign we are able to showcase examples of best practice
to reduce greenhouse gas emissions, highlighting the need for collaborative
action and the clear business benefits to a strategic approach. Indeed, one
of the gurus featured in this book, Tony Juniper, is a member of the Advisory
Group that is helping to shape the direction of the Network.

The individuals in this book are great examples of leaders who, early on,
were determined to make the case for taking important steps to improve the
way we use the valuable resources around us, and the very way that we do
business. There are many other examples of the ways in which strong leadership in this area can inspire change for good. Polar explorer Pen Hadow
is, at the time of publishing, leading the Catlin Arctic Survey; a pioneering
expedition to measure the thickness of the remaining Arctic ice and determine how long it will continue to be a permanent feature on the planet.

I hope that you will read the stories that follow and be inspired, as I was.
If you have a similar story to tell, I would urge you to do so. In the words of
Nelson Mandela, 'When you let your light shine, you unconsciously give
other people permission to do the same.'

Jim Haywood
Environment Director
Business in the Community

Acknowledgements

Apart from thanking our contributors for generously giving us their valuable time and thoughtful contributions, we have a number of people to thank for what was at times a daunting logistical challenge.

In no particular order, they are: Marilyn Fike of the Bullitt Foundation; Jo Ann Bachman and Linda Sutton of Interface, Inc.; Lisa Cope Lilienthal for help with Interface; Jenni Hagland and Joanna Lee of the Carbon Disclosure Project; Clare Freeman of Climate Change Capital; Sam Lakha of Volans; Carmelle Druchniak of Stonyfield Farm; Fiona Davis of Friends of the Earth; Mary Kent of Rocky Mountain Institute; Wanjira Mathai and the Green Belt Movement; Margaret and Priya of Dr Shiva's office; Karen Eveleigh of Oxford's Smith School of Enterprise and the Environment; Robin Giampa and Cyndi Mielke of Timberland; Sue Lee of Sir Crispin Tickell's office; and all the nice people at the Gaia Foundation in London.

We also owe heartfelt thanks to Anne Morton, and to everyone who has helped us so much at John Wiley & Sons, including Claire Plimmer, Nick Mannion, Viv Wickham, Samantha Hartley, Jo Golesworthy, Michaela Fay and Louise Cheer.

About the Authors

Laura Mazur and Louella Miles are business writers and partners in Writers 4 Management, a professional writing firm. Since they formed it in 2004, Laura and Louella have worked with a range of organisations and individuals. Activities have included writing white papers, running writing training courses, newsletters and acting as ghost writers/editors on a number of books. Their previous book was *Conversations with Marketing Masters* (Wiley, 2007).

Laura has been a business journalist since 1978 and was editor of the UK's *Marketing* magazine from 1986 to 1989. She has written for a range of publications, including a weekly column for *Marketing* magazine for five years, and is also the author of management guides on international marketing and communications published by the Economist Intelligence Unit and Financial Times Reports. In addition, she also worked for six years for the Conference Board Europe, acting as project director for both the European Council on Marketing, and the Futures Council, which brought together corporate strategists from around Europe for regular meetings.

Louella started in consumer journalism in 1976, with the Consumer's Association, before moving over to business writing in 1980. She was managing editor of *Marketing* magazine through the mid to late 1980s. Her portfolio includes management reports on topics as diverse as corporate reputation and sponsorship, published by *Management Today* and *International Marketing Reports* respectively. She also edited a weekly media newsletter for seven years, and produces a range of titles on qualitative research.

Introduction

Words and phrases like climate change, sustainability and the green agenda have all become part of the everyday currency of life. But there are so many conflicting ideas and arguments about what sort of threat we as the human race face and what we can do about it, it is hardly surprising that many people stop listening and hope it all goes away.

That's why we decided to do this book. We wanted to talk to those people who early on began to warn that we were heading for environmental disaster if we didn't change course. All the people in this book are pioneers in identifying the dangers but, much more importantly, trying to find the solutions.

These conversations have been held with people from different continents, different sectors and different professions. They represent business, government, academics, finance, private foundations and non-Governmental Organisations (NGOs). Despite this variety, one big common theme emerges: there really is no option but to act more sustainably. We have to not only stop harming the environment, but also try and reverse the damage we have done to the planet. Their arguments are both convincing and perturbing.

Nevertheless, there is also a guarded sense of optimism that, if businesses, government and consumers begin to embrace this thinking and change behaviour collectively, we might – just – avert what one of our interviewees calls a planetary emergency.

This message should resonate particularly with businesses, since, along with the risk they face from climate change, there are endless opportunities to prosper from working in a much more environmentally-friendly way. Indeed, the businesses in this book have found just that.

What shines through all these conversations is the humanity of every one of this disparate group of people. Looking at what set them on the paths they chose throws up some interesting and at times moving answers. Each, in his or her own way, is trying to make this world a better place to live.

We really enjoyed our conversations with them. We hope you do too.

1

....

Ray Anderson

Ray Anderson is the founder of Interface, Inc. An honours graduate of Georgia Institute of Technology, Ray learned the carpet trade through 14-plus years at various positions at Deering-Milliken and Callaway Mills; and, in 1973, set about founding a company to produce the first free-lay carpet tiles in America. Interface has since diversified and globalized its businesses, with sales in 110 countries and manufacturing facilities on four continents. It is the world's largest producer of commercial floor coverings.

In 1994 Ray had what he calls a 'spear in the chest' epiphany when he first read Paul Hawken's The Ecology of Commerce, *seeking inspiration for a speech to an Interface task force on the company's environmental vision. Fourteen years and a sea change later, Interface, Inc, is more than 50% towards the vision of 'Mission Zero'. This is the company's promise to eliminate any negative impact it might have on the environment by the year 2020, through the redesign of processes and products, the pioneering of new technologies and efforts to reduce or eliminate waste and harmful emissions while increasing the use of renewable materials and sources of energy.*

He has authored a book chronicling his journey, Mid-Course Correction: Toward a Sustainable Enterprise: the Interface Model, *and become an unlikely screen hero in the 2004 Canadian documentary, 'The Corporation' and Leonardo DiCaprio's 'The 11th Hour'. He is a master commentator on the Sundance Channel's series, 'Big Ideas for a Small Planet', and was named one of* TIME *magazine's Heroes of the Environment in 2007, with a similar honour from* Elle *magazine that year. He is a sought-after speaker and adviser on environmental issues and was co-chair of the President's Council on Sustainable Development during President Clinton's administration.*

Ray has been lauded by government, environmental and business groups alike. In 2007, he was honoured as a recipient of the Purpose Prize from Civic Ventures, a think tank and an incubator, generating ideas and inventing programs to help society to achieve the greatest return on experience, and by Auburn University with its International Quality of Life Award. In 1996 he received the Inaugural Millennium Award from Global Green, presented by Mikhail Gorbachev, and won recognition from Forbes *magazine and Ernst & Young, which named him Entrepreneur of the Year – among many other honours.*

Ray is former Board Chair for The Georgia Conservancy and serves on the boards of the Ida Cason Callaway Foundation, Rocky Mountain Institute, the David Suzuki Foundation, Emory University Board of Visitors, the ASID Foundation, Worldwatch Institute and Melaver, Inc. He is on the Advisory Boards of

the Harvard Medical School Center for Health and the Global Environment and
the Upper Chattahoochee Riverkeeper. He holds eight honorary doctorates from
Northland College (public service), LaGrange College (business), N.C. State
University (humane letters), University of Southern Maine (humane letters), The
University of the South (civil law), Colby College (law), Kendall College (art)
and Emory University (science).

The professional journey

What, in your view, are you best known for?

I think probably as the founder of Interface, which brought European carpet
tile technology to America and effectively pioneered this new concept
here. And then, 21 years later, for changing course towards environmental
responsibility.

Let's talk about the founding of the business first. Why carpet tiles?

Back in the 1950s a family-owned Dutch company called Van Heugten
invented carpet tiles, or modular carpet, which it sold under the name of
Heuga. This improved technology was also being pursued by an English and
a German company. So you had these three companies focusing on carpet
tiles, with each one doing a little better than the last one. We then decided
to team up with the British and the Germans to bring their technology to
America, starting Interface from scratch with the idea of producing carpet
tiles in America for the emerging so-called 'office of the future', which provided the perfect market for modular carpet – even demanded modular
carpet.

What was your educational background?

I graduated from the Georgia Institute of Technology as an industrial engineer. After two years with a major food company, I moved into the carpet
and textile business at Callaway Mills. I spent nine years there climbing the
corporate ladder to the point where I was heading a number of corporate
functions such as engineering and quality control.

Deering-Milliken then acquired Callaway, and all of the functions that I was responsible for at Callaway were absorbed into the larger company. I was assigned to the carpet business of Milliken as director of development, which is to say director of innovation. That's where I first came across the technology for carpet tiles. We ended up bringing some of that technology to America under Milliken's name.

When I saw that this was going to be a big thing I found my own European partners and we set out to create a company from scratch to develop this marketplace. It turned out that our technology was better than the Milliken technology and we were able to steal a march on Milliken and then quickly become the leader in America. By 1988, 15 years into our existence, we were number two in the world. We then acquired Heuga, which was number one, thus combining the three leading technologies in the world into one global company. We became number one in the world by a wide margin.

And then, in 1994, we began to hear a question from our customers that we'd never heard before. "What is your company doing for the environment?" But we had no answers.

What was the context for this?

I think there was a handful of people in the architecture and the interior design fields who were becoming really sensitised to the issue of the environment. They were early movers who realised that they had great power over the specifications that they developed for the buildings they built. So they began to ask these questions just to see what responses they would get from their suppliers. And we listened. I think that's maybe what set us apart from our competitors. We listened very carefully and we said, hell, we don't have any answers and we need some. Our customers care; we have to care, too.

So we created a taskforce made up of people from our divisions around the world to see what we were doing. And the organisers of the taskforce asked me to launch it with a kick-off speech about my environmental vision. Well, I didn't have an environmental vision, except to comply with the law! I'd spent 21 years building a company from scratch with survival in mind and, by 1994, when we'd succeeded beyond anybody's wildest dreams, I was 60 years old – the time people start thinking about retirement.

But the request to speak was there. Because I didn't have the vision (I knew 'comply' was not a vision) I knew they were looking for, I was really worried about what I should say. And at that propitious moment a book landed on my desk. It was Paul Hawken's book, *The Ecology of Commerce*.

Was that serendipity?

Pure serendipity. And there's a back story there that's almost kind of spooky. One of our sales managers in southern California was pursuing the carpet order for a new demonstration green building that was being built in a Los Angeles suburb, and she kept running into this environmental consultant who rejected everything she put forward by way of product proposals. And he finally said to her, 'Look, Interface just doesn't get it.' And that word got back to me. And my response, so help me God, was: 'Interface doesn't get what?' Which sort of confirmed the consultant's point of view, I think.

And then, more or less simultaneously, a young woman living in Seattle, Washington, working for the state of Washington's environmental protection division, hears this guy speak, likes what he has to say and buys his book. She reads it. She sends it to her mother. Her mother is the sales manager in southern California who has had to convey the message that Interface just doesn't get it, and has had to choke on her CEO's response: 'Interface doesn't get what?' So courageously she sends the book to her CEO, me, and it lands on my desk at that propitious moment.

I picked it up with no idea who Paul Hawken was or what the book was about or anything. I began to thumb the thing, as you would do with a new book. On page 19, I came to a chapter heading, 'The Death of Birth'. I began to read and I found very quickly that the death of birth is a phrase to describe species extinction – species disappearing, never again to experience the miracle of birth.

And it was like a spear in the chest.

As I got more deeply into the book, I found that Hawken's central point was that the living systems, the life support systems, the biosphere itself that supports and nurtures all of life, is in decline, serious decline, long-term, systemic decline. And the biggest culprit in this is the industrial system – the way we make stuff, this linear take–make–waste system that we're all part of – digging up the earth and turning it into products that become scrap or waste for landfills in very short order.

He then goes on to say there's only one institution on earth that is large enough, powerful enough, pervasive enough *and* wealthy enough to change that course. And that's the same institution that's doing the damage: the institution of business. Well, I took that very seriously and used Hawken's material in the speech. In fact, he gave me almost more vision than I could handle! And I made that speech to that tiny taskforce and challenged them to lead our company to sustainability and beyond. To make Interface a restorative company. To put back more than we take and do good for the earth, not just 'do no harm'.

Did you have to face a lot of scepticism initially?

It began right there with that taskforce. They listened and they went away shaking their heads and were almost in revolt, you know? We make carpet tiles, what is this sustainability stuff? They'd maybe expected something along the lines of 'how do we keep our reputation clean and how do we deal with the regulators', and more of that sort of compliance kind of thinking. But this went so far beyond compliance it left them breathless.

There was one person in the taskforce, however, from Britain, who had come over with some of the earliest of our processing machinery and decided to stay in America. And he said something to the effect that, you know, all my life I've made compromises for the sake of putting bread on the table and taking care of my family. If we can do this and really do it well we'd set an example for the whole world. If we can do it, anybody can. And we would make up for all those compromises we've ever made.

Brave words.

Strong stuff. And then the taskforce gained some traction and they each went back to their individual businesses and began with the mantra: do something. Just do something.

But, still, you've got a company of 5000 people and none of them had ever heard the word sustainability and had no idea what it meant. And this little handful of people, each going back to their individual businesses, were like voices in the wilderness, straws in the wind, so to speak. It took fully a year for us to gain real traction and during that period I spoke at every opportunity to our people at plant meetings, sales meetings, any time I could get an audience. I talked about this environmental vision and our environmental stewardship responsibility and gradually, one mind at a time, they came around. That's the way it happened.

Over the course of that year we devised a plan and articulated the vision in very clear and hopefully understandable words: that we've got this mountain to climb and it's named 'Mount Sustainability'. And the point at the top, if you can visualise the point at the top of a mountain, symbolises zero footprint, zero environmental impact. That's sustainability and that's where we're going. We've got to climb this whole mountain and there are at least seven faces to the mountain. So, we spent that first year defining the seven faces of Mount Sustainability and how you would go about climbing them.

> *Over the course of that year we devised a plan and articulated the vision in very clear and hopefully understandable words: that we've got this mountain to climb and it's named 'Mount Sustainability'. And the point at the top, if you can visualise the point at the top of a mountain, symbolises zero footprint, zero environmental impact. That's sustainability and that's where we're going. We've got to climb this whole mountain and there are at least seven faces to the mountain.*

Why seven?

Well, when we thought about the mountain and the broad areas of activity that we had to tackle, it seemed to sort itself out into seven fronts. The first of those was to eliminate waste, to eliminate the very concept. There's no waste in nature. One organism's waste is another's food. So we looked at nature to show us how to do this. The next face of the mountain is energy. Nature runs on sunlight. How do you run an industrial enterprise on sunlight? Everything in nature is cyclical. How do you then take these linear processes, the take-make-waste processes, and bend them into cyclical processes? In nature there are no emissions that are harmful to anybody. So how do we create factories that have no emissions? Or at least so that what goes out is harmless to the biosphere? And then you've got the whole area of transportation to deal with, which is separate unto itself. So we've got five faces there. Waste, emissions, energy, material flows and transportation. And then the sixth face we realised probably ought to be first on the list because nothing of any lasting value happens without it, and that is the culture shift.

That's quite a big challenge, isn't it?

Right! It's huge; it's changing minds. It's changing the world view of 5000 people from the notion that we can take it for granted that there are infinite resources, to a realisation that the earth is finite. It's finite as a source, in terms of what it can provide. It's finite as a sink, as to what it can absorb and assimilate and endure. So we have to think beyond the next quarter and we have to think beyond our own lifetime. The timeframe has to shift here beyond our brief time on earth to our grandchildren, their grandchildren and their grandchildren.

So, over time, one mind at a time we made the shift. And we spent a lot of energy and effort to create the opportunity for people to change their minds.

Did you apply this approach to your shareholders as well?

When we talked to Wall Street we talked about waste elimination and we gave this particular issue a name, QUEST (Quality Utilising Employee Suggestions and Teamwork). How can you argue with that?

So that's what we talked to Wall Street about until the rest of the plan was not only conceived and in place, but things were actually happening. And in the annual report to our shareholders for the year 2000, which came out in early 2001, the tagline was: a better way to bigger profits.

We spelled out the whole initiative there, all seven faces of the mountain, with the ultimate objective being the seventh face of the mountain: to change the way we go to market and re-invent commerce. Instead of selling products and stuff we would sell the service that the product delivered: the colour, the texture, the comfort underfoot, the acoustical value, the ambience, the functionality – all the reasons anybody would want a carpet. We would satisfy those reasons but retain ownership of the means – that is, the stuff itself – and give that stuff life after life in closed loop material flows.

And how did you propose to do that?

When we began the technology did not exist. This is about recycling – getting our products back at the end of their first useful life and giving them life after life by separating them into their individual components and putting each of those components back into its own closed loop. We've just now, over the last year, put the technology in place to close the loop on the most difficult of all material components to recycle: the nylon, the polyamide face of the carpet.

It's ironic. DuPont invented nylon and DuPont says it's impossible to recycle it. But we and another supplier figured out how to do it.

You were saying that it was the questioning of the people who were commissioning for premises, for hotels, for offices and so on, that prompted you to go start this journey

Right.

So obviously they were asking this question of other suppliers too?

Oh, I'm sure they were.

In your experience, what was it that made you listen?

Well, that's an interesting question. There was a day in August in 1974, in our start-up year. We had spent 1973 building and equipping the factory and training our initial workforce and in early 1974 we launched our first product line. And that, you may remember, was in the middle of a horrific recession.

I remember one day in August of 1974. Here we are, with our factory built and equipped, our workforce hired and trained, raw materials bought and paid for, products developed and I looked at the order book and there was not a single order. And that is a traumatic experience. It says you're one order away from being out of business. If you don't get the next order, it's like the next heartbeat. If you don't get it, you die. So, with my life savings invested in this new company, I was looking at failure: corporate death and financial ruin for myself, personally.

Well, we got the next order and then the next one and the next one and so forth. We survived. But from that day on, the customer has been the single most important person in our company. I remember having conversations with our plant people when we were still a very small company, like meeting with them at Christmas time and asking, who do you think is the most important person in this company? And they would say, well, you. Or

Joe Kyle, who was our manufacturing guy or Mr Russell, our marketing guy. And I said no, no, no, no. The most important person is our customer and don't you forget it. We'll do anything for our customers. From that traumatic experience of an empty order book, we were a customer-intimate company from that day forward. So, 21 yeas later, when our customers were asking these questions to which we had no answers, we listened and said, you know, this is important.

That led to the taskforce and then the speech and all of that. It was an epiphanal experience for me personally. And then, over the course of the next year or two, I'd say, that epiphany spread one mind at a time through our company so that we began to really gain traction. From the beginning, though, we made real progress on the waste elimination front; we saved a lot of money and we took the view that we could save this money and put it in the bank, or we could re-invest some of it in the mountain-climbing plan.

And we did. We took the more holistic view that said: we don't want to optimise just this part of the company or that part of the company or another part of the company. We want to optimise the whole thing, and move the company from where it is today to a totally different place.

Where are you now in terms of the mountain?

Well, we're at different places on different faces of the mountain and it depends on how you weigh the individual faces. For example, our greenhouse gas emissions have been reduced by a net 82%, in absolute tonnage. Our carbon intensity has been reduced at Interface by 89%. This is phenomenal. I doubt if there's another company on earth which has done that over the same period of time. And we're a petro-intensive company; so if we can do it, anybody can.

In terms of using renewable and recycled materials, we're at 25% and growing very rapidly. We've reduced fossil fuel energy intensity by 60%; and something like 27% of our total energy today is coming from renewable sources; 88% of our electricity is from renewable sources. We've shut down a third of our smoke stacks and 71% of our effluent pipes by creating process changes that obviate the need for them. So, depending on how you weigh all this out, we're somewhere better than halfway to that objective. The ideal objective is a zero footprint.

And QUEST has saved the company $393 million.

That's an amazing figure

Absolutely. It has paid for all the rest of this mountain climb, all the R&D, all the capital expenditures, all of the training, everything – more than paid for by the waste elimination alone. And this is not a small company. This is a $1 billion company.

How do you view other companies which make excuses about why they are not making the same stringent efforts that you are?

Do you know the name Deepak Chopra? Deepak has this wonderful saying. He says that people are really doing the best they can, given their level of awareness. This whole environmental and social equity movement is about awareness, about raising levels of awareness. And there's always a higher level for anybody. Even for Deepak himself there's a higher level of awareness, and that is the name of the game. It doesn't make me mad. It makes me sad that others have not achieved a level of awareness about what to me is so obvious: that we're destroying the biosphere.

Current views

How do you define sustainability? Because it seems that different people have different ways of defining it.

That's true. What we did is take all of it in and ask, well, how does this apply to us? And we concluded that sustainability for us means taking from the earth only that which is naturally and rapidly renewable – not another fresh drop of oil – and doing no harm to the biosphere. That's sustainability for us. And then there's the fairness part of it too.

What do you mean by that?

Fairness is in our bones. We know that that means diversity and, certainly in the United States, it means cultural, ethnic and racial diversity. And we operate most everywhere in what is a very complex world, so adapting to local customs and treating people right everywhere is very important. But fundamentally we are focused on the environment and that means take nothing and do no harm. We believe strongly that resource efficiency is the way we help to create a rising tide that will float everybody's boat higher.

And from that everything else flows?

Yes. And then beyond sustainable is restorative, which is to put back more than we take. Do good, not just do no harm. When I first put that to our people in that first taskforce meeting they came back to me and said, 'You know, we think we understand sustainability and how we can begin to move in that direction, but this thing called restorative seems to us like perpetual motion. And how do you do that?' As we talked about it, we realised if we could really begin to move in a demonstrable, credible, measurable way towards sustainability, get a really clear fix of what that meant to us and begin to move in that direction, something else just might happen. We might influence somebody else to move, too.

We really felt that we could attract other businesses to a better business model. And that's how we have become restorative: through the power of influence. It's not just what we do, but what we influence others to do. That's how we become restorative.

And I would say today that Interface is a restorative company. Even though we're a bit over halfway to sustainability, the influence that we've had in the world is amazing. We have companies coming to us every day asking, 'How do you do this?' And we've even created a consulting arm within Interface to deal with those companies, which, by the way, we call InterfaceRAISE – raise expectations, standards, awareness and profits. We realised that 14 years of this has created a lot of value. It's a furtherance of the restorative initiative.

Would you say that, overall, you feel optimistic about where we are headed?

Well, I'm deeply concerned. People ask me all the time, are you optimistic? And I cannot say I am. I think there's going to be a lot of pain before humankind figures this out and we reverse the wrong course that we're on. That's why I wrote my book, *Mid-Course Correction*, because the whole damn system has got to have a mid-course correction.

So business has a big role to play?

Paul Hawken was absolutely right. Business has to lead. Well, I say absolutely right because I've slightly modified my own view of that over time

to the point that I'd say today if business does not come aboard, where its
influence is so powerful in the world
for good or for ill, and have that
mid-course correction collectively as
an industrial system, it's over for
humankind. It's just a matter of
time.

If business does not come
aboard, where its influence is so
powerful in the world for good or
for ill, and have that mid-course
correction collectively as an
industrial system, it's over for
humankind. It's just a matter of
time.

What role can governments and ordinary people play?

Well, business is undoubtedly the most powerful institution on earth. Governments follow, they don't lead. People? Well, if people could institution-
alise themselves to speak with one voice it would be the people that would
be the most powerful because business responds to its customers. Politicians
respond to their voters. So it's people ultimately who have the power, but
the people don't yet speak with one voice. If they did it would move markets,
move governments and move the whole thing.

Look at Jeff Immelt at GE. He has committed GE to doubling its R&D
in clean technologies from $750 million to $1.5 billion and expects to
double his revenues from $10 billion to $20 billion from those same clean
technologies. He's not doing it for altruism. He's doing it because he's heard
his customers say, we want the clean technologies.

**Anita Roddick of the Body Shop used to talk about the second bottom
line. Is that what you mean?**

Well, my view on this is that the triple bottom line, done right, comes
together in one truly superior, totally ethical, better financial bottom line.
It's financial, social and environment. This is John Elkington's phrase. He
has pioneered the notion of three bottom lines, which is great. But I really
do believe that beyond the triple bottom line lies that one truly superior,
totally ethical, financial bottom line that will hopefully attract companies
everywhere to a better business model. I think more in terms of a three-stage
rocket. The payload is profits.

You make a very powerful business case for taking this route.

Well, in our experience the business case is crystal clear. Our costs are down, not up. We have to dispel the myth that there's a trade-off – a choice. It's a false choice between the environment and the economy. Our products are the best they've ever been. When our product designers began to approach product design through the lens of sustainable design it opened up a whole new world. It's been a wellspring of innovation. Nobody could have anticipated it. It was a total surprise. Because of that, our products are innovative and they're the best in the world in our category. Our people are just galvanised around this shared higher purpose.

In our experience the business case is crystal clear. Our costs are down, not up. We have to dispel the myth that there's a trade-off – a choice. It's a false choice between the environment and the economy.

I'll tell you a quick story. I mentioned the consulting business. One of our first clients was a big international company that sent 15 of its top management people to us here in La Grange, Georgia, to a carpet factory for a cultural immersion experience! They were in a conference room that's deliberately out in the middle of the factory, where you can see the products and the processes going on all around you.

There was one woman among those 15. And she did not want to be there. She was belligerent, sceptical, disruptive; she challenged everything and clearly did not understand why her company was spending this time and money to send 15 people to this little rinky-dink carpet factory in Georgia.

During the mid-morning break everybody had to find their way to the restrooms by going through the factory. So she finds the ladies' room and on her way back encounters a fork truck driver who has this big roll of carpet on his fork truck. She stops him and says: 'What do you do here?' And, so help me, his response was: 'Ma'am, I come to work every day to help save the earth.' It just stunned her. She then began to draw him out, to ask him more questions. After a couple of minutes of this he said: 'Ma'am, I hate to be rude, but if I don't get this roll of carpet to that machine over there in the next minute our waste figures and our emissions figures will go completely out of control. I've got to go.'

She came back and sat down. No one knew that this had happened, but our person running the meeting said that when she took her seat, she was a visibly different person. She sat there very quietly, not saying anything. And she then began to challenge her people. Why aren't we doing this, why aren't we doing that? And then she told the story of her encounter on the factory floor. She said, 'I've never seen anything like it before to demonstrate alignment from the very top of an organisation clear to the factory floor.' Then she says, 'The only word I can think of that describes it is love.'

So you can see the galvanising effect this has had on our people and the way our people have taken on this higher purpose.

The final element in the business case is certainly as important as any of the others and that is the goodwill of the marketplace. It has just been astonishing. No amount of money we could have spent on advertising or marketing would have created the goodwill that this single initiative has.

So does this approach help with marketing your products, do you think?

We have been very, very careful and actually reticent to put much in the hands of our sales force because we didn't want to raise too many expectations. For the first eight, nine years we wouldn't even let our sales force talk about it. We just said, look, you go and do your job and every time you make a sale you can be sure that the work being done in the factory is going to be reflected in the product you sell.

But in the last few years we have begun to put the marketing literature together to help the sales force present what we're doing. At the end of the day, people deal as often with the company behind the product as they do with a product. And so it's too valuable *not* to incorporate somehow into the marketing, and present that face of the company to the public.

Do you think one of the problems is that there has been a certain amount of greenwashing, where people mount initiatives just to show that they're doing something when they're not?

That happens all the time. That's the typical competitive response, a knee-jerk reaction. You know: 'We're losing position in the marketplace, we've got to do something.' What you get is greenwash, using 'green' in a way that's transparently self-serving.

Is it a case of carrot or stick to get companies to change?

What I hope to do in Interface is create such a powerful example that no-one can ignore it; so it draws other companies to the example. I suspect that we're going to have regulations that begin to create a more insistent stick, particularly with regard to climate change. With a change of administration in Washington, almost certainly something's going to emerge to deal with climate change. If it doesn't, then it really is over.

So you'd be quite keen to see that emerge?

Well, I think that businesses in general, much larger businesses than ours, are looking for a level playing field; and regulation in a way creates that. Just give us the goal and leave it to us to get to it. The goal, of course, will eventually be translated into a cap on emissions, which will be ratcheted down, down, down until companies everywhere are where we are today, at 82% reduction.

How are we going to resolve the different competing needs of nationalism and globalism to come up with regulations, and who will police them?

Well, I presume it's going to be one nation at a time, each doing its own thing and there's going to be a huge amount of negotiation, the give and take, the push and pull. It's a many-sided issue. It's an equation with so many variables. And I don't know. I'm not smart enough in the political sense to know how it all gets done. I do know, though, where it all has to end up. It has to end up with an 80% reduction in greenhouse gases in absolute terms. Or maybe more. We've got to get the emissions down below the earth's absorption or sequestration rate so that we can begin to reverse the trend – not just reduce the upward trend but turn it downward and drive it *below* where we are today, at a CO_2 concentration of roughly 387 ppm, to 350 ppm or less.

You said you're not overly optimistic. Can technology save us?

Well, technology's got to be part of the solution, absolutely. It's the contrast between the technologies of the first industrial revolution, which, by the way is still going on today, and the technologies of the new industrial revolution. The contrast will be pretty dramatic. The first industrial revolution technologies are basically extractive and the new technology will have to be renewable. The technologies are basically linear today, and in the future they've got to be cyclical. Today, they are driven by fossil fuels; tomorrow they must be driven by renewables. Today they are wasteful and abusive; tomorrow they must be waste-free and benign and focused on resource-efficiency.

What do you reckon the world will be like for your grandchildren?

Less unsustainable, we hope.

Looking into your crystal ball, in 10 or 15 years, can you see other businesses climbing the mountain?

Definitely. People ask me all the time, when you get to the top of the mountain, what do you hope to see? I say, aside from the fact the view is going to be wonderful, I want to look down that mountain in all directions and see other companies climbing right behind us because there's plenty of room at the top.

And, of course, you spend a lot of time spreading the message, don't you?

I spend a lot of time talking to people, that's for sure. People everywhere want to hear the story of Interface. I relinquished the CEO role years ago, so that I'm freed up from the day-to-day of the business and I can do this. I can talk to people. I made 150 speeches in 2007. Actually it was 108 speeches and 42 interviews. Put it this way: I never seek an invitation but they do keep finding me!

The cumulative effect of all of this has created enormous goodwill in the marketplace and prepared the way for our sales people to now lay the goods on the table. Here we are and this is what I can tell you about this product.

Its footprint has been reduced by half and the company behind it has reduced its footprint by half. So the cumulative effect of third-party endorsement, plus what our sales force is able to generate, has put us in a whole different place with regard to the public and our marketplace.

Getting more personal

What is it about you as a person that has brought you here? When you were very young were you very much into nature, for instance?

Well, as a kid growing up in a small town in Georgia, sure, I spent summers outdoors, but I was an athlete too. During the school year I was involved in football, basketball and baseball and I eventually went to college on an athletic scholarship. So I was not particularly a naturalist or a nature person growing up. Ultimately it was my five grandchildren who prepared me for that spear in the chest experience. In fact, I'll give you another anecdote. Have you heard of Yvon Chouinard? He's a founder of Patagonia, which makes outdoor wear.

Yvon was a blacksmith in his early years and he was a mountain climber and made his own gear. And his friends said, 'Look, your stuff's better than my stuff, would you make me one of those?' And that's how Patagonia started. It then moved into clothing and so forth. It's a very successful company and has been committed to sustainability longer than I have, going way, way back.

Well, I was invited to make a speech to Patagonia's supply chain. They had a green-the-supply chain meeting years ago and I went to California and talked about the Interface example. Then, over dinner one evening, I was sitting across the table from Yvon and he started quizzing me. He asked me, 'Do you climb mountains?' I said, 'Oh, no. No, I don't climb mountains. That's too dangerous for me.' He said, 'Well, what about fishing? Do you like to fish?' I said, 'Well, when I was a boy I went with my father, but since I've been an adult I haven't been fishing very much.' He said, 'Well, what about hunting?' I said, 'Well, yeah, I went dove hunting when I was 16 years old. I hit a dove, but it didn't die. I had to pull its head off. And since then I haven't wanted to go hunting.' He said, 'Well, what about hiking? Do you like to hike?' I said, 'Well, that's pretty strenuous, Yvon.' And in total frustration he said, 'Then why the hell do you do this?'

And I said, 'Yvon, I have five grandchildren.' He said, 'Oh, right.' That was a whole new reason for him.

That's a great story. So what would you say you are proudest of in terms of your work?

Oh, what Interface has become. This paragon of sustainability. And we're not done. We're only halfway there. And I hope to live to see the top of that mountain. It's a good thing I come from long-lived people.

We're only halfway there. And I hope to live to see the top of that mountain. It's a good thing I come from long-lived people.

Finally, do you have what you might call a defining moment in your life?

It was Hawken's book. In that chapter on 'The Death of Birth' he uses the example of the reindeer of St Matthew Island as a metaphor.

St Matthew Island, in the Bering Sea, was a deserted island except for a coastguard weather station. So somebody had the bright idea of putting reindeer on the island so that if the food supply ships couldn't get in there the men could at least shoot a reindeer for dinner. And in 1944 they put 29 reindeer on the island.

Over the years the coastguard abandoned the weather station, but one biologist stayed in touch with what was happening on the island. By 1963 the reindeer population had grown from 29 to 6000 reindeer. But he had calculated that the island could support between 1600 and 2300 animals. So 6000 was an overshoot in biological terms. On his return to the island three years later, though, the biologist found that the population had crashed to 42. From 29 to 6000 to 42! This was way below the original carrying capacity of the island because the environment had been so destroyed by the overshoot. Carrying capacity, overshoot, collapse. Three very important ecological concepts.

Well, I read that and I said, 'My God, that's a metaphor for humankind and the earth.' We are in overshoot already and getting worse, and this is what lies before us if we don't get it under control.

2

....

James Cameron

James Cameron is the Founder, Executive Director and Vice-Chairman of Climate Change Capital (CCC). CCC is an investment manager and adviser specialising in the opportunities that are generated by the global transition to the low-carbon economy. It advises and invests in companies which recognise that combating global warming is both a necessity and an economic opportunity. As of November 2008, it had $1.6 billion under management.

CCC has advised, raised and deployed capital for numerous low-carbon activities on a global basis. These include financing renewable energy installations in the United Kingdom; destroying industrial greenhouse gases in India and China; advice on the acquisition and divestiture strategies for private equity funds and the carbon-intensive industry in Europe and the US; and waste-to-energy projects in China and Hungary.

Previously, James was Counsel to international law firm, Baker & McKenzie, where he founded and led its Global Climate, Clean Energy and Emissions Trading Group.

As a barrister he has spent much of his career specialising in trade law, environmental law and human rights and been involved in a number of high profile cases ranging from Brent Spar to the arrest and extradition of General Pinochet.

In 1989, with three others, he established the Centre for International Environmental Law (CIEL), which pioneered the development of academic and research tools needed to initiate environmental legislation and negotiate international agreements. In 1990, the CIEL broke off into two organisations: the London-based Foundation for International Environmental Law and Development (FIELD) and Washington-based CIEL.

He helped to negotiate the 1992 UN Framework Convention on Climate Change (UNFCCC) at the UN Conference on Environment and Development (UNCED) where he championed the 'flexibility mechanisms' now enshrined in the 1997 Kyoto protocol. He provided legal assistance and representation to the Alliance of Small Island States (AOSIS) throughout these negotiations.

James was a member of the Green Global Network (formerly the Green Globe Task Force), which advised the then-UK Foreign Minister, Robin Cook, on global environmental policy. He was also a special adviser to the House of Commons Select Committee on the Environment during its enquiry into world trade and environment and its enquiry on multilateral environmental agreements. He is a member of the International Union for Conservation of Nature's Commission on Environmental Law and has been engaged as a consultant to advise

*governments, inter-governmental organisations and non-governmental organis-
ations on the development and implementation of international environmental
policy and law.*

*He is chairman of the Carbon Disclosure Project, launched in December 2000.
This is recognised as the largest registry of GHG emissions in the world and has
established the primary global corporate greenhouse gases reporting process which
can be used to set target levels and rate companies' performances.*

*James is treasurer/member of the governing board of the Renewable Energy and
Energy Efficient Partnership (REEEP); and a member of the steering committee
of Renewable Energy Policy Network for the 21st Century (REN21), a network
that was born out of the International Conference for Renewable Energies in Bonn
(2004) and aims to provide a forum for international leadership on renewable
energy. He is chairman of the international publishing company, Cameron May,
and was a founder/non-executive director of Solar Century, the UK's leading solar
photovoltaics company.*

*He has held academic positions at Cambridge, London, Bruges and Sydney, is
a Fellow of the Yale Center for Environmental Law and Policy, and a board
member of the Center for Business and the Environment at Yale. He is a member
of the board of GE Ecomagination and a member of the Copenhagen Climate
Council.*

The professional journey

What do you feel you're best known for?

I think that I have built up quite a rounded perspective on abuse of power.
I figured out, after years and years of working on climate change, and human
rights and trade issues, that it wasn't enough to focus on public expressions
of power, on governments and public policy-making, treaty-making and law
courts and dispute settlement. Many environmental problems stem from
abuse of power in private hands.

However, it became very obvious to me that too many of the people in
the environment movement comfort themselves – which I think is
lazy – that the corporation is the enemy. Well, it's not, because the corporation is just another society and you can make it do things that are in
the interests of the whole, even if its principal motivation is to further
the interest of its own society. And there is no point vilifying shareholders,

because we are all, in the working world, in some way or another, shareholders.

Is that the thinking that motivated you to start CCC?

Absolutely. We feel strongly that our work denies the absurd separation between the economy and the environment that people have made over the years. Four of us started the company and now there are 160. We started as a small advisory practice and we now manage about $1.6 billion of assets, with offices in China and the US.

It's interesting. I was often described, especially in a commercial law firm, as 'uncommercial' – a ghastly word meant as an insult. Now I love the fact that this is a successful commercial business, driven by the ideals that I helped to set. I proved that it's possible to combine my particular strengths with people who really care about making money, who care about the discipline of investment and the processes involved in looking after large institutional investors' money so that they get healthy returns. There are many different types of people in this business and we all work together. It's a great atmosphere.

So you must have to be careful to choose the right people?

They have to have the right attitude. They don't need to be experts in climate change or even passionate about the environment, although it helps. I don't mind taking on people who care more about making their fortune here. But they've got to fit in. They've got to be able to have coffee with someone who actually ran Friends of the Earth's climate campaign for years, for example.

What is it about you, as a person, that's made you get involved in this area?

I'm reasonably self-aware and I have some attributes that enable people to follow my lead. It's to do with having a vision that can be articulated so that it's an attractive vision, but mostly it's to do with being encouraging to others and to give them space and responsibility to be a part of the enterprise rather than owning it all myself.

Let's look back at your career. What are some of the major events that have had an impact on where you are now?

The story really begins with law. I was a young international lawyer at Cambridge and, in the aftermath of the Chernobyl accident/incident, the first piece of work that I did on the environment was looking at the international law on sovereignty issues associated with the passage of a plume of radioactivity across northern Europe. Note that it wasn't the governments who told us that we were at risk as citizens. It was revealed by a privately-owned satellite. The Soviet Union certainly didn't tell the neighbouring states.

It raised big issues such as: why did nobody bring a claim? It was such an obvious harm caused by somebody. Why couldn't a claim be brought – which is what would normally happen within a jurisdiction – between jurisdictions? And then you figure out that, in fact, countries don't do this because they worry about somebody else doing it to them. So you have to ask the question: well, what is this legal system that's supposed to bind countries together to do things in the public interest of their own citizens?

That tied in perfectly with the work that I was doing at Cambridge with my long-time friend and colleague Philippe Sands, now Professor of International Law at University College, London, and Philip Allott, who taught us both and who is Professor of International Law at Trinity College, Cambridge. We were discussing a revolutionary re-thinking, a re-imagining of what international law is and what its purpose is and how we could improve it.

Were you studying at the time?

Yes. That was during a phase of graduate work and my first academic appointments. I was Director of Studies in Law at Clare Hall, Cambridge, and a research assistant at the Research Centre for International Law. There was a little group of us there, including Philippe and myself, who have stayed connected in some way or other ever since. We were imagining what we were going to do with our lives.

What you need to understand is that in international law there are various traditions and cultures that require academic credibility. Whether it lasts like that I don't know and there's probably a lot of change taking place now in the profession, but throughout my career it has been necessary to establish your credentials in academia in order to be effective as a practitioner.

Is that particular to international law?

It is in some other areas of law that are discrete, arcane, different and away from the mainstream. And then, of course, international law has long been connected with international diplomacy and, therefore, politics. The connections are in the sphere of public discourse about politics and morality as much as they are about private settlement or disputes and resolution of economic conflicts – but that's a broader conversation.

Anyway, when in 1985 I wrote down what I saw as an ideal law practice, I had written on that list the environment. Because we recognised that here was a problem that transcended national boundaries, that required international cooperation and the order and discipline of rules and the fairness and justice associated with the administration of those rules in international institutions.

So our theoretical discussions, our idealistic discussions, met a desire to have a real practice in international law. And, in setting out what those areas were so that we could get a real practice that was consistent with our ideals, the environment stood out. But so did human rights, as did international trade, international movements of money and disputes settlement.

So how did you formulate this list?

It was broken up into bits, with European law as a subset of international law. Let me give you a sense, though, of how different things were back in 1980. When I was looking for chambers to join and came to have my first interviews at the Bar, senior barristers would say, you've expressed an interest in international law and European law, but we don't do European law. I just looked at them and said, what are you talking about? You can't choose. European law will be part of English law and there will still be a specialist practice that is distinct. You haven't got any option.

And these were very, very able people at the top of their profession, yet they couldn't see that the material with which they worked was changing in front of them. So there were some irritable exchanges. And they'd say things like, name three recent contract law cases. And I'd say, well, I haven't got a clue about that. I'm an international lawyer.

So are you saying that international law was really at an embryonic stage then?

Well, it's a relatively young subject, but you can trace it back many hundreds of years. Indeed, you could look at the way that states have always organised their relations between each other. But there has been a very remarkable development in international law in my lifetime. In the 20-odd years that I've been working it has reached into people's ordinary lives much more obviously. It's now much harder to segregate international law into state-to-state diplomatic affairs, with rules of etiquette and conduct between states in their contractual relations. It's now, in part, integral to European law, human rights law and the ways in which laws reorientate the relationships that develop through a globalised economy.

There's no doubt that the World Trade Organisation rules have accelerated the processes of globalisation that were happening anyway. So, whereas when I started out international law was obviously very distinct and people could comfortably argue, 'We don't do that' or 'It's separate from', or would say you can only do that by being an academic, things have moved on.

Why did your interest in environmental issues grow?

Well, I had a reason for entering into the environment debate through international law, not the other way round. I didn't spend a childhood campaigning on environmental issues. I wasn't overly sensitised to the green debate. I was aware, but it wasn't driving me when I was a student. The things that have always driven me have been a deep, deep belief in the value of law, in the need for what I imagine to be international society to be governed by law, and a really, very, very sensitive antenna for abuse of power. This is very easy to translate into environmental issues because so many of the problems associated with the environment are connected to abuse of power, whether in public or private hands.

> *The things that have always driven me have been a deep, deep belief in the value of law, in the need for what I imagine to be international society to be governed by law, and a really, very, very sensitive antenna for abuse of power.*

How does this manifest itself?

States that just don't care. Companies which just don't care. People who are prepared to put their own advantage against the interests of others. These are all versions of abuse of power. And they're frequently connected to other abuses. It's no mistake that human rights issues and environment issues are connected, or that revolutionary movements to remove abusive power in government often begin in the environment arena.

And people's fear of the declining value of the world in which they live is often sensitive to the air they breathe, the water they drink and all these fundamentals of life. So I didn't begin with the environment. My way into all of this came through idealism about international law, about international society – that sense of the need to seek justice by looking directly at the face of power and having the confidence that you get from the law to represent the weak against the strong.

There is a consistent theme in my working life, which I hope is true in all of my life, which is that I have a real determination to confront and prevent abuse of power in any form, including personal. I abhor bullies of any type and I've learnt that I'm pretty good at dealing with them. You've got to acknowledge power – you can't walk away from it. You can't pretend it's not there just because you don't like it. The one thing you do with bullies is take them on, so you find techniques to ensure that you stay true to yourself in doing that without turning into one of them.

So that's the background.

How did you start?

The first thing Philippe and I did together was to match theory and practice by looking for ways in which to use the law in order to protect the environment. We did that first through an organisation called the Centre for International Environmental Law (CIEL), which we founded in 1989. Cambridge was a little bit too conservative for us, but it was a rather more dynamic dean at King's College Law School, Ian Kennedy, who had been at Berkeley and understood what we were on about, and took it on.

This was quite pioneering then, setting this up?

Nobody had done it before but we did a deal with him and we said, we'll teach for nothing – but only if we have autonomy in developing this new centre. We brought two people – Durwood Zaelke and Wendy Dinner – across from the US whom we'd met in Washington at an event discussing Chernobyl and legal issues. This was really led by Philippe because he'd written this book called *Chernobyl Law and Communications*.

After I'd delivered a speech there we all went and had several beers and finished up starting a new organisation. They took a huge risk by leaving the US, where they worked for the Sierra Company of Defence Fund, and yet they came over and we started work in London. For a period we operated on two fronts: US and UK. But in time we went our separate ways and, rather than fight over the name, we started again in London in 1990 but gave ourselves a new name.

We called it the Foundation for International Environmental Law and Development (FIELD), which still exists at the University College London. In 2005 FIELD got together with the International Institute for Environmental Development (IIED) which is a wonderful organisation, does superb work and has done so for many years.

Interestingly, we also had talked about merging FIELD and IIED early on in 1990 because when we started CIEL the previous year we were the first organisation to be funded by the Ford Foundation outside the US to do international work. And if it weren't for IIED we wouldn't have got that money, and never have got started. We also had connections with Sir Brian Urquhart, who was an under-secretary of the UN and a figurehead for the Ford Foundation, and went to see him.

We also went to see Sir Crispin Tickell at the same time, when he was UK ambassador to the UN. It was very gracious of him to see us bearing in mind that we were, basically, kids who said we've got this idea that we might want to start an organisation. I'd read a lot of his speeches, because it was just after the Falklands problem and both Philippe and I had done a lot of work as international lawyers on that issue.

It created a good context in which to say to him: well, we've got this idea that we might want to start an organisation to use international law to protect the environment. What do you think? And there's this particular issue that we think is going to be huge that needs international law: it's called climate change. We should have done better research ourselves, because at this point he reached behind him and pulled out his book on climate change which he had written in the 1970s!

Why do you think the Ford Foundation decided to give you funds?

The thesis was pretty straightforward. A global problem needs a global solution backed by law. Otherwise you won't get adequate change in behaviour by states, let alone companies. Who is at risk? Who is least able to represent their interests and therefore most in need of a bunch of idealistic lawyers to look after their interests? We wanted to carry out research and development for an international agreement on climate change for the benefit of low-lying developing countries.

We said that there's got to be an international agreement. It has to have certain principles that we understand very well because we're young and idealistic international lawyers and the beneficiaries of our charitable work have to be those most at risk and least able to represent themselves, with no power other than the law. So without economic power, or political power, their best hope is to use the law. Who are they?

We latched on to everybody who's exposed to sea-level rise, the most certain consequence of climate change. In 1988 I'd written an opinion piece for Greenpeace, which is why I had the idea. It was on state responsibility for climate change because way back then it had asked my opinion on whether it could bring a case before the International Court of Justice against the US for not doing anything about climate change. I turned that into a *Law Review* article, which I wrote with Durwood, which was finally published in 1990. This was the first piece of writing in the legal literature on climate change and the law.

And the programme officer at the Ford Foundation, Janet Maughan, was a remarkable woman. She looked at us and said: 'You know what? It doesn't fit, but if I get my colleagues in here and we go right to the top of the organisation we'll go round this and find a way of funding this.'

So we built the Centre of International Environmental Law on the back of that Ford Foundation $200 000-odd grant into a really powerful influencing group. One of our biggest achievements was to develop a coalition which became the Alliance of Small Island States. We first got together in November 1990 at the Second World Climate Conference in Geneva to work together as a group of small island states. By the time of the UN's Earth Summit in Rio in 1992, we had 43 countries.

Imagine all these tiny countries that nobody pays any attention to at all, suddenly organised. We had written a manifesto for them for the Geneva conference in 1990. We prepared them as if we were the Foreign Office lawyers but with much more clout. And we negotiated on their behalf, wrote their speeches and interventions, we crafted text, we brought precedents.

The US State Department lawyers would come out and say, no, you can't do things that way. And we'd say, well, really? And you'd only have to look at them and think, my education's just as good as yours. If you're an international lawyer it's a small club: you know who taught me and I know who taught you, so let the games begin. You'd better be good. And we soon realised that ultimately there was power behind that United States banner and, boy, did they try to exercise it.

What were you trying to get out of this?

To get a political commitment and a declaration to create an international agreement on climate change, and limit greenhouse gas emissions globally. Incidentally, Margaret Thatcher was the most prominent figure in the world at that event. She said at the time, in November 1990, that the science is so clear and the need for international cooperation is so obvious that we shouldn't be spending our time squabbling over who pays for it. So it's interesting how long it's taken us to get to grips with this problem.

We worked really hard to build that coalition of small island states. At the Geneva conference their representatives came in one after the other to support the precautionary principle which we'd drafted for them. It was a really good way of applying the principle that you don't wait until you've proved beyond doubt that you have catastrophic climate change, because by then it will be too late. You take your evidence, intervene early and you avoid risk because you're facing serious and irreversible harm.

The small island states made it an article of faith that it had to be in the agreement in November 1990 in order to get an agreement soon thereafter. And we got it in. In the end the whole regime was, and is, based on the precautionary principle. It was the first time they'd worked together and it was wonderful to watch. You can imagine how striking it would have been to other people in powerful countries who would never have heard these people speak up before. Jeremy Leggett's book *The Carbon War* documents this moment very accurately.

What drove you in all this?

I'm very idealistic and unashamedly so. But I also like to get things done. I'm somebody capable of connecting the world of ideas and the world of action. I'm not a scholar philosopher. I'm not disciplined enough. I'm quite good at understanding and articulating complex ideas, including those of other people, but I haven't got the dedication and commitment to work just on that. I'm interested in making change possible when the status quo isn't good enough.

Current views

What, in your view, is the way to tackle environmental challenges?

Let's just focus on the climate change issue, though you could apply the same model to other parts of the environment sphere. There's a very simple triangle: policy, finance and technology. To deal with a situation where business as usual cannot be allowed to continue, you have to have some kind of intervention. And with the current financial crisis, we now have a chance to rethink our relationship with money, to realise that it matters how we create wealth as well as how much of it we create.

There's a very simple triangle: policy, finance and technology. To deal with a situation where business as usual cannot be allowed to continue, you have to have some kind of intervention. And with the current financial crisis, we now have a chance to rethink our relationship with money, to realise that it matters how we create wealth as well as how much of it we create.

My view is that that liberal democratic markets, with the right regulatory framework, are the best way to distribute wealth and deliver the public good. But we must admit that we have failed properly to value many of the things that count most – a stable climate, thriving ecosystems, good soil quality and clean water, for example. The best evidence of the physical consequences of climate change shows that we face catastrophic losses over a century and real economic losses within years. So

The best evidence of the physical consequences of climate change shows that we face catastrophic losses over a century and real economic losses within years. So we have no option but to turn our economic system towards solutions to the problem.

we have no option but to turn our economic system towards solutions to the problem.

Who should be driving this?

Leadership, though difficult to define, is critical because we need a big societal shift in a short period of time. It will be very disruptive and difficult, so you have to have people whom others can look up to. People have to feel that if they make sacrifices it will be worthwhile.

Have we got the leaders who could actually do this?

I don't think so. We still choose the wrong type. The model leadership in my view is the working-mother leadership. It's the people who can multitask and juggle a million things and have a deep sense of responsibility and don't need credit for having solved it. And those people don't go into politics, because they don't want to be in it and it's a real problem.

Can others help to find solutions?

Absolutely. When you go to some of these multilateral conferences it's exasperating how slow things are. But you can always be comforted by a conversation you have around the edges with someone who's doing something interesting, getting stuff done – maybe in the NGO movement or maybe in business. And then you've got to figure out better ways of getting them involved, to convince them that it's a good thing they're there.

The ritual still involves heads of state signing agreements, but if you look at who's there, how the ideas are circulating, where they're going in and out – it's more than mere ritual. That's one of the reasons why our market mechanisms are one of the right places to concentrate effort because they can distribute decision-making very widely without a commanding hand. And a commanding hand will not solve the climate change problem – not anywhere, not even in China or in the States.

Do consumers have a role here?

Of course they do, but you can't expect them to change the world by consumption. That will always be marginal. And I know from doing the shopping that there are so many other forces that affect how you behave at the moment of consumption that it's unrealistic to expect consumption to be the solution. But it's a part of the story and you want to make it easy for people to choose the right option. Of course, if you include governments and businesses as consumers you get a different answer.

Aren't consumers very sceptical about green marketing anyway?

It's the wrong part to focus on. It's important, but not the most important place. In many instances we do actually need to take away what has been an important part of the consumer culture all of my adult life, which is choice. There's an assumption that choice is always better. No, it's not. Ask a practical woman. Do you want to choose between these two fridges? One that's environmentally damaging and one that's not? No. I don't want that choice. I want to choose between these two fridges in some other way such as whether it fits in this space in my kitchen, but I don't want the option that one is environmentally damaging and one is not.

So there is a myth about consumer choice here that needs to be confronted. We've tended to approach green consumerism by saying, we should have another choice. Well, that's good. My kids will pick out Fair Trade this or organic that, and the labelling certainly helps, but that's really only a small part of the story. This is a systemic problem that needs a system correction, and you can't do that simply through consumer choice.

You can also intervene with regulation by cutting out choice and saying that only those things that meet these standards can be sold. But in the middle you've got to deal with a business culture that has quarterly reporting. It has institutional investors, and has to behave rationally towards them and also think about their own career paths. Eventually I think that these environment issues will be taken into account by monetarising them. We've got to get these environmental values built in to the way in which we do business.

Look at GE's Ecomagination, where I sit on the board. It's a brilliant initiative and great fun because we get to look at the whole technology pipeline. In essence, it's a business initiative to help to meet customer demand for more energy-efficient products and to drive reliable growth for GE, one that delivers for investors long term. It's really quite exciting.

Is that very influential for other businesses?

Oh yes. Everybody needs validation. Right? You get insecurities at every stage of your life and you need validation from somebody you trust. Nobody knows everything. So they're always looking for somebody else who might know better. Even if I were to disguise the fact that I don't know, I still think that probably somebody knows better than I do so I need to find that person.

People don't like being made fools of, so they mostly like to follow. And they're sort of the same in the business world, too, particularly in financial services, apart from entrepreneurs who are in a different category. So big businesses, structured businesses are mostly followers. They tend to follow someone bigger. Or there's a brand that they recognise and value, or a business leader who they trust. GE has got all that. It's probably the most trusted brand in the world among business decision-makers. It's highly respected for its business processes. It's a hard business. So all those folks who might think environment is a soft issue have nothing to say when GE says it's not.

What sort of discussions do you have with prospective clients, in terms of this issue?

I have a few themes, although of course it depends on what we're promoting at the time. And don't forget we're still a very young, entrepreneurial company and we're learning as we go. There's a certain effort that goes into raising funds, so you're selling a strategy for investors to make returns that meet their expectations. Now, of course, that varies from fund to fund, but in categories like private equity, or our carbon fund – which is extremely unusual and the first of its kind – there's quite a bit of risk involved. Investors are looking for a high rate of return to match that risk, and if they don't see it they won't invest.

There is a structure for that conversation, governed by what you want at the end of it. Then there are different communications that are more to do with selling the ideas, such as wealth worth having, and deploying capital at scale in the low-carbon economy of the future. Or how to build a carbon market, because one of the obvious reasons for having such a market is that it enters business consciousness.

And it really works, although we won't be able to know how successfully for years. It has certainly entered business consciousness that there is a problem that needs fixing and it's a problem because it's so dispersed, it's so huge in scale, that no government can intervene and command a solution on its own. They can only intervene and enable the solution to emerge by setting the right incentives.

What are the right incentives?

They come, not exclusively but largely, through pricing mechanisms – at least in a capitalist economy. Such mechanisms also cross borders much better than regulation or taxation does. And it's a global problem. It's a global language that people understand. So if you say there is a price for emitting carbon and a value associated with not emitting it, it works. Eventually. Once people get the hang of it and once people stop resisting it.

Are there common themes that companies you're trying to help throw up as objections?

Of course. They're mostly to do with timing or threat and fear. So many of the arguments are: we get your point, but not now.

And if not now, then when?

Exactly. So then you have to add that to the conversation. There is a logic behind those arguments. For example, you find many investors saying: until you can show me what price for carbon you're going to be achieving after 2012 I can't rationally make this investment. My investment has to make returns over 20 years, not anything shorter.

You say, there's going to be one. Their answer is, well, that's not good enough. I want to know what it is. Well, you don't know what the interest rates are going to be at this time either, do you? So there are lots of reasons for 'not now'. And then there are alternative fears like, if I do this my competitor will beat me. I have absolutely no time for these arguments at all.

There is an imperative to respond rationally to climate change; that is what the lead scientists tell us. I am only interested in the best ways of responding to that imperative, including ensuring that life is pleasurable and beautiful. Doing nothing isn't rational or interesting. I don't like to hear the words 'you can't'. Lots of people who start businesses or enterprises feel like that.

Getting more personal

Is there anything in particular you're proudest of that you've done in your career?

I'm very, very proud of the work we did in the early days of climate agreements, arguing for them, building up the Alliance of Small Island States coalition and then working with them and getting that agreement. I think the framework I mentioned is often not talked about because everybody talks about Kyoto. We were a very effective group in Kyoto as well, but for me the 1992 agreements in Rio were really important.

This forged lifelong connections with people who have stayed with the debate. Then there are one or two cases that I did as a barrister that I'm proud of – landmark cases. There was a whole cluster of cases around the representation of people harmed by the poor behaviour of companies in South Africa and Namibia. Bringing their cases in the UK, in the English courts for the first time, and winning them, was very satisfying. There's a whole series, such as Connolly against RTZ, and a whole cluster I did with a law firm called Leigh, Day & Co., which did a lot of environment cases. And, of course, founding CCC.

Was your background a big influence on you?

There is an adventurer history in my family. The Camerons went everywhere and my great grandfather was governor of Tasmania as well as the Falkland Islands. That's why my father was born in Australia and there's definitely pioneer blood in there. My mother was English, so I'm half Australian, half English.

My father was a pilot, a wandering aviator. He moved around from place to place, running away and joining the cavalry in Western Australia when he was under-age. Then he flew in pretty much every major conflict from the Second World War onwards. I'm proud of what he did.

I grew up in Lebanon, Singapore and Australia. I travelled on my own. I was definitely driven by an adventurous spirit. But my father was also bloody hard to be the son of and not very responsible. And my mother died relatively young. So there was a contest between a sense of responsibility and duty on the one hand and sense of adventure and risk taking on the other.

And my strong sense of idealism is the reason why so much of what I do in my life is paradoxical. There is a blurring of boundaries all the time.

And my strong sense of idealism is the reason why so much of what I do in my life is paradoxical. There is a blurring of boundaries all the time.

Is there one defining moment that set you on your path, do you think?

If I try to pick one there's no doubt that it's my mother's death, when I was 24. She had motor neurone disease. It was an appalling, appalling illness to be a part of, to look after. And she was a very lovely woman, very beautiful, kind and patient. It was just awful to watch the decline and sense the injustice of it all. So that has engendered a really strong commitment to family which is central to my life. There's no doubt that my mother's death and my marriage have been defining moments.

What keeps you grounded?

My wife and my children. My wife has been a huge help to me. And she figured out how to be successful as a parent as well as an individual because she's now a QC and a judge. It's quite an achievement to have done that. Finding a balance, over and again as things change, once the basic needs for life are met ... that's critical. Ultimately though, it is, of course, love that counts.

3

....

Paul Dickinson

Paul Dickinson is CEO of the Carbon Disclosure Project, which he co-founded in 2000, with the aim of engaging the investment and corporate communities to work together to tackle the issues of climate change. The CDP is an independent not-for-profit organisation which acts as an intermediary between shareholders and corporations on all climate change-related issues, providing primary climate change data from the world's largest corporations to the global marketplace.

The data is obtained from responses to CDP's annual Information Request, sent on behalf of institutional investors and purchasing organisations. Leading a small team, Paul has built up a global collaboration of over 385 of the world's largest institutional investors, holding over $57 trillion in assets under management.

Paul is also co-founder and Chair of EyeNetwork – a video-conferencing system which offers corporations the ability to meet clients globally, from the comfort of their own office. He has conducted extensive research into how increased use of video-conferencing can be incorporated into business strategy to make a considerable reduction in corporate emissions generated through travel.

In addition, he is a member of the Environmental Research Group of the UK Faculty and Institute of Actuaries.

Prior to founding CDP, Paul co-founded and built a corporate communications company, Rufus Leonard, into a multi-million turnover company, working with clients such as Shell and the Prudential. He is also an established author and expert on business development, corporate branding and the role the corporate community can play in bringing about positive change. His book, Beautiful Corporations, was published in 2000.

The professional journey

Let's start by looking at the Carbon Disclosure Project (CDP). Where did the idea come from, because there doesn't seem to have been anything like it before?

I don't think so, no. The original genesis of the idea for this organisation stemmed from discussions I was having with our founding chair, Tessa Tennant. I had put it to her that climate change was a very serious problem and it was going to become more so. This was in the summer of the year 2000.

We realised that the largest fund managers in effect control the world's largest companies – or that they could exercise control if they wanted to – and that what investors needed then, and what they still need, is information to help them to develop a rational response to the risks and opportunities that companies face from climate change. So in 2001 we set about looking at how those investors could best collaborate in terms of asking the corporations that they own to provide information on these risks and opportunities and specifically to give indications of their greenhouse gas emissions. And that is what we have been doing ever since. The CDP now represents 385 institutional investors with $57 trillion in assets under management.

That is a very big number and so now has the attention of the world. We were delighted that a figure as distinguished as Madeleine Albright, the former US Secretary of State, came forward to chair our first launch event in March 2003 in New York. At the time she was a director of the New York Exchange and was quoted in the *Financial Times* that day as saying that our business is to help investors to vote with their money. Well, we now have 57 000 million votes in terms of companies' activities.

But when you started it can't have been so straightforward. What was the reaction, for example, of that first company you contacted or the first fund manager?

Well, many of the first fund managers said, who on earth are you people and what makes you think we're going to sign this piece of paper? But in the end the reason why 35 institutions put their names to the first Carbon Disclosure Project was because they'd worked with us on the development of the documentation and we had followed their advice.

So you did a lot of consultation before you set it up?

Yes, we did. And we also had some amazing friends. Perhaps the most notable was Lord Adair Turner who, on his own authority, brought Merrill

Lynch as the first major US signatory to the project back in 2002. People looked at that and said, well, Merrill Lynch is part of this so it can't be all that bad. And a few other leaders like UBS, Credit Suisse, Munich Re and Swiss Re all put their name to it too. I think Legal & General was our very first signatory. That band of pioneers led a group that has doubled in size almost every year.

Did you feel at first as if you were a voice in the wilderness?

Our first-ever documentation didn't actually say that climate change was necessarily real, but what it did make clear was that actions in response to the *perception* of climate change were real. So even if you couldn't prove climate change was real, you could prove that policy responses to climate change were real. There was significant debate about the EU emissions trading scheme at that time, while the Kyoto Protocol was a gathering force. It was actually intriguing to remember what Secretary Albright said at our New York launch. She said that the Kyoto Protocol was negotiated under her supervision and the only reason we had an emissions trading scheme in Europe was because we in the United States insisted on it – and now the US wasn't part of Kyoto! And she was almost shaking with anger when she said that.

So we did start off softly, softly. We felt that it was reasonable to say that climate change was an active phenomenon in the world and that it was growing in importance. But it was a while before we felt we really had a kind of a mandate to be more demanding of the responding corporations. However, I think it's probably fair to say that each year we've tried to improve the process and to get closer to the nub of the problem and we do see the naysayers falling by the wayside.

You mean the sort of people who say that climate change doesn't exist?

Yes, the ones who say we can't do anything about it or it's too expensive to do anything about it or it's hopeless to do anything about it. They say it's almost an act of egotism to believe you can do anything to stop climate change. It's too late. We should spend the money, and I never know where this money comes from, but we should spend the money stopping HIV or something. There are a thousand ways to interfere with action taken in defence of the obvious.

Tell us a bit about your career and how you got to be here.

Well, I've always been interested in politics, but I had never found any particular cause that was sufficiently dramatic to shake me out of the private sector. After school the first job I did was in retail. I'd wanted to work in the John Lewis Partnership because it struck me as an interesting business, being owned by its staff. I was turned down by them but accepted by Harrods so I spent three and a half years training there. It was initially rather junior training, but I then had the opportunity to enter the graduate course when I was 19 and I completed that by the time I was 21.

I then left Harrods and went and worked in various odd jobs in areas like market research and the fashion industry. For instance, I was secretary for the English designer Katherine Hamnett. That was very interesting. She had famously been photographed with the UK Prime Minister, Margaret Thatcher, at Downing Street in 1983 wearing a T-shirt protesting against basing US Pershing missiles in the UK. It said '58% don't want Pershing' and it became the most used press photo in the world that year.

I thought it was quite interesting the way that there was a convergence of wealth creation and political sloganeering. I had by this time won a place at university to study politics, but at the same time I was working at an annual report design company. And I did actually leave in the first term of my politics degree because it struck me that what we call politics, the way the world is being run, was much more in the hands of the corporations I was working with as a consultant than it was in the historical traditions of the legislatures of the world and the parliaments. So I became involved in founding and building up a business over the next 10 years, which was very educative.

Was this Rufus Leonard?

That's correct. I co-founded it.

What was the rationale behind founding it?

Well, because I felt that there was something about communications that was intrinsic to politics, I suppose, and also I had worked in the design industry at Wolff Olins, which was a great company. I'd learned a lot there about this notion of corporate identity and I'd been particularly interested in the idea of the corporate citizen. This culminated, in fact, in a book I wrote which was published in 2000 by Financial Times/Prentice Hall and called *Beautiful Corporations*. There was a thesis in it about sustainability and product marketing which is an area I built up over my 10 years at Rufus Leonard. And this argued that products and services were increasingly the same, but the real opportunity to differentiate was not based on the quality of your advertising or marketing, which is the shallowest differentiator, but on the character of your corporation – what you do and how you do it.

The other thing to mention is that Rufus Leonard had got very much into electronic media quite early on and developing electronic media products. So by the time the internet came along in 1995 we were very well positioned and made a lot of money out of that. But I was looking for the next big thing. I was in a research role by that time and it struck me that corporate sustainability and responsibility were going to be pivotal.

What happened then?

Well, I went to do what was a new MSc degree at the University of Bath in responsibility and business practice. I met a chap there in 1997 called Stephan Harding who is a brilliant ecologist, and an assistant and friend of James Lovelock. By the way, he has written a wonderful book called *Animate Earth*.

Anyway, in 1997 Stephan said to me that Kyoto's coming up and it's our last chance. I said to him what people say to me now: facetious comments like, so what if Bangladesh floods, it's always been too cold here! To which he replied, well, look out because it's going to be freezing here, the Gulf Stream will shut off and we haven't got any snow ploughs. And somehow or other he kind of got under my radar. Since then I've been looking into what's going to be happening and is happening already in Bangladesh and I regret the facetiousness of my joke, but I didn't actually realise at that time how serious it was and is.

But the key moment for me was really in 1999. I'd come into a small amount of money and so I took some time off and started looking at what I wanted to do with my career because I felt that I needed to get more directly engaged with these issues. And I stuck up on my wall a graph from a document from the Clinton administration called 'The Kyoto Protocol and the President's policies to address climate change'. It's the famous graph of CO_2 emissions versus temperature changes over 150 000 years where you see the two moving in lockstep and then you see the CO_2 shoot up dramatically. And you know that the temperature must, of course, follow. After having that stuck on my wall for a few weeks I then took a decision in early 2000 that I was going to spend the rest of my life working on climate change and I've stuck to that ever since.

That was quite a decision.

Well, it decided me really. I think that if you immerse yourself in the statistics for any length of time and you look at the severity of the warnings from the scientists – this is my personal opinion, I'm not speaking for my organisation here – this is a war. It's a war against catastrophe and the good news is that we're not being shot at and we can live a civil kind of existence. But it would be an enormous mistake to underestimate the severity of the situation if climate change starts to occur at a speed that we cannot retard in any useful way. The Earth system is not necessarily characterised entirely by gradual changes. The history of the Earth system shows there have been quite dramatic changes before.

And say there is a release of methane from permafrost, increased heat from a reduced albedo effect from the white ice at the North and South Poles, and a dying back of the Amazon rainforest. In combination, all these impacts could cause the Earth system to change dramatically. The impact on food productivity could be absolutely breathtaking, spectacular and in plain terms, catastrophic. In those circumstances any number of people could be killed, and it would somewhat dwarf all previous wars put together. So I think in response to such a circumstance it's not unreasonable to dedicate oneself to the absolutely supreme task of protecting this rather ill-advised generation from – I wish I could use less loaded language – well, slaughtering their children.

But why this organisation? You could have easily started up a communications consultancy, say, or a lobbying group.

Let's go back to what corporations are. They are much more mysterious, I think, than we realise. The way to look at it is that they are not conscious entities but are represented by some traditions like a certificate of incorporation. That is probably the defining legal document that lies at the heart of the corporation. And it expresses the legal mission for the corporation to maximise return to shareholders as the sole object of the corporation. Now, under that particular legal framework, an organisation begins to function and very often on a larger and larger and larger scale. It's not conscious, but it has a kind of life.

Let's take, for example, the Coca-Cola Corporation. It's 120 years old, it's bigger now than it's ever been before, it's stronger now than it's ever been before and it's one of thousands of large corporations that operate throughout the world. These corporations are creations of humans and they are actually owned by us. We own them, we work at them, we buy their products. I've probably got Coca-Cola shares through my insurance policies and my investments and my pension. And so I'm intimately involved with that company and all the other thousands of companies in so many different ways.

Global investors and global corporations are perhaps best capable of responding rationally to a global problem like climate change, whereas national governments display a kind of responsibility-deficit and bicker in a rather unhelpful way about it, So what we've done, rather than start a communications consultancy, is to ask if it's possible to develop a system whereby all the world's largest investors will sign the same piece of paper.

We started it on a small scale and it's got bigger and bigger and bigger. It's a controlled process. I believe we're reasonably well-trusted around the world because we deliver on what we say we will do. And that has given us authority in this controlled process wherein capital can speak to corporations and can require certain behaviours. And that process can continue to serve as an increasingly important response to climate change. So I think what we've been trying to do is enact an Italian phrase: 'it's the union that makes the force'.

So are you the voice of the shareholders for this in a way?

I think that's a fair comment. We've put together a voice that they are happy to have. We've done this in discussion with them. And now a total of 385 shareholders have decided to put their names to that document to give them a collective voice. By the way, it's not just shareholders any more. We have colleagues now working with 29 of the world's largest corporations, sending the same questions to their suppliers.

Wal-Mart led the way here when it said in 2007 that it was sending our Carbon Disclosure Project questions to its suppliers. Three weeks later, in London, Sir Terry Leahy of Tesco announced that he was sending the questions to his suppliers. Now we have Carrefour, Pepsi-Cola, Dell, Hewlett-Packard, Nestlé, Procter & Gamble, Unilever and a host of others all sending our questions to their suppliers. So we're increasingly capturing the authority of shareholders and the authority of purchasing organisations and aggregating that together into a single unified global process.

And has there been a measurable outcome since you started?

Sure. The primary deliverable for us has been that more than 1500 of the world's largest corporations report on their responses to climate change, their greenhouse gas emissions and the risks and opportunities they face through our website – and that's by far the largest registry of greenhouse gas emissions in the world. It's all free, everyone can download these reports and the capital markets across the world buy and sell based upon that data. Banks consider loans based upon those responses. Insurance companies consider who they want to insure based on those responses. Governments and academics pore over them, working out the most cost-effective policies for responding to climate change.

So I think that the engagement of so many corporations is particularly valuable. There is a story from Wal-Mart which illustrates the impact. When it originally responded to the Carbon Disclosure Project, its relevant operative put together the figures and sent them off to the legal department. The legal department asked, what's the margin of error here? And he said, oh, I don't know, 10%, 20% maybe. And they said, look, you can't give our shareholders a figure with that kind of margin of error. It has to be within 5% accuracy. So he had to recalculate with increased accuracy.

The point being that this is a formal legal communication from shareholders to corporations. I find it outrageous that there are still many large corporations which don't answer these questions. I don't know what on earth they've got to hide, but the ones that do answer are doing something that Adair Turner describes brilliantly: they're measuring, and what gets measured gets managed.

Do you think that there should be some sort of regulatory framework whereby companies have to report on their emissions?

Yes, absolutely.

Because they don't have to do it, do they?

In terms of reporting, under the European Union (EU) emissions trading scheme since 2005, I believe more than 11 000 installations in the EU have had to report their emissions. Clearly, as the Carbon Disclosure Project, we'd be in favour of all legislation in all the countries of the world that suggested that corporations have to report their greenhouse gas emissions. There's a lot of other data in the Carbon Disclosure Project responses that legislation will probably in due course require.

We've operated globally since we started and there are certain countries that seem to be catching up, and that's a good thing. We are very much in favour of that. Speaking as what you might call a climate change worker I am absolutely convinced, along with people like former President Bill Clinton, Angela Merkel of Germany, Lord Stern in the United Kingdom and numerous others that it is not acceptable for there to be anything but an absolutely dramatic reduction in the production of CO_2 and its equivalent gases. That's a huge and urgent requirement for the world and we support all efforts in that direction.

Current views

How do you define sustainability generally?

Well, there are two definitions of sustainability. There's the one from the Brundtland Report and my own. The Brundtland Report says sustainable development is providing for the needs of people in the present without compromising the ability of future generations to meet their own needs. But it often seems as if sustainable development is a dustbin for those contemporary world problems which can't be resolved within the competence of the political system. There's this sort of 'difficult cupboard' where things can be put away.

Of course, there are tremendous challenges for modern governments operating nationally in a world increasingly defined by international or global problems and where national governments are under-performers. There also appears to be a systemic constriction of debate brought on by self-regulating and somewhat unrestricted commerce. A couple of examples of that include the massive investment in coal-fired electricity generation across the world at the moment and the huge investment in relatively inefficient unconventional oil recovery. There is massive airport expansion, the volumes of new roads being built in China and India and so on.

The examples of unsustainable expansion of industry without the emissions being captured are too numerous to mention at the moment. So back to your point: what is sustainable development? You could write several books on the meaning of it, but if you wanted to simplify it I would say that it's behaviour that would be described as not suicidal.

We're in the early stages, geologically speaking, of a kind of explosion. The CO_2 density in the atmosphere is outside of the range of the last 500 000 years, perhaps many millions of years. We're in entirely uncharted areas in terms of the way the Earth system operates and it's extremely frightening.

When you meet heads of companies don't they, in general, have a very short-term agenda geared to their quarterly results?

Well, if the heads of companies are serving for three or five years or something, are they really the heads of the companies? Maybe the companies don't have heads.

So how does a company like Coke last 120 years?

By the aggregation of thousands of processes combined with people's ingenuity and intelligence applied to the development of the Coca-Cola system. And sector-wide responses to climate change may be what becomes very interesting. Great companies like Cisco, British Telecom and Vodafone need to help to dematerialise our economies. A founder of the Carbon Disclosure Project, a very distinguished Dutch businessman called Eckart Wintzen, who unfortunately died in March 2008 at the relatively young age of 68, told me a story a while ago about how his 16-year-old daughter wanted to chat up some boy at the other side of her classroom. He said, five years ago she would have gone to the shops and got fancy clothes flown over from China or wherever with the associated emissions, but instead she was sending him flirtatious text messages with effectively zero emissions. The objective was achieved either way, though!

Is this what you mean by dematerialise?

Exactly. And there are certain activities which simply can't grow and others that must grow. The great mistake is to believe that, as a result of climate change, money is going to have to disappear off into space or there'll be unemployment. No. If you want employment, if you want growth, you want to invest in, and back, the solutions to the problem and not be the creator of it.

Because there are great opportunities?

Yes. And in the end the true people running companies, the real bosses who are there today and will be there tomorrow, are the consumers. And they will simply not invest ever larger amounts of their money endangering their children. It is absolutely inevitable that finding solutions to the problems will become the defining creator of market share and profitability in the twenty-first century. The race is on and it's absolutely unavoidable. I often say to business audiences that climate change is like the internet. It arrives one day and gets bigger every year; it never goes away and you have to learn to make money from it or you're in trouble.

The beautiful thing about business is that it doesn't have any ideology except to make money. If you can demonstrate that you make more money by saving the world, then businesses will save the world really quickly. And so all we have to do is wake up the consumer to stop putting money into their own endangerment. And that shouldn't be very difficult.

The beautiful thing about business is that it doesn't have any ideology except to make money. If you can demonstrate that you make more money by saving the world, then businesses will save the world really quickly. And so all we have to do is wake up the consumer to stop putting money into their own endangerment. And that shouldn't be very difficult.

So it comes down to the consumer?

In the end, yes. If turkeys carry on voting for Christmas, in the end Christmas will come and they will get cooked. However, if turkeys stop voting for Christmas and vote instead for the Turkey Liberation Front, they'll run free and happy forever!

Do you think, though, that consumers are very sceptical of anyone – people or companies – who profess their greenness?

People use peculiarly imprecise clichés like 'make a difference', 'it's good to be green', 'be environmentally friendly', and I think maybe this is a way of doing a little dance with a theme without having to get one's hands dirty. The reality of working on climate change is that one looks at graphs of CO_2 density against temperature changes over hundreds of thousands of years and one begins to realise that there is a serious risk of an abrupt climate change event that could wipe an awful lot of people out. And I mean an awful lot.

So you're denied the easy simplicities on whether plastic bags in supermarkets are a good or a bad thing. Instead, one finds oneself challenged at every corner. Your flights on holiday, your food flown in, your home heating, your computers being left on, what you buy, whom you fund – it's a difficult philosophical engagement to come to terms with and people don't particularly want to do that, so they dabble with green and keep it trite and then they can drop it just as quickly as they've adopted it.

Don't people also grumble at the idea of 'green' taxes as just a way of getting more of our money?

Do people say Gucci just wants more money from us? Do people say Mercedes just wants more money? Does Lamborghini just want more money from us? Does Coca-Cola just want more money from us for coloured water? Yes. But we don't mind because we're not cross with them. We like them. And who we like gets our money. I do agree that there'll be a thousand backlashes on the road to salvation.

I personally have some business interests in the video-conferencing industry. As oil prices rise, and as business travel becomes less and less acceptable, our business just makes more and more money. There's more than one way something can be done and as things change, new customers are just sitting there waiting to be snapped up. You can even say that all this greenwashing confusion creates opportunities for serious, honourable, authentic companies to come in and say, look, this is all a sham, so we are actually going to do the right thing and win customers on that basis.

Do you think companies should be offered incentives: the carrot instead of the stick? So rather than tell them you must do this, the regulations say this, is there some way you can persuade companies?

I happen to know of a mobile phone company which generates 200 times the profit per tonne of carbon dioxide in comparison to a certain airline. I met its chief executive last year and asked him, why doesn't the government not just tax air fuel, but also remove all taxation from information and communication technology? That would go a long way to solving the problem and would make these very rich information and communication technology companies a lot richer. Currently there's no tax on air fuel. Relatively speaking, we're all subsidising the airlines to fly half-empty planes around the world, thereby threatening the integrity of the biosphere on which we all depend.

So there are lots of examples of where you could tax something bad to encourage something good. There are significant taxes on tobacco because it's very widely perceived, in the more developed world, as not a terribly good thing. But you can also offer incentives. There are feed-in tariffs for renewable generation, subsidies for low-carbon solutions, no congestion charge for the Toyota Prius and so on.

What sort of tips would you offer a company which knows it needs to address this but is avoiding the issue?

I would say try to imagine when email came along, try to imagine when telephones came along, when plastics came along, try to imagine when democracy came along, try to imagine when equal votes for women came along, try to imagine when slavery was abolished. You can say that you don't like these things because you don't believe women should have the vote, that you're in favour of slavery and that you don't like telephones – but you're just going to get bowled over by the great waves of progress.

It is unthinkable that humans won't respond to the challenge of climate change. They will. If you fail to ensure that your business marches along with the rest of the world towards safety you will be flattened or ignored and it is your job to attend to this. If you don't, you'll go bust.

Just as I wouldn't encourage anyone to go into a new financial year without a business plan or a budget, I wouldn't encourage them to go into the new year without paying very close attention to climate change.

Do you think that during a financial downturn it is harder to get companies to listen to your message about the urgency of dealing with climate change?

The financial downturn is proof that we need to change, and bring into action the next great phase in our technology and society. The best way out of the downturn is to reduce waste, and to sell the technology of tomorrow. Have fuel-efficient car sales suffered in the financial downturn? No, they sell better. That is the lesson.

Are you optimistic?

Yes. I remember reading at the end of Winston Churchill's book about the Second World War, US President Roosevelt asked what the war should be called, because it didn't really have a name. And Churchill answered, without a moment's hesitation, the entirely avoidable war. An avoidable war *is easy to avoid*. And it's exactly the same with climate change. It's perfectly possible for this species, with our incredible technology and organisation, to protect our children. I know that everybody wants to protect their children. I'm optimistic, therefore, that we will protect them. But you could be forgiven for feeling pretty nervous if you looked at the way the land lies at the moment. There's going to be a lot of change. There must be.

Do you see an end point for your organisation? Does there come a point when you're no longer needed?

Well, when the risk of accelerating or abrupt climate change has diminished to the statistically irrelevant I think I and other colleagues will go back to the private sector and concentrate on making money, just as if a war was over and we had been demobbed from the army. But it looks like action stations at the moment.

Where do you see us in five years' time in terms of progress?

Well, there is a little balloon that goes up from an atoll in the Pacific that measures the CO_2 density in the atmosphere, and that balloon has been showing an increase in density for every year since its records began in the 1950s. CO_2 concentration in the atmosphere will continue for the next decade or so. Or more. And that is going to attract more and more heat which will threaten accelerating climate change and that is serious. I would summarise, in answer to your question, that in five years we – and I mean society, citizens, corporations, investors, the governments and the non-governmental organisations – will all start knuckling down to this most phenomenal challenge. We haven't even started yet.

What about people who say technology will solve the problem?

Well, they're right. But I wouldn't go thinking that technology is necessarily cheap or easy. For example, probably the most promising technology is carbon capture and storage – pumping CO_2 underground. There is, however, no large-scale demonstration of that anywhere in the world at the moment. So retro-fitting the entire world's power stations wouldn't seem like something for today, tomorrow or the week after.

Getting more personal

What drives you?

Well, I've never seen anything like this before. I basically was just like everybody else – a happy-go-lucky person. I didn't really worry too much about anything, I worked for private business all my life up until 2000. So I don't think I can hold myself up as any kind of paragon of virtue. If I have one particular capability – which amazingly seems to be denied to most other people I meet – it's that I can understand a simple graph!

But most people wouldn't have gone as far as setting up something like CDP, which must have been hard work.

Everyone here could earn more working anywhere else. They've also seen it the same way I see it: that we're in a tough spot and this is no time to do anything but focus on trying as hard as possible to ring the alarm.

But you're doing it in a very business-effective way.

Well, there's a nice phrase from Lovelock where he said that we are so intrinsically part of the technosphere that a reactionary back-to-nature campaign would be like diving off an ocean liner mid-Atlantic, and swimming the rest of the journey in glorious independence of the technology that had taken you to that particular point. We cannot pretend the modern world hasn't happened. I don't think I'd want to. I think the application of good technology is going to be very, very helpful. But people are going to have to think a bit more about how to deal with this and they're going to have to think quite hard and they're going to have to think quite often. It's frightening, but it's exciting.

Is there any one thing you're proudest of in your career so far?

Pride comes before a fall, isn't that what they say? But I think it's really touching for me that Chancellor Merkel, as chair of the G8, made a statement in support of the work of this organization; that people like Bill Clinton and Al Gore give up their time to talk at our events, or that the

Swedish prime minister hosts events for us; and that pretty much all the world's largest investors, from Goldman Sachs to Mitsubishi UFJ, will put their name to what we're doing, will write reports with us and will help to accelerate this. And then there is the kindness, generosity and intelligence of the staff who work here.

How many staff do you have?

There are 27 full-time people in this organisation and we have partner organisations all over the world. And many volunteers.

Finally, was there a defining moment in your life? Was it seeing that graph on CO_2 emissions vs temperature change?

Yes, the graph is what got me into this. There would appear to be absolutely incontrovertible evidence. Nobody, believe me, nobody, contests the fact that increasing concentrations of CO_2 attract more heat. The Earth is also warming and that warming is accelerating. That's all you need to know. And there is no plan at all to deal with it as far as we can gather on any kind of scale except for the Kyoto Protocol, which is a far from perfect instrument.

The UK government's former chief scientist, Sir David King, said it would be a mistake not to believe we are in difficulties. A former chairman of Shell said that without carbon capture and storage he sees very little hope for our species. I don't know why more people aren't really worried about this and focusing on it. I promise you they will be. Because it's incredibly irresponsible to do anything but.

I don't know why more people aren't really worried about this and focusing on it. I promise you they will be. Because it's incredibly irresponsible to do anything but.

4

....

John Elkington

John Elkington is a Founding Partner and Director of Volans, a business launched in April 2008. It aims to find, explore, advise on and build innovative scalable solutions to the great global divides that overshadow our future. A co-founder of SustainAbility in 1987 (Chair from 1995 to 2005), John is seen as a world authority on corporate responsibility and sustainable development. In 2004, Business Week *described him as 'a dean of the corporate responsibility movement for three decades', and in 2008, the* Evening Standard *named him among the '1000 Most Influential People' in London, describing him as 'a true green business guru', and as 'an evangelist for corporate social and environmental responsibility long before it was fashionable.'*

John has authored or co-authored 17 books, including 1988's million-selling Green Consumer Guide *and* Cannibals with Forks: The Triple Bottom Line of 21st Century Business *(1997), and has written or co-written some 40 published reports. His latest book,* The Power of Unreasonable People: How Social Entrepreneurs Create Markets That Change the World, *was co-authored with Pamela Hartigan, and published by Harvard Business School Press in February, 2008. Through SustainAbility and Volans, he has been working with The Skoll Foundation on a $1 million, 3-year field-building program in relation to social entrepreneurship.*

Since 1974, he has undertaken consultancy work for a wide range of national and international government and non-governmental agencies, including Greenpeace International, USAID, WRI and WWF. He has visited hundreds of companies world wide and worked for corporate clients such as Anglian Water, ASG, Astra, BAA, BP, BP Chemicals, British Airways, British Airways Holidays, British Telecom, Danone, Dow Europe, the Ford Motor Company, GlaxoSmith-Kline, IBM, a range of ICI companies, Nissan, Novo Nordisk and Shell.

John is a visiting professor at the Doughty Centre for Corporate Responsibility, Cranfield School of Management. He also chairs The Environment Foundation and the Aflatoun Impact and Policy Analysis Steering Group, and sits on boards for the Global Reporting Initiative (GRI), SustainAbility and Volans, and advisory boards for organisations like the Dow Jones Sustainability Indexes, EcoVadis, Zouk Ventures, the Cleantech Innovation Council, Physic Ventures, LP, 2degrees, and Instituto Ethos, Brazil. He was chairman of the Export Credits Guarantee Department's Advisory Council for several years and is a member of the WWF Council of Ambassadors, the Evian Group Brain Trust and the United Nations

Global Compact Cities Programme (UNGCCP) International Advisory Council. He was a faculty member of the World Economic Forum between 2002 and 2008. In 2008, he picked up the Fast Company *'Social Capitalist' Award for Sustain-Ability's efforts in related fields.*

John has written hundreds of articles for newspapers, magazines and journals, and was Editor of Biotechnology Bulletin *from 1982 to 1995, producing over 170 issues. He has also been a regular contributor to* New Scientist *on environmental, energy and development issues (1975–78),* Tomorrow *magazine (1995–2000) and the* Guardian *(1981–2001). He contributes regular columns to* Nikkei Ecology *in Japan,* chinadialogue *in China, Brazil's* Época Negócios, *and* Director *magazine in the UK.*

For a full list of his achievements, see www.johnelkington.com

The professional journey

What would you say you are best known for?

Insofar as I'm known for anything, I suppose I am known as one of a very small group of people who early on, in the mid-1970s, became interested in the realm of business and markets. This was not about treating business like some sort of Gulliver, strapping it down with lots of rules and regulations. It was more about how you could inspire business, how you could motivate and incentivise business to become creative rather than defensive about issues like the environment.

In 1978, with a couple of other people, one of whom was Max Nicholson, who co-founded the World Wildlife Fund and many, many other organisations, we set up an organisation called Environmental Data Services or ENDS. So I ran that for five years. I visited probably about 250 to 300 companies around the world in that five-year period, trying to get a sense of how they saw the environmental challenge. It was bought subsequently by the publishing company Haymarket and has recently celebrated its 30th anniversary

What prompted you to go down that route?

To some extent it goes back to my *New Scientist* era, to which I had contributed for a number of years. I had started to visit companies like BP, which was exploring for and developing oil and gas in Alaska. At the time BP was, in a sense, pioneering because it was being forced to some degree to move into areas like environmental impact assessment and environmental auditing. I then started to look through the same lens at companies like British Gas, which was doing a lot of work in environmental impact assessment, and English China Clays, which was making huge holes in the British South West landscape. Ironically, the Eden Project, with its biomes creating eco-climates, is now occupying one of the clay pits in which I walked around, I think, in 1976.

But actually my interest in what business can do goes way deeper and way earlier than that. I think back to when I was away at prep school in the late 1950s/early 1960s, and I used to write off to aircraft manufacturers because I loved getting their catalogues. I just liked aircraft and aviation – my father was a pilot. And reading those publications when I must have been 9, 10, 11, that sort of age, helped me to build my interest in business.

But I didn't really think of doing anything about it until the *New Scientist* period. The writing that I did for the publication then, over four or five years, led to me being invited by Max and David Layton to set up ENDS. And then, once I started visiting companies, I found it fascinating because it's like lion-taming. Those companies, certainly at that stage, had absolutely zero interest in talking to what they saw as troublemakers, environmentalists – whatever we called ourselves.

It was literally nine months before we got through the door of the first company. And this was despite the fact that ENDS had a parent company at that stage, Incomes Data Services, which had a profoundly respected role in industrial relations. So you would have thought we would have been seen to be a little bit more legitimate. But the first door that I got through, I think, was a chemical company called Albright & Wilson. And then very quickly, within 18 months of having finally got through the first door and having by then visited well over 100 companies around the world, I was asked to help BP with its first written environmental policy statement. And ditto with ICI.

And earlier I had worked for organisations like the United Nations doing some of the very early environmental impact assessments on dams, refineries and things like that in such countries as Egypt. This was where the most interesting interface between business and the environment was to be found at the time.

So what did ENDS actually do?

Well, at that stage we published every fortnight, although it's now monthly, and there are various other products. I edited what was called the *ENDS Report* for five years about all of the market-shaping trends concerning politics, regulation, economics, technology, NGO activity and so on. But what I particularly specialised in, and found most interesting, was company profiles. And it wasn't easy. Again, even when you got through the front door, companies were very particular about what you would say about them. And one of the things on which I always insisted was that where we published a profile it would always be cleared with the company beforehand. Not that they would be able to remove lots of material, although some certainly tried.

When you were asked by companies like BP and ICI to help with an environmental policy statement, did they do it because of external pressures or because people like you had got them listening to the arguments?

Outside pressure, almost exclusively at that stage. What you found with these very big companies was that they tended to have a reflexive response to strategies in health and safety, in the environment, or in whatever areas they were feeling the pressure. So at times they would set up a dedicated unit and then they'd think, ah, well, this actually ought to be distributed out to the business units, and then they would find that it didn't always work terribly well and there were elements that needed to be re-concentrated – so it would be almost like an accordion effect.

But what really caught companies' attention was when US President Nixon set up the Environmental Protection Agency in 1970 and suddenly the landscape became a regulated landscape, with the potential for a lot more regulation. In BP's case, because it was an outsider playing in the highly controversial Alaskan oil game, it was probably a bit more sensitive than some of the American oil companies at that stage to community and activist pressure.

Through one of BP's senior people on the health, safety and environmental side, I very quickly met people at board level. This wasn't usual. It was probably about seven or eight years later that it became standard to meet board-level people. At that early stage it was still primarily a set of reflexive activities that were meant to defend the companies' flanks against what were seen as nuisance attacks.

So were these companies moving beyond simply 'greenwashing'?

No, I think there is always greenwash. Companies are like people. We always tend to mythologise a bit and paint a better picture of some aspects of what we do and who we are. Companies do that too. I think greenwashing began to be a real problem when the agenda accelerated and went off in unexpected directions, which left companies feeling exposed. If you had left companies themselves to decide what they said or how they presented themselves they would not have been quite as egregiously idiotic. But marketing and advertising agencies were briefed, in a sense, to fend off some of the problems of the late 1980s, such as the ozone depletion issue and the lead in petrol issue. So you would get ads like the ones that appeared in this country where one car manufacturer was claiming that if you used unleaded petrol you could save the ozone layer.

I think greenwashing began to be a real problem when the agenda accelerated and went off in unexpected directions, which left companies feeling exposed. If you had left companies themselves to decide what they said or how they presented themselves they would not have been quite as egregiously idiotic.

Some of that was just scientific illiteracy, but some of it was more wilful. There were many CEOs who, because they felt it was expected of them, gave their vision which others helped them to construct and made promises and set targets when they had no way of knowing whether those targets were reachable. And very often they weren't because a recession or other problems came along.

So the greenwashing is always there. In reality it's always a part of business. It's something that we should always be aware of, but, having said that, it has worried me a lot less than it has a lot of leading activists for the obvious reason that, for them, it's a problem if companies can almost create this lubricant effect through greenwashing, slithering past the roadblocks that activists try to erect against them. Whereas I feel that if you at least get people in companies talking about some of these issues, it encourages them to figure out what they really think about them.

What did you do after leaving ENDS in 1983?

Well, before that, in 1981 I started to edit *Biotechnology Bulletin* because by that stage I was also interested in bioscience and biotechnology. I had done a report with ENDS for the UK Department of Environment called *Pollution 1990* which, I think, was published in 1980. This was helping the Department to think through longer-term technology and market trends. And one of the things I got quite excited about through doing that work was biotechnology. So out of the blue, and partly because of the writing I was doing for *New Scientist* and *The Guardian* newspaper, I was asked to create and edit the Bulletin. I did that for about 15 years.

That again involved visiting several hundred companies around the world which were, in one way or another, into bioscience and biotechnology. It was more or less a hobby. I tended to do it in the evenings and weekends. And from that came my book, *The Gene Factory*, in 1985. But I was also writing a number of other books at the same time. There was one on solar energy, *Sun Traps*, and another called *The Poisoned Womb*, which was about human reproduction in a polluted world.

Meanwhile, in 1983 I also joined an organisation as a trustee/director called the Earthlife Foundation. It was an odd hybrid combination of property development – including trying to develop an early eco-science park in the Docklands – and environmental projects. So, for example, one of the directors made films about rainforests, with a major rainforest conservation project being developed in Cameroon. We tried to look at how you could sensibly and sustainably exploit the resources of the rainforest to put revenue back into the pockets of people who at that time were simply being exploited or nudged aside.

Earthlife was a pretty visionary organisation. However, it eventually imploded because of financing problems. When I look back at that, I see it almost like a neutron star that blew up and then seeded the universe with the seeds of life and new life forms.

In what way?

Well, out of that came SustainAbility, among other things. I had raised funds for two projects at Earthlife. One was almost like an encyclopaedia of the green economy, called *Green Pages*. I'd raised money to do it from the

European Union, as well as from BP, ICI, the old Central Electricity Generating Board, and others. But all that money had gone into the black hole at the heart of Earthlife and been swallowed up.

That must have been a difficult experience.

Well, it wasn't the high point in my life and I thought, well, what do I do? Do I simply say, put it down to experience, the money's gone? Happily, in the meantime, a young woman, Julia Hailes, had joined me to work on *Green Pages*. The reason why she wanted to work with me primarily, I think, was that in our first conversation we talked about the idea of a *Green Consumer Guide*, which was another idea I had been toying with. And she was very excited about that.

She had just walked through the door – and we ended up setting up SustainAbility together. One of the glories about this area is that people do that. I remember about 10 years ago, when I was in Australia, I was asked, what is your most important strategic tool? And I said, our sofa. And that's true. Conversation is what guides us, and the stimulus and pleasure of being with interesting people. It is where ideas surface and where testing of those ideas is done. It's no accident that the first two bits of furniture we got here at Volans were sofas.

It sounds as though in terms of your spreading your ideas, people have come to you just as much as you put yourself out there?

It's both. And when I look back at myself I see somebody who was paralytically shy in some strange ways and yet now I speak to many thousands of people every year and actually quite enjoy it. I don't get nervous before doing it in the way that I once would have done, and far prefer now to get into the act of conversation with an audience than do a presentation piece, whereas it used to be quite different.

What led to your founding SustainAbility in 1987?

Sheer blind panic, I think. The experience with Earthlife was also one of the reasons that we set SustainAbility up as a limited company. This wasn't really something that was done at that stage. People set up those sorts of organisations as not-for-profits such as charities or foundations.

I remember that we were struggling to get some sort of name for the organisation and I had been thinking about animal names and a number of others. Then I was flying back from Brussels one day and the name just came into my brain with the capitalised A and everything. That was a breakthrough moment. And it was at a time when nobody used the word sustainability.

Weren't you lucky that you got it before anyone?

Yes, although there is one prior reference that I have found in the sense in which it is used now which goes back to about 1974, to a French Canadian priest who used the word in the modern sense. But if you go through the *Our Common Future,* the Brundtland Report published in 1987, you won't find the word sustainability once.

We did suffer a bit from that. For about the first three or four years we spent the whole time spelling the word and we got things addressed to Survivability, Stainability and so on. But in the event, it has worked very well.

What sort of services were you offering?

Well, I had clients already because, alongside Earthlife, when I left ENDS I had set up my own consultancy, John Elkington Associates, and worked for many of the companies that I've talked about already such as BP, ICI, Shell and Monsanto. I was working in areas like environmental audits, strategy and early forms of stakeholder engagement.

So when Julia came on the scene I already had two people working with me. When we set up SustainAbility the consulting side continued, but I also had started to work on the *Green Consumer Guide* from 1986 onwards. One of the ironic things about the *Green Consumer Guide* was that I had come up with an idea for an exhibition in 1986, helping to put it together and writing the catalogue. At the end I came up with 10 questions to ask a 'green' designer, and the tenth was: after you've done all the designing, will whatever you've done appeal to the green consumer? So that was the first time that the phrase was coined. And it was ICI's Group Environment

Adviser who beat me up around the time of the exhibition, saying that they had developed a number of the products and technologies spotlighted at the exhibition, but too few people were buying them. So I thought of doing the *Guide* – and, here's the irony: ICI almost sued us on three points covered in the book. In all cases we were right, but they didn't like the conclusions.

Current views

So how would you define sustainability?

Somebody who was involved in the early stages of SustainAbility said something which has always stuck with me: that sustainability is like a compass point. It gives you a broad sense of direction. It doesn't necessarily specify exactly what you do if you're in a chemical company or a Department of Industry or whatever it happens to be. And that's why, in 1994, I came up with the notion of the triple bottom line, something I had been struggling towards for about 18 months. A couple of years on, I wrote *Cannibals with Forks: The Triple Bottom Line of 21st Century Business*. At that point the goals of social equity, environmental protection and economic prosperity – or People, Planet, Profit as I put it in a slightly more populist formulation – were treated as quite separate. So that is one of the concepts I am still best known for.

Have others in the environmental arena ever criticised your ideas about the role that business should play?

Before the *Green Consumer Guide* I did a book called *Green Capitalists* in 1987 and it really got up the noses of many green activists. They basically felt you shouldn't put green and capitalism in the same phrase. There was also a period when papers like *The Independent* would do pieces on me, one of which featured a very large cartoon of a wolf underneath a sheep's skin.

So there can be a big divide between people like you and what we might call the purists?

Yes, although I actually can be quite fundamentalist at times. I think of civilisation as somehow cruising for a bruising – I think it's going to go down in flames or into a great soggy mess of ecological destruction. But at the same time I think capitalism has a crucial role to play in driving change. I see capitalism as a nuclear process. You've got to shield it with the lead of cultural expectations, standards, hard regulation and all sorts of things that contain it.

Hadn't you been warning of a major financial meltdown well before it happened?

I think of civilisation as somehow cruising for a bruising – I think it's going to go down in flames or into a great soggy mess of ecological destruction. But at the same time I think capitalism has a crucial role to play in driving change. I see capitalism as a nuclear process. You've got to shield it with the lead of cultural expectations, standards, hard regulation and all sorts of things that contain it.

Yes, I have been saying that for a couple of years. It wasn't hard to see it coming. To some degree I believe in the work of people like Nikolai Kondratieff and Joseph Schumpeter, who talked about these cycles or waves of economic evolution and creative destruction. I had felt that every time you have a boom period that runs longer than you would expect, and politicians start to say we have moved beyond boom and bust, you start to worry because in that environment all sorts of things proliferate, like spooky derivative devices which no one really understands. Then that is followed by a sort of searing cauterisation process where you burn a lot of that stuff out of the system and some of it survives and rises like the phoenix, while some of it disappears forever. That's why I increasingly talk of the need to build the 'Phoenix Economy'.

How does the set up of your recent venture, Volans, fit into the evolution of your thinking?

Well, this is different in a way. What happened right at the beginning of this century was that I started to go to the World Economic Forum events. Actually, before that, in 2001, I met Pamela Hartigan who was managing director of the Schwab Foundation for Social Entrepreneurship in Switzerland, which had been set up by the creator of the World Economic Forum. And I had started to work with her.

Then there were people I had known from about 30 years ago when there was a previous sort of flush of entrepreneurship in the environmental space, when people were into whole foods and early forms of renewable energy – but most of that stuff burned out relatively quickly. I started to find I was getting back into touch with these people who weren't corporate – although I know many nice people in the corporate space – and whose whole mindset was different. They wanted to go out and break things. They wanted to create things that were disruptive.

I started to try to bring some of that back into SustainAbility, where the focus is primarily on working with major multinational corporations and, at least to begin with, I found it a bit difficult. It was hard to see where the money was going to come from. Then two years ago we got a grant from the Skoll Foundation, set up by the co-founder of eBay, and whose mission is to bring about change by encouraging social entrepreneurs. They came to us and basically said, we like what you've been doing with the business world and we'd like to help you to do more of that in terms of entrepreneurship and sustainability.

So part of Volans is a place where we can explore, but with a solid business model that hopefully will keep us going year on year. I want it to be a set of rolling conversations with people who are really quite unlike us. So, for example, the first member of our advisory board was David Puttnam, the film-maker. Others are Tim Brown of IDEO, Tim Smit of the Eden Project, and Jerry Linenger, who flew missions of the *Atlantis* and *Discovery* space shuttles, and then served five months on the Russian space station *Mir*. We want to keep the horizons open here.

It sounds like quite a different approach to business-as-usual?

The tagline that we've chosen for Volans is 'the business of social innovation'. What we're saying is that business has to become much more thoughtful about how, in a world headed towards nine billion people, where the global ecosystem is starting to come apart at the seams, you have to create business structures, business models, economic models and technologies that don't just do things better, but are transformative. Paul Hawken said – around the time he wrote *The Ecology of Commerce* – that even if every company in the world is a Body Shop, a Ben & Jerry's or a Patagonia, we're still screwed. We're still going down the tubes. And in effect what we need to do is to come up with technologies that are very actively not just less harmful but are actually regenerative. A tall order.

But I think we're at one of those extraordinary inflection points where we're going to see all sorts of connections being made in ways that will be quite amazing.

What we're saying is that business has to become much more thoughtful about how, in a world headed towards nine billion people, where the global ecosystem is starting to come apart at the seams, you have to create business structures, business models, economic models and technologies that don't just do things better, but are transformative.

Is Volans somewhere you can have people coming in from completely different areas who will be able to meet and brainstorm about all sorts of ideas?

A key part of what we're planning to be is a sort of dating agency between entrepreneurs interested in building the Phoenix Economy and mainstream actors in business and government. We want to find, explore, advise on and build innovative scalable solutions to some of our big problems that threaten us. A lot of it will be experimental.

I remember reading a book on the early years of aviation about people like Geoffrey de Havilland and the Wright brothers. If you go back to the early years of aviation, what you see is a landscape populated by people who'd crashed and burned and been crippled or killed. I actually think we're going into a period of radically accelerated innovation.

One of the problems that NGOs have in this new order is that they can point the way towards some of the solutions but they don't like failures. They don't like being associated with companies that fail. But I think that the rate of failure is going to go off the scale in the next 20 or 30 years. It has to, because we don't know how we are going to dig ourselves out of this particular hole.

So that's what we're doing at Volans: starting a process that will result in a mapping of the landscape of innovation, innovative thinking and practice in different areas. It's that thinking that led to my latest book, with Pamela Hartigan, called *The Power of Unreasonable People: How Social Entrepreneurs Create Markets That Change the World.*

In addition, although we're not going to be a traditional venture fund to start with, we are talking about creating an investable portfolio where we take a range of social, environmental and mainstream entrepreneurs and put them together in a portfolio in which people can invest. We're also doing a growing range of consultancy projects, in addition to which there are now nearly 40 organisations where we sit either on the board or advisory board, which is a huge privilege – and responsibility!

In your experience, what is the best way to persuade business to take on board these new ideas for solving what look like intractable problems? Stick or carrot?

You have to be prepared to crucify companies if they get things wrong – and I think we find that very difficult. If companies are doing destructive things, for example, too often we tend to protect them for as long as we possibly can. I think of asbestos, I think of the chlorofluorocarbon (CFC) industry and now the fossil fuels industry. I think we have got to be prepared to wade in and shut down entire sectors of industry at times.

What should governments be doing?

Governments play a really crucial role in shaping markets That was something that the government of Japan used to be very good at: being strategic and realising that, although it was good at metal-bashing and shipbuilding, the competitive landscape was changing. And so for a period of time Japan was profoundly strategic. Another thing I've always enormously respected the Japanese for historically is that they would often – and strategically – invest in the teeth of an oncoming recession. They had a sufficient sense of where the market was going to not shut everything down in hard times, but to invest through them, although that has changed a bit now.

Governments are enormously important in all of this – and likely to become more so after what has happened in the financial markets. If you think about President John F. Kennedy and the Man on the Moon promise, that shows one extreme end of what governments potentially can do. They can invest in underpinning the science and technology infrastructure. As the human species increasingly crowds into mega-cities, the infrastructural side of all this is going to be one of the fundamentally important issues to deal with. Not just in terms of windmills and things like that, but to get all the things like sewerage and the water supply and air conditioning to work in appropriate ways.

Actually, one of the projects that we're doing on the consulting side is working with the World Energy Council on what may become an annual survey of 50 to 60 countries. We're looking at how government policy does or does not shape markets in a way that incentivises energy investment and performance in terms of accessibility, availability and acceptability criteria.

Getting more personal

What is it about you as a person that has brought you here, do you think?

I see myself as an outsider. I was brought up to some degree outside England because of my father's job. We went to Northern Ireland first and for three years, as children, we were trapped between the Protestants and Catholics, in the midst of countryside which was phenomenally wonderful. In some ways, it was vicious. We then went on to Cyprus where exactly the same thing happened. We also visited Israel. I had been to all these places by the time I was 9 and I guess it caused something in my brain to throw out religion in all of its various forms. But it also meant that I was looking for a different way of structuring the world. And perhaps environmentalism provided some of that systemic framing of the world.

I remember that when I was 11, in 1961, I stood up at school and did a speech for the World Wildlife Fund, which had just been formed. I asked all the pupils for their pocket money for two weeks – and got it. And this was at a time when I was absolutely terrified of anything to do with public speaking.

I had no idea why I did it. Ironically, Max Nicholson, who co-founded WWF and ENDS, and I were driving down to the WWF headquarters in the late 1970s when he asked me the same question. And I said, well, what I remember is aged 11, in 1961, standing up and doing this. I can't remember for the life of me where that came from.

He said, I know exactly where that came from. And as soon as he said that WWF had got a 24-page article in a major national newspaper that year, I could just remember going into the school library, seeing the newspaper on a lectern or whatever, reading it and thinking: well, I've got to do something.

What else has influenced you?

One of the most interesting people I ever met was Frank Herbert, who wrote the *Dune* series of science fiction novels. I had tried to meet him for years and finally succeeded in the early 1980s. He had a huge impact on my thinking. He was able to think not just in the generational timescale, but over millennia about how societies and civilisations build and decay.

If there is one subject that I really adore it's history. You may have seen the mapping of societies where they do a bubble for the past, a bubble for the present and a bubble for the future. The States has got a very big future bubble, quite a big present one, but a very small one for the past. Whereas this country, the UK, tends to have a very big past bubble and nowadays quite a consumerist big middle bubble, but we're a bit confused about the future. I love history and, perhaps oddly, I also love the future.

The two go together though, don't they?

Well, I think Churchill once said the further you can see back into history the further you can see forwards into the future. There are discontinuities which make it very difficult sometimes to project, but there's an element of truth there.

What are you proudest of?

I don't know. I think it would probably be the friendships that I have built up over a period of time in this space and it's been an astonishing privilege to be a part of this series of interlinking global movements as they've morphed and mutated and evolved over the last 40 years or so. I was extraordinarily lucky to be in early on.

I also think I've been extraordinarily lucky to have the capacity to write and perhaps to have developed the capacity to speak. And there are certain books that I've done which are very close to my heart. *The Green Consumer Guide* is one of them. The *Young Green Consumer Guide* is another. I still get paintings done by children at schools in places like the USA, even after all these years. And *Cannibals with Forks,* which talked about the triple bottom line. I'm also very proud of our latest book, *The Power of Unreasonable People,* because it's an attempt to capture some of the stuff that's at the cutting edge of what may become tomorrow's capitalism.

I'm also really happy to have held a marriage together for 40 years, thanks to my wife Elaine. And our two daughters, who at 31 and 29 have now started to write film scripts together.

Finally, do you have a defining moment in your life? One that stands out?

There have been literally many. For instance, there were moments when we were being sued by McDonald's in 1988/89, after *The Green Consumer Guide* came out. The lawyers said, you'd better cave in. If we didn't, we were told that SustainAbility would be destroyed. But as I walked out of the lawyer's office, he said to me: unless, of course, you'd like to play poker. Well, I've never played poker in my life but I knew exactly what he was speaking about.

And that evening I went down to Cardiff to appear on a panel for a BBC radio programme, apparently with eight million people listening. And someone else on the panel brought up the subject of *The Green Consumer Guide* and McDonald's – and we started to discuss it. But there were people from McDonald's in the audience who ran up and said, you can't do this, you're under a legal injunction. And I thought, no, we're going to fight this. I said we had decided to fight the case, we'll see you in court. The company's president rang me the next morning. It was profoundly stressful, but in the end we pretty much came out on top.

Further back, when I was six or seven, I had another defining moment – this was in Northern Ireland. At least it seemed definitive later, although scientists say that our memories are constantly regenerated every time we tell a story. Anyway, walking home in the pitch dark from a farm labourer's cottage where I used to have dinner once a week, I was between disused flax ponds when I suddenly felt a lot of astonishing elastic activity around my ankles and found myself surrounded by migrating silver eels, or elvers. I have no idea now whether they were headed to or from the ponds, but there was a moment of profound connection with Nature that has never quite left me.

At the time I was one of the few notionally Protestant children at a Catholic convent school. A day or so later I asked the Mother Superior, do animals go to heaven? And she exploded. She said to me: you're either a pantheist or a pagan – and she didn't know which was worse. I had to ask my mother that evening what those words meant!

I have a pretty visual imagination – and my main memory of the conversation with Mother Superior is this mental image of a pair of clawed hands ripping through a curtain in my brain.

Walking home in the pitch dark from a farm labourer's cottage where I used to have dinner once a week, I was between disused flax ponds when I suddenly felt a lot of astonishing elastic activity around my ankles and found myself surrounded by migrating silver eels, or elvers. I have no idea now whether they were headed to or from the ponds, but there was a moment of profound connection with Nature that has never quite left me.

And, in that moment, everything I felt I knew about religion and faith went out of the window. All of which left me pretty receptive, it now seems, to the notions that began to surface a few years later around environmentalism and, later still, sustainability.

5

....

John Grant

John Grant is author of the award-winning book, The Green Marketing Manifesto, *which has been described as a road map for companies needing help finding their way through the subtleties and complexities of the green marketplace. He has had a long association with sustainability projects, think tanks, consultancies, committees and reports stretching back to the mid-1990s.*

What makes his advice to companies particularly pertinent is that he comes to this with a background in brand, innovation, web 2.0 and new marketing. Where the two strands meet in John's work is the thorny question being raised in governments, businesses, social ventures and NGOs: how to change people's behaviour and values?

He is a former co-founder of socially-aware communications agency St Luke's, which was formed in 1995. Working with clients such as the Body Shop as well as mainstream brands, St Luke's pioneered the view of a company's 'Total Role in Society' and operated as an employee-shareholder. It was described by the New York Times *as a 'culture that seeks to stir the creative juices by making every employee an owner, with no corporate ladder to climb or glass ceiling to break through.'*

Since leaving in 1999, he has worked as an independent consultant. John has advised diverse groups on sustainability and related marketing, communication and innovation issues (including the BBC, IKEA, Unilever, Philips, Cisco, the Eco-logist magazine, The Co-operative Bank *and London City Council. John has also been an adviser to numerous social ventures (including Onzo, 2 Degrees, School of Everything,* The Nag, Do the Green Thing *and Unchained).*

As a strategy, innovation and brand consultant John has worked with organisations such as the BBC, BT, IBM, IKEA, Heidrick & Struggles, innocent, LEGO, O$_2$, Sony Ericsson and the Swedish government. He is an Associate of Forum for the Future and Demos, and a contributor to The Young Foundation, Social Innovation Camp, The Campaign for Learning, Tomorrow's Company *and the London College of Communications.*

His previous books have all dealt with the theme of 'what's new?' and have earned popular and critical acclaim. They include The New Marketing Manifesto, *which was named one of the 10 best business books of 1999 by Amazon,* After Image *(2002) and* The Brand Innovation Manifesto *(2006).*

John has also founded a collective of green, creative entrepreneurs called 'London United'. He is a frequent conference speaker, commentator and writer of articles and also a prolific blogger (www.greenormal.blogspot.com).

The professional journey

Let's start by looking at your latest book, *The Green Marketing Manifesto,* **which has been received with such acclaim. What is the main message you want to get across?**

I wrote the book (originally it started as a paper for a potential client project) to try to make sense of the torrent of recent green marketing initiatives. I wanted to sift out what was greenwash and what had substance – and also try to get to what was actually working, and why; and to map out the terrain. The structure that emerged from this research into the main types of approach turned out to be a 3 × 3 grid.

One axis simply describes what is being marketed: is it a public/corporate task, a brand/social identity/community sort of thing, or is it about products, practicalities, inconspicuous consumption and everyday habits? It becomes much simpler to talk about green marketing when you don't mix up these different levels. Corporate, brand and product marketing are always different. The only thing Du Pont, the Toyota Prius and lagging your loft have in common is the aim to reduce carbon emissions; but in different contexts, and obviously with very different types of marketing, in different media, to different audiences.

The other axis discriminates between three broad types of objectives. The first is Green, which is when a company or brand or product is setting new standards. It might be a corporate programme like 'Plan A' from Marks & Spencer, a brand conforming to an eco-labelling scheme; or a product which is simply made in a better way. The marketing in this category tends to be quite straightforward and factual.

Next comes Greener. In many markets the main impact comes from how the product or service is used rather than its manufacture or disposal. Hence the potential to work with customers to achieve a bigger result together. The most prominent example in the UK has been Ariel detergent asking people to 'turn to 30' when they run their washing machines. That's a very simple, common-sense request. But in other cases, getting people to cut or switch can require education.

Did you know that one-third of food bought in the UK is wasted? Apart from all the resources that went into production and transportation, food waste produces methane (a much more powerful greenhouse gas than CO_2).

Emissions associated with wasted food are reckoned to be equivalent to one-fifth of all car use. There's a government education campaign called Waste & Resources Action Programme (WRAP) that has been launched in the UK to tackle this, and retailers and manufacturers are getting involved, too. It's a really interesting cultural issue and incidentally points out how limited is the 'leave it all to us' attitude taken by some brands.

Finally, the third type of objective I describe as Greenest. Gradual improvements and efficiencies are not going to get us to the 90% reduction in carbon emissions that many are now saying are needed. Nor will they tackle the many other sustainability crises with water, agriculture, loss of biodiversity, social justice or economics. There are going to have to be much bigger changes. Some will involve giving stuff up – low-cost flights for one. Some research found that 80% feel guilty every time they fly. And also that 41% are already using their cars less.

Gradual improvements and efficiencies are not going to get us to the 90% reductions in carbon emissions that many are now saying are needed. Nor tackle the many other sustainability crises with water, agriculture, loss of biodiversity, social justice or economics. There are going to have to be much bigger changes.

There will also be instances where people's needs can be met just as well or better, while doing dramatically less damage. Home grocery delivery is a much greener option, if it becomes widespread enough to drive out-of-town shopping out of business. Home delivery is becoming quite well established, but what about sharing clubs, libraries, rental and so on, for most consumer durables? How about making it normal to go back to the launderette? What if every gym had a launderette, and the treadmills generated some of the electricity? This is where we need bold 'Trojan horse' ideas to help us all over our greenophobia.

Where are we currently, do you think?

Overall, where the conversation has got to is that we have inherited and consolidated a man-made world that isn't working and is reaching crises in many fields at the same time as our culture of 'more, more, more' hits natural limits. We need to design a new world, which works regeneratively in partnership with nature. The 'cradle to cradle' philosophy is one such view, which literally sees what is ahead as a redesign task – an attempt to ensure that there is no waste, only 'food' for natural or technological processes.

However, I am not convinced by the view that we can still have 'more' of everything if we redesign the material flows in this way, because it doesn't take into account the issues of absolute shortages in resources and energy, nor the looming crisis of climate change. In my view we will each need to live better, happier lives with less. As far as marketing is concerned, I think it's simply a matter of recognising that this is the way the world is going. Marketing is always a process of working faster than others in the direction the world is going. It's a bit like sailing in that respect: you still have a destination, but you have to work with the winds, tides and around the obstacles. In future it will not be economic to produce goods and services that are harmful in any way. Your carbon emissions, to take one example, will fundamentally determine your costs, share price and ability to attract talent. The best position is prospective: to sense that this a paradigm shift and there are new markets to be created.

So have you become deeply involved in this whole area?

First, let me point out that the area is in rapid redefinition. But yes, you could say that. My platform for the last 18 months has been sustainability in marketing and that has divided into two areas. First, helping new, often-social, ventures and start-ups. Somebody called this area 'g-commerce'. There is certainly a boom in new and green and social businesses. I've worked with about 20 of those over the last two or three years and, in many senses, St Luke's was an education in starting a business which also had a social mission. That's one of my key areas of interest now.

The other half of what I've been doing is educating corporations about how to integrate this great 'sustainability thing' which has, in many ways, worked like – and I don't want to say this in a negative way – a management fad, in the same way that you've seen with concepts like re-engineering the corporation and total quality management

For instance, a recent conversation I had with a marketing client of mine is typical: 'Our CEO has just got religion about sustainability. Now we're all going to have to work out how to fit it into everything we're doing.' In most cases it's not about changing their business into a socially-focused business like Timberland. It's more a matter of reform and integration. Unilever, for example, is going through its entire portfolio, brand by brand, and working out how to integrate the sustainability agenda that is right for the audience, product type and region.

But my absolute passion increasingly is for these social ventures that are starting afresh. There is barely a market that couldn't be re-invented if you started again, thinking about planet, people and profit together. You have to find business concepts that have a chance of scaling because the problems are too great to be fixed by a cottage industry 'purist' approach. But the new entrants have a chance to come at it fresh and are not held back by legacy considerations, like an existing manufacturing process or supply chain.

Let's look back at your career. What did you study?

I went to university to study Natural Sciences with the intention of doing psychology in the second year when, as head of the university yoga society and a vegetarian and card-carrying member of the hippy party, I discovered that to take this course I would need to do experiments with lab rats and that the whole subject was very 'behaviourist' and grounded in statistics. So I rethought my career, ditched psychology and continued to study theoretical physics and mathematics.

What my career has in common with my scientific education is that while I am happiest with the theoretical approach, when it came to practical experiments things often (in some cases literally) blew up: I would regard any success I've had as coming from process of screwing stuff up and having to compensate and invent a system that will patch up and repair. For instance, I messed up a geophysics experiment by not realising I had to plant the explosive charges in a field in one direction and then the other direction, so you could triangulate the results. So instead I had to write a computer program to crunch the results from an incomplete set of data.

That describes my relationship over 20 years with the theory of brands, which was born out of an utter inability to understand what people meant when they drew all those usual charts. Plus my experience of many experiments – the ones I learned most from being those that didn't quite work as intended. So I've invented a number of my own systems – some of which are half put together and some of which arrive back at the same conclusions!

What did you do after your degree?

Well, I did two things which were quite formative. The first was to spend the summer working at War on Want as a volunteer. The second, after leaving the laboratory, was based on an ambition to go into advertising and marketing for three or four years, gain some skills and then go to work in the charity's marketing department. I think it's quite important to remember that 20 years ago you did one or the other – business or doing good – and I lost a lot of friends after university because they considered that I'd 'sold out'. Even back then many of my friends were becoming green anarchists, or going to work for local councils, printing unions or wherever. In their minds I had gone into this Porsche-driving world of exploitative capitalist consumerism.

And it was absolutely true, too. At my first agency, JWT, I had probably some of the worst times of my life. I really didn't fit in. I was an account manager and, for somebody who's not very organised, it was really stressful. I got shingles (a disease most associated with old age) at the age of 23. And so I had to rethink things.

That sounds dreadful!

Well, life is a difficult teacher. And later, when we were planning St Luke's, my key criterion for thinking about the radical new way of working we were developing was 'would this give a much better experience to our 23 year olds than I had had?' But after two years at JWT I went on to become a planner at BMP for five years, which was a much more conducive way of life.

Then I decided to join the London office of Chiat/Day. It had been founded by Jay Chiat in 1969 in California, and had created some world-famous ads. It was also a virtual office long before that became popular. I'd been told when considering the job that Chiat/Day London was about to fold, but I'd had a personal tragedy at that point involving a relationship break-up and I was just looking for the equivalent of a French Foreign Legion. That's why the idea of joining this thing called Chiat/Day London – which was in a precarious situation but had an exciting new team and was into this new thing called new media in a big way – sounded like just what I needed.

At the time when I was talking to them, Andy and David – Andy Law and David Abraham were co-founders of St Luke's – were working on a report on companies' total role in society, where ethics becomes not an option but a requirement. We also, as a condition for working with the Body Shop, did a sustainability audit, looking not only at material issues but also at the ethical impact of our work and the degree to which we really lived up to our 'no hierarchy' aspirations.

So I arrived and was just thrown into sustainability issues because this was the time of the global anti-capitalist demos and all that kind of stuff. It was a very political time. I liked the prospect of bringing some of that into the workplace. And many of our campaigns picked up on what we saw as a 'return to community' values in society at large.

Was this bringing anarchy into marketing in a way?

I did have profound misgivings about the net social impact of marketing but took the line with myself that it's possible to do more from inside. Sure, it can be an intrinsically-compromised position. But are there any ethics-free zones? There are always ethical dilemmas, no matter what you do. Even if you are an activist you have to consider 'what if people get hurt?'

Yes, we're going to have to change things but we can't do that by walking off into some pure place. At the height of what we were trying to do with St Luke's, I was at an academic conference where somebody stood up and just said, I just think consumerism is all wrong. And I said, you're an academic and you're supposed to provide critical tools so that people working in a discipline can operate and make better decisions. So that's not really all that helpful. After all, there are plenty of grounds for questioning academia and its distortion by external funding and internal politics but I don't say that it's 'all wrong'.

It sounds like St Luke's was the right place for you to be.

I was very at home there. We inherited our philosophy from Chiat/Day and it was initially very Californian, but over time we adapted it. We owed a huge debt to them and to Jay Chiat in particular who, at this stage of his career, was much more interested in flying over to London and hanging out with people like Anita Roddick or talking about the potential of the internet to change everything than being at his showcase advertising agencies in Los Angeles.

We did some amazing things there. The biggest commercial success was probably IKEA's 'Chuck out your chintz', which doubled sales through its existing stores. But that was a success because we got the cultural mood right. We tuned into something that wanted saying (in this case that Britain was ready for change) and there were many other examples where we said something that resonated in that way – like 'Act your age, not your shoe size' for Clark's Shoes, which gave a different view of being middle-aged than that presented by the media.

Why the name St Luke's?

We wanted it to be a brand turnaround agency and originally we were going to call it St Elsewhere and the slogan was: 'a hospital for sick brands'. But the new business guy said no brand wants to think of themselves as sick! We were then going to call it St Jude's because it sounded cool, a bit like a Beatles song. And then somebody looked up a list of saints and said, well, Jude is the patron saint of lost causes. So we looked for another saint. Then we found that St Luke is the patron saint of doctors and artists. And we liked the idea of healing – something that runs quite deep for me as well, I think.

One of the things I like about this slant today is the concept of ideas which can heal the world. When I've worked with companies, particularly on internal issues that need reconciling, I've often found that what is needed is an idea that everybody can move forward with together. There is a shift I've made in terms of creativity. Before, it was the creativity of an iconoclasm that's smashing up what exists. For instance, our 'Chuck out your chintz' campaign was quite violent in a way and quite young. But now I've moved, I think, to the idea of creativity as trying to find a bigger common ground and a broader space where things can co-exist and move together. This is about reconciliation by coming to a broader view, within which former conflicts are put into perspective.

What do you think you learned from your time at St Luke's?

It was great. It was my '1960s experience' and an engine for personal development. It's still one of those fixed reference points in my life, like going to college. But I came to a point after five years where the opportunities to leave and do other things were so compelling it was hard to justify staying. But I also felt that if I stayed another five years I wouldn't grow and change as much as I had in the first five. I would have missed 'the new economy' for one thing.

And when did you start getting much more involved with environmental issues?

Well, politically I had always been very attracted to developing world issues. I had volunteered at War on Want, for example, and I was the account manager, when I worked in advertising, for the Disasters Emergency Committee when there were seven natural disasters in one year, 1989. And for Amnesty, the Red Cross and other such causes.

Then various events occurred. Around 2000/2001, I was sitting on a Department of Trade and Industry committee on intangible values – nicknamed the imponderable values committee – headed by one of my clients. The person sitting next to me was Jonathon Porritt, who was absolutely banging his head against a brick wall. He said, look, I've just been through this whole thing with Unilever on sustainable farming and we've got the chairman on board but we've just hit a complete brick wall of incomprehension with the marketing department. I can't get my head around them and they can't get their head around me. So I lent him the book that I'd just written, *After Image*, which was all about the demise of image advertising for building brands and how companies needed to find new ways to work based upon lifelong learning, which was a much better way to understand the new internet brands like eBay, Amazon and Google, for one thing.

He read that and said: 'Do you know what? This makes total sense. There would be no difficulty in translating what we're doing into these terms.' Porritt's summary now of green marketing is to innovate and educate, which is sort of where I come out too. So he called me on to a committee he was putting together called Limited Edition to work with the marketing industry. Various people joined us and I started to see my world through his eyes. I really got into it.

Totally coincidentally, at the time I was doing a night shift at the Samaritans alongside the managing editor of the *Ecologist* magazine. He was marking up page proofs and I said: 'What are you doing?' He said, 'Oh, a magazine, it's late, and these are the galley proofs.' Then he asked me: 'What are you doing?' And I said, 'I've just written a business book.' And he said, 'So, what do you do?' 'Marketing', I said. 'Well,' he replied, 'we're quite anti-marketing, but, boy, have we got some problems with our circulation. Could you just come in and help us? But we haven't got any money.' Who could resist such a challenge – to market something that was anti-marketing?

So, through a series of such relationships, I became much more educated. And in the last two to four years, with Al Gore's 'Inconvenient Truth', the Stern Report moment, and a whole load of things like that, I think a number of people, including me, have gone through a big mind shift. It's a matter of degree. I used to think this stuff was important in the way that certain values are important to me – like tolerance, learning, creativity, democracy. Now I think it's much more important than that (although those values are still important). Now it's a question of survival.

How big an issue is climate change, do you think?

Somebody wrote a theory of consciousness and said that the psychological experience we describe as consciousness consists of constantly finding new pathways between an unbearable present and the image we hold in mind of a beautiful future. And hence it's always working in a dynamic way; between the current awareness of problems and the current set of ideas we have, not only for solutions, but our vision of a better place as destination. That author told a story about somebody who was going to an important meeting – let's say it was a hot date. You've got your mind on where you're going and then, just as you're stepping off the kerb at the lights, you see a hurtling truck out of the corner of your eye. All of your attention goes on avoiding being hit by the truck, and your entire frame shifts. However, you haven't changed direction. You're still going to that meeting or that date. You're just incorporating something that's more urgent.

I think that's where a number of people running companies and in marketing have got to with sustainability. They actually accept what the environmentalists have been saying forever, that they need to put sustainability first – but they do so not because of a political or personal allegiance with the old green romantic ideals ('back to nature') but because they now recognise that climate change is like a hurtling truck. There is a global crisis. It's the sort of thing (as Thomas Homer Dixon argues) that really brought down the Roman Empire.

We are in a system which is in imminent danger of being hit by a number of these trucks. What we're recognising is that the way to work with this stuff is to focus on the truck first and everything else that you're doing second. Lots of people in business think you can incorporate it as a sub-issue but that never really works. Paradoxically, if you do put sustainability first you often do come up with better business ideas. Because while you have been looking for innovations that work for people and profit for 40 years, you hadn't looked seriously at the larger space for innovation marked out by people, profit and planet – which is one definition of sustainability. The practical result is that you find great new ideas that you never would have thought of otherwise.

Paradoxically, if you do put sustainability first you often do come up with better business ideas. Because while you have been looking for innovations that work for people and profit for forty years, you hadn't looked seriously at the larger space for innovation marked out by people, profit and planet – which is one definition of sustainability. The practical result is that you find great new ideas that you never would have thought of otherwise.

Here's an example. I was hired to give a view to the company that makes PG Tips tea bags on two topics. One was about new marketing stuff, like interactive. The other was on sustainability and how to apply it to PG Tips. I went to a meeting with three ideas and the marketing director said that this is so obvious, we could do it next week.

And the three ideas were first, don't overfill your kettle. The kettle uses a third of cooking energy. Secondly, start composting. People in the UK have a real hang up about this topic. They think it's wormy, smelly and that the neighbours won't like it. So just do lovely great big PG Tips composting bins. The fact that you're a household name brand can make this seem normal. And the third idea was loose leaf tea. Why have bleached paper for tea bags? Making a pot of tea and sharing it could become a desirable community activity. It could be fashionable too; it's a version of 'cider over ice', which re-invigorated the cider industry.

I have concluded that the challenge is not to make normal things look green, it's to make green things look normal. And that's where big household name brands can really help – they bring that sense of cosy familiarity; they really could make things like composting look normal, not weird.

Have you been pleased by the reaction to your ideas?

Not always. For instance, I worked on a really big project with a major company which was all about developing e-commerce as well as ideas for sustainability. I was looking at building sustainability into the heart of the e-commerce platform. The company, however, felt it didn't fit its strategy and wasn't right for where it was going. So all of that got axed.

The problem isn't just with sustainable innovation. It's that corporate innovation can often be a boulevard of broken dreams. You do have to celebrate that you got somewhere with the thinking and it can plant some seeds and so forth. But actually, so often an established corporation lacks the appetite and the will for true innovation. If there's any value in what I've been doing for the last few years, it's actually been things like simply being an educator. I often speak at two or three events a week telling the same story again and again. I calculated recently that I have probably spoken to a larger audience in person than I have reached with the book and the blog together.

I'll pop up anywhere and tell people not to greenwash, what the alternative is and – where I see the opportunity – talk to them about everything we've talked about here in terms of business. Lots of people come up to me and say that it finally makes sense, that they can see there are things they can do.

Current views

What do you think the role of business, government and/or consumers should be in terms of sustainability?

It's the 'who's going to blink first' question. Some authoritative surveys – for instance, by the Stockholm Environmental Institute – have shown that there is no decoupling between economic growth and climate damage. For example, the gains that were made by the substantial sustainability commitments made by companies were all wiped out by economic growth in America over the last three years, according to a study by environmental strategist Joel Makower's team.

Look at the UK. We claim to have reduced our carbon emissions by 5% or 15%, depending on which measure you choose, since 1990. And we call ourselves the green growth economy and are inviting others to the table to show them how to do it. We are proud of the UK's Stern report, for instance.

But actually it's just not true. It's false accounting. People talk about flying but that's a small fraction of the problem. What we're not counting is net imports of carbon – the impact of the goods which happen outside our territory in terms of raw materials, the manufacturing and the transport – principally from China. And so, unfortunately, a potentially deep recession is probably the only thing that could put the brakes on. Although it's also a bit like trying to slow a car down by crashing into a tree – there is nothing sustainable about ripping apart companies and communities.

But isn't the fact that a company like Wal-Mart has made a big commitment to lowering its carbon footprint a good thing?

But the net effect is neutral. Of course, it could have been worse if it hadn't done so. We're currently exceeding the worst-case scenario, according to the latest survey of carbon emissions. We are not only failing to slow down; we are actually accelerating. If you just look at greenhouse gas emissions, we have all these targets but we're on the absolute road to hell, whether the temperature rises by two degrees, four degrees or six degrees. Or goes into positive feedback and unstoppable runaway climate change. We have not succeeded in turning the big ship yet.

Many recent discussions do return to this question of economics. For instance, banks have the only proven method of lowering carbon emissions and that's called a savings account. In most circumstances, people who save money doing one thing (for instance,

We're currently exceeding the worst-case scenario, according to the latest survey of carbon emissions. We are not only failing to slow down; we are actually accelerating. If you just look at greenhouse gas emissions, we have all these targets but we're on the absolute road to hell, whether the temperature rises by two degrees, four degrees or six degrees ... We have not succeeded in turning the big ship yet.

saving on fuel bills) tend to spend it on another, like a weekend break in Amsterdam. It's not that they make a conscious decision, it's just that they spend their whole disposable income and whatever it is spent on, €1 = 1 kg of carbon, roughly. That 'indirect' rebound effect is a worry. A recession, though, takes out some of the rebound effect by making people inclined to hoard money and save, which is one reason why there are difficulties in the money supply in a recession.

What I think will drive the solution is community citizen engagement. I think we can create mirror images of Wikipedia in markets among consumers. A contact of mine runs a site called the Nag. It is a lovely little activist website that gets you to make a commitment and then nags you until you've done it. She also has a business called Worn Again which makes new trainers out of things like parachutes, old prams and all sorts of stuff. She was in the news, for example, because she secured a load of Virgin Atlantic plane seats to turn into handy washing bags.

We had a brainstorming session and one of my ideas for the Nag was that a million of us, through an extended network of recruiting people, will move our current accounts to the first bank that commits to dropping all direct mail and paper-based data.

What do you think the reaction of banks would be to that?

I've spoken to a number of them, including those with green commitments and they just said: 'We can't do that. Direct mail makes us more than it costs, our competitors do it, it brings in sales and we can't drop it. We can't drop it until it's banned or something like that.' So we want to create a consumer activist rationale for doing the right thing.

For example, there is a movement called Carrotmob which organises consumers to make purchases that give financial rewards to those businesses that agree to make socially beneficial choices. They did a version of this in a small city block in San Francisco where they brought together lots and lots of people to spend $27 000 in an afternoon in a Korean grocery store. The store owners then spent 30% of their take from that day on energy efficiency improvements and now have one of the most energy efficient corner grocery stores in the world.

So this is about consumer citizen engagement and linking that to the government policies and generally getting behind things, I was working on something with the previous London mayor's administration to look at adopting LED lighting technology. Although an LED bulb is quite expensive at £10, it will last for 50 years. We talked about filming celebrities on YouTube telling the last light bulb jokes, because these jokes would become extinct since we'd never have to change a light bulb again. It would also get rid of the mercury elimination problem we now have from the current low-energy bulbs. Our idea was to say we're going to ask citizens to adopt this. 'Don't think of it as a consumer purchase, think of it like a wristband.' If a million Londoners did so, then big companies like GE and Philips are going to have to get into this market, like it or not.

How realistic is that, do you think?

Realism is the enemy of all my work. Realism is the thing that kills most of my favourite ideas because if you haven't seen it before it doesn't look like it's made out of fragments of the real world. And I spend my whole time trying to repaint things as realistic, describing it as like a Wikipedia, or a Facebook group

I think that the epicentre of change in the world – and we have to change – is going to be like the 20-person village meeting absorbing all of these ideas and deciding what we're going to do. The Transition town movement is one good example of that. What I've learned about ethics – and I've got a great deal more to learn – is that ethics are the product of that process of deliberating, taking in information, having a group around you – almost like a WeightWatchers support group.

The next stage is making decisions, whether popular or unpopular. It goes back to the origins of Athenian democracy: decisions made by being grounded in conversation and debate. I believe that given sufficient information people tend to do the right thing.

What advice would you give to a business person, say, who's thinking, where do I start? It's just too confusing.

Well, it doesn't get any less confusing. Honestly. The more you learn the more confusing it is. First, let's look at people in business. I think to be effective in business in times of disruption you need the mind and view of an entrepreneur. All entrepreneurs are obsessed with the customer. If you have to spend even one day not talking to customers you're an administrator, not a manager. Your contact with reality has to be the market and the communities you're serving.

Another thing in the mind of the entrepreneur is a way of thinking: you hold a model of the world in your head and you continually challenge it. You're always testing it and you're always seeking conversations to strengthen it or force you to evolve it, because I think a lot of the answers to the challenges we face are actually going to be quite structural. They'll be to do with different formats and ownership structures and the way that you involve stakeholders. All those trendy words are actually about designing institutions that can support us in the directions that we need to go, but if we try to make the journey without attending to those structures we'll fail.

So what advice would I give? I don't know. Because it is a continual struggle. I gave some advice at a talk for a business audience where I asked simply: do you want to live your lives and business careers and not to have struggled? This is your wartime, this is your adventure. At last our generation has something to care about that isn't the next PDA screen, the next holiday or whatever.

Think of many of the social ills, the levels of anxiety and depression in the West and the lack of basic commodities and rights elsewhere, and the global destruction of the environment. Isn't that something really worth tackling with innovation? I read recently that there is no community without an objective. It's the objective that pulls people together. That's what creates the blitz spirit. And if you don't have a shared objective you're just a bunch of people with neighbour conflicts. At last we have found our objective. That's a start at least.

Getting more personal

What are you proudest of, do you think?

That's not an easy question. My first thought in response is my son, Cosmo, who is six. I'm so proud of what he sees, what he understands and also his imagination and how he is as a human being. My son and I have some of the most amazing conversations about everything from – if you translated it to adult terms – quantum cosmology, social justice, why shadows are long at a certain time to talks about hunting, primitive science and so forth. Plus big conversations about mortality. Many people say that they got into sustainability because of their children. For me that's not it but I am certainly inspired by the way he looks at things.

What is it about you as a person that has brought you to where you are?

Well, it is ironically probably a lack of planning. It's the type of personality where you read the preface of a book and you think you've got the whole argument or where somebody speaks for 10 seconds and you've actually got their whole thing – or you haven't, but you think you have. I'm a jumper to conclusions; and I tend to leap into things more than being held by any commitments to past thoughts, to commonly accepted beliefs. The result is that my life and career are a case of 'one thing that led to another'. I'm not saying there is no pattern or consistency at a deeper level of values. It's just that everything I am doing now is the result of an accumulation of instances of leaping into things, without much reflection or pause for thought.

Were you like that as a child as well? Always just getting into things?

I guess so. The formative thing from my childhood was that I went to a Catholic experimental school, where most of the teachers were nuns but, because it was a 1970s experimental school, it decided not to have lessons and a timetable but 'resource centres' instead. So, like most of the boys, I skived off and played a lot of football while forging teachers' signatures from each resource centre!

What also became apparent in that time is that one of the things that crushes me is boredom. Being bored, I started reading for myself. I read every book in the kids' library and then got permission to get stuck into the adult library. The school scrapped the experiment after two or three years because clearly most of the kids didn't spend their whole time in books from the town library. But it made me into what I am now: a bookworm. And I love the incredible diversity of thoughts and ideas that you get when you just read things to find out stuff.

The school also gave me the experience – which I think is one of the most important ones you can have – of falling and catching yourself. What I like about my son's primary school is that while they do have a little more structure, when I first arrived, I was given a tour by two pupils all round the building, explaining to me how it worked and asking if I had any questions. It was about children finding self and group responsibility, working as a community and taking an equal part in running the school.

In a time of change and innovation you need an open and communitarian process of inquiry because there are so many different aspects to getting something to work and which involves everybody. There are no experts, only enquirers.

This was very much the founding principle of St Luke's. In a time of change and innovation you need an open and communitarian process of inquiry because there are so many different aspects to getting something to work and which involves everybody. There are no experts, only enquirers.

6

Denis Hayes

Denis Hayes is President and CEO of The Bullitt Foundation. He directs the Foundation, which he joined in 1992, from the perspective of a practical visionary who has devoted his life to conservation. He acknowledges, albeit with mixed feelings, that he is probably still best known for having been National Coordinator of the first Earth Day when he was 25. But he also is the seasoned veteran of many environmental, legislative, and litigation victories over the years.

He was born in Wisconsin though raised mainly in the small town of Camas, Washington, where in 2007 Hayes Freedom High School was named in his honour. His experiences growing up in the Pacific Northwest instilled in him a lifelong love of nature. He received his undergraduate degree in history from Stanford University, where he was president of the student body and an activist against the Vietnam War. During those years, he spent significant time backpacking to remote corners of the world.

Denis later enrolled at the Kennedy School of Government at Harvard University. He left Harvard after being selected by Senator Gaylord Nelson to serve as National Coordinator of the first Earth Day. Earth Day, on 22 April 1970, had participants and celebrants in 2000 colleges and universities, about 10 000 primary and secondary schools, and thousands of communities. The Associated Press estimated that more than 20 million demonstrators participated.

He became head of the Solar Energy Research Institute (now the National Renewable Energy Laboratory) where clean power became his passion, but left this position when the Reagan administration cut funding for the programme. Denis went back to school and completed a Juris Doctor degree at Stanford in 1985, later becoming an adjunct professor of engineering at the university.

In 1989, he helped to found Green Seal, in response to the lack of a US-based third-party, ecolabelling organisation and became its first Chair & CEO. Today Green Seal continues to be one of the most respected ecolabels: it has developed more than 30 environmental leadership standards and certified more than 2500 products and services.

Denis served as international chairman for Earth Day's anniversaries in 1990 and 2000. Internationally, he is recognised for expanding the Earth Day Network to more than 180 nations. It is now the world's most widely-observed secular holiday. He serves as Honourary Chair of the international Earth Day Network.

He has also been a visiting scholar at the Woodrow Wilson Center, a senior fellow at the Worldwatch Institute, and a Silicon Valley lawyer. He has received the national Jefferson Medal for Outstanding Public Service as well as the highest awards bestowed by the Sierra Club, The Humane Society of the United States, *the National Wildlife Federation, the Natural Resources Council of America, the Global Environmental Facility of the World Bank, the inter-faith Center for Corporate Responsibility, the American Solar Energy Society, and the Commonwealth Club.*

He has served on dozens of governing boards, including those of Stanford University, the World Resources Institute, the Federation of American Scientists, The Energy Foundation, Children Now, the National Programming Council for Public Television, the American Solar Energy Society, Greenpeace, CERES, and the Environmental Grantmakers Association. He is the author of Rays of Hope: The Transition to a Post-Petroleum World. *In 1999,* Time *magazine named him as 'Hero of the Planet'.*

Mobilizing the resources of The Bullitt Foundation, which was founded in 1952 by Dorothy Bullitt, a prominent Seattle businesswoman and philanthropist, Denis intends to help make the Pacific Northwest the best-educated, most environmentally aware, most progressive corner of America – a global model for sustainable development.

The professional journey

What, in your view, do you think you're best known for? This is probably difficult because you've done so many things. But if you reflect for a minute, what do you think is associated with your name most prominently?

Perhaps, unfortunately, it doesn't require much introspection. At 25 I was the national coordinator of a huge event in the US called Earth Day, which is often credited with launching the modern phase of the environmental movement. Almost 40 years later, every time I'm introduced to give a talk, Earth Day is mentioned. You could say I peaked at 25!

Which is obviously not the case! But tell us more how it all came about.

Some years earlier, in the midst of trekking around the world for a few years, I came to a decision that what I wanted to do with my life was to figure out ways to reorganise human society along ecological principles, although there wasn't a vocabulary then for what we now call urban ecology or industrial ecology. After graduating from Stanford I went off to Harvard and, as part of the curriculum, I had to carry out an external assignment such as interning in a government office.

Meanwhile, Senator Gaylord Nelson from Wisconsin gave several speeches calling for an environmental teach-in on college campuses across the country, akin to the teach-ins that we had in the early days of the civil rights movement and the movement against the war in Vietnam. He gave one of those talks at a conference in Virginia. It happened that Gladwin Hill, a very senior reporter from the *New York Times*, was attending the conference. He was expected to file a story after spending four days at the conference, so he wrote about the proposed 'teach-in'. It must have been the slowest news day of the twentieth century, because *The Times* put his story on the front page and distributed the article to its nationwide syndicate.

I read about the teach-in idea up in Boston and, with all the arrogance of youth, I flew down to Washington, DC, to have a five-minute courtesy interview with the senator. I wanted to get the charter to organise the teach-in for Cambridge, or even perhaps for Boston, since this was the kind of project that I needed to do for the Kennedy School. And it turned out that Senator Nelson didn't have anyone who was working on it in Cambridge, the city of Boston, the state of Massachusetts, the region of New England, or anywhere else.

He'd given this speech at several college campuses, and then the story in *The Times* made it 'real'. Suddenly mail began pouring into his office. So we sat down and instead of five minutes I spent a couple of hours with him, talking about how a nationwide event could be organised. I returned home with the mandate to organise Boston. Two days later, I got a telephone call from the senator asking whether I'd be willing to drop out of school and come to Washington to organise America.

And you had no hesitation about taking this leap into the unknown?

Well, this was in the 1960s. I was part of a generation that was, frankly, pretty full of itself. It never occurred to us that we really needed a college degree or that we might be unemployed. Many of us thought that the world was likely to come to a swift end, one way or the other, and the most important thing we could do was to leap onto the barricades. I was

convinced that, in the big picture, environmental issues dwarfed and sub-
sumed the others.

Why did it resonate with you so strongly, do you think?

When I was in high school I had gone to a summer institute sponsored by
the National Science Foundation on, of all things, ecology. Before I was
recruited to do this I'd never heard the word. Nobody talked about ecology
back then. I was, what, 15 or 16 years old. We used an early edition of
Eugene Odum's book, *Principles of Ecology*. I was introduced to the science
of how all plants and animals interact with one another to form healthy,
resilient, sustainable ecosystems.

By the time I was 19, I was in a deep, teenaged state of *weltschmertz*,
looking for some meaning to my life and not finding it. The super powers
faced off against one another with tens of thousands of nuclear weapons.
Authorities in the American south turned police dogs and fire hoses on
people who only wanted to get a decent education, a good job, or the right
to vote. I was convinced that my country was on the wrong side of the war
in Vietnam.

For a couple of years I attended a community college where I read Marx,
Adam Smith, Freud, Herbert Marcuse and Frantz Fanon – all the fashionable theorists who were trying to make sense of the world. I wasn't sure I
believed any of their theories. So I strapped on a big backpack full of books
and started travelling a lot because I wanted to see what was actually going
on in Russia, in Eastern Europe, and in the emerging former colonies in
Africa, and whether any of the grand theories were actually panning out. It
was ultimately frustrating, because I didn't find any success stories.

One night, as I was hitchhiking around Africa, I found myself dropped off at a lonely crossroads in what is now Namibia. I walked out over a hill and laid out my sleeping bag. And that night, for whatever reasons, all sorts of things came together in my mind. I began thinking about how the principles of ecology applied to every-thing: the principles governed the behaviour of amoeba and elk, polar

I began thinking about how the principles of ecology applied to everything: the principles governed the behaviour of amoeba and elk, polar bears and monkeys, orang-utans and chimpanzees. I thought that if these principles explained all the other animals, including primates, they probably explained human beings as well.

bears and monkeys, orang-utans and chimpanzees. I thought that if these principles explained all the other animals, including primates, they probably explained human beings as well.

These thoughts might sound a bit trite now, but they were not a common way to view the world back then. I spent much of that night speculating about how humans had managed to evade some of those fundamental laws. For instance, we tap into stocks of energy – oil, gas, coal – buried deep in the earth, while other life forms depend upon flows of energy from the sun. Oil, gas, and coal caused a lot of problems, and their supply wasn't infinite. Could we design a human society to prosper from the flow of energy from the sun? I began recalling concepts like carrying capacity, homeostasis and collapse, and applied them to the human prospect.

The following morning, I arose with a sense of direction. I came back to America and enrolled at Stanford, where I attended lectures by professors such as Paul Ehrlich and Don Kennedy, got engaged in some of these issues, and kept looking for opportunities. But mostly I figured that I needed to get some credentials before I could have real impact.

So then came Stanford, Harvard and eventually, Earth Day.
Was Earth Day an all-consuming project?

It happened really, really fast. It was like drinking from a fire hose. We had only about five months to organise the event. What was to have been the core of the event – college teach-ins – turned out to be peripheral. Although many colleges had some sort of 'teach-in', the major events had a distinctly more activist character. We put together a huge outpouring of protest demonstrations from urban areas, focusing on air pollution, water pollution, toxic waste, nuclear power, coal mining, lead paint, leaded petrol, etc. More than 10 000 schools in our database sent kids out to study nature, pick up litter, or talk to their parents about recycling. Perhaps the most important thing I did was to change the name from National Environmental Teach-in to Earth Day, which, among other things, translates into every language in the world. It made it more an activist thing and less of a passive, teach-in kind of event.

After Earth Day I stayed for a year running a lobbying group that coordinated all the citizen-led environmental lobbying around the Clean Air Act of 1970. Then I went to a new institution just being set up, called the Woodrow Wilson International Center for Scholars, where I dug deeply into energy issues from a human ecology perspective. This, by the way, was at a time when 'energy policy' was not in the popular lexicon. We had a coal policy, an oil policy, a hydropower policy. ... But I was trying to think in terms of energy quality and quantity, with the sources of energy being fairly interchangeable.

While I was at the Wilson Center, I met some scientists who helped me to understand that we actually had some renewable energy technologies that could, with some successful research and some good fortune, be made afford-able and ubiquitous, tapping power directly from the sun and the wind. It was an important year for me.

When my fellowship at the Center ended, I returned to Stanford as a graduate student in business and economics. I was interested in learning how conventional accounting and finance could be moulded to promote what we would now call sustainability values. Then, in 1973, King Faisal of Saudi Arabia graciously made all my energy theories extremely relevant by launch-ing the Arab oil embargo!

About that time a Democratic governor of Illinois named Dan Walker came calling. He appeared, at the time, to be an attractive person who might well rise to the presidency, and he was assembling a team in Illinois drawn from across the country. I was asked if I would like to be the founding direc-tor of Illinois' brand new energy office, as well as special assistant to the governor for natural resources. So I dropped out of school – yet again – and went off to Illinois.

Walker was subsequently defeated in his own party's primary by the Daley machine in Chicago, Illinois' dominant city. I moved to Washington, DC, and joined the Worldwatch Institute, which was being set up by Lester Brown. I ran the Worldwatch energy programme. After Jimmy Carter was elected President in 1977, I was chosen to head the new Solar Energy Research Institute (SERI).

How did that happen?

That's kind of an interesting story. The very first secretary of the new Department of Energy was Jim Schlesinger. Previously, he had been the chairman of the Atomic Energy Commission. Secretary of Defense, director of the CIA, and head of the Budget Office. In other words, he had done almost everything. He was not viewed by anyone as being particularly liberal. Carter's decision to appoint Schlesinger as Secretary of Energy was seen by many in the environmental community as a betrayal of the support they had given Carter in the election.

After becoming Secretary of Energy, Schlesinger went on a trip to Saudi Arabia and was invited to dinner at the house of Zaki Yamani, then Minister of Petroleum for Saudi Arabia. Schlesinger turned up at Yamani's house with his press aide, was shown in by a servant, and deposited in a parlour. Schlesinger has a restless mind. He always wants to be engaged in something, but there were no newspapers or magazines to read. Sitting in the middle of the room, though, on a table, was a book I had written: *Rays of Hope*.

I'd sent the book to Yamani a day or two earlier, and it happened to end up in this room. When researching *Rays of Hope*, I'd travelled around the world talking to many energy experts. As a thank you for their time, I later sent each of these experts a copy of my book. I had spent maybe an hour, an hour and a half, with Yamani, and subsequently wrote an editorial in *Science* describing some rather clever ideas he had about building a Saudi solar industry. When I sent him the book, I had written something flowery like, 'To my dear friend Zaki Yamani. Thank you very much for all the insights you gave me. I hope our countries will find ways to work together to promote a clean energy future.' Schlesinger picked the book up, read this inscription and said: 'Who the hell is Denis Hayes?'

To my good fortune, the guy who was with him, the former *Newsweek* Washington bureau chief Jim Bishop, happened to know the answer. So when they came back to the US, Schlesinger invited me out for lunch, and then for dinner. While we disagreed on a huge number of things, we sort of hit it off; we were both relatively blunt and straightforward and driven by data.

The Carter Administration had set up SERI, but its first director, a distinguished scientist, had been weakened by cancer. Consequently, he had been beaten up in bureaucratic battles with the other national labs, and SERI was being pushed around by former Atomic Energy Commission bureaucrats at the Department of Energy. Schlesinger had this idea that SERI really needed someone who was a strong advocate for solar energy, to balance the strong nuclear, coal, and oil advocates. So he appointed me to lead SERI. I quickly got in a couple of very public battles with senior officials at the Energy Department, and won – buying the lab some breathing room.

Throughout your career you have come across as someone who feels very strongly about what you believe. What have been some of the challenges that you faced in getting your ideas across?

Well, let me tell you the theory that guided a lot of early things I did. In college I had an experience that, writ large, characterised a couple of decades of my life. I was the student body president in my last year at Stanford. We were always protesting this and that and seizing and occupying buildings. We seized the Applied Electronics Laboratory at Stanford because it was doing highly classified research on the guidance systems for anti-ballistic missiles (ABMs).

We occupied that lab for some weeks and, as the debate evolved on campus, we framed the issue as a protest about the proper mission of an academic institution. We argued that universities should be about gaining knowledge, teaching students, and providing general wisdom to society. Universities should not be doing secret, classified research, which is inimical to the freedom of inquiry and expression.

While we were in the Applied Electronics Laboratory, the then-governor of California, Ronald Reagan, massed a bunch of National Guard troops in a nearby city. He held a press conference and announced that he was pre-pared to move them in and take those radicals out of that building as soon as he was given the nod by the Stanford's president. The president of the university had just arrived there a few months earlier from a much smaller college. He was a very nice guy, but was sort of in over his head. He was being buffeted on the one side by a very conservative board of trustees, and on the other by a liberal/radical faculty and student body. He was paralysed with indecision. So I called a press conference to announce that Stanford could handle its own affairs, thank you, and suggested that the Governor should butt out.

A few days later, plans leaked that the National Guard intended to move onto the campus to arrest everyone in the lab. Frankly, some of the pro-testers from off campus were a little crazy, and a Kent State situation could have easily occurred.

There was an obscure little section in the constitution of the student body that said that the president could call a meeting of the Stanford community on issues of community-wide importance. No one had ever used it. Nobody knew what it meant. But I decided to call a meeting of 'the Stanford community' in a huge amphitheatre to vote on whether classified research should be banned. This was not without its own risks, but I wanted to see what would really happen. At that point this issue had been front-page news in the student newspaper for weeks. People who would just as soon never think about anti-ballistic missiles had been forced to, because there was this huge disruptive protest going on right in the heart of the campus, with rallies every night.

Well, *everyone* showed up: faculty, students, staff, and even a couple of trustees. It was standing room only in this huge amphitheatre and we had a debate. Some professors and graduate students in the school of engineering explained why they thought it was important to do classified research on campus. Other professors and students explained why classified research was contrary to the essential nature of a university. I called for a vote to ban classified research at Stanford, and at least 90% of the crowd voted in favour of a ban. Although the vote carried no authority at all, the fact was that the 'university community' did have real power. In a matter of months, the board of trustees banned classified research and phased out all the existing classified research on campus. Then several other universities across the country also began to ban classified research.

The lessons I took away from that experience were these: first, the toughest step is to get people's attention. We did that by seizing and occupying a building! But one way or another, you need to do something that forces people to think about the *issue*. Then, once people are focused on the subject, and if they are exposed to rational arguments from all sides, the majority will come to a sensible conclusion. Democracy works when people are paying attention to the facts. That, in fact, became the underlying rationale for Earth Day, which, once we got people to focus their attention on the issues, produced a tidal wave of public support for smart, cost-effective legislation that dramatically improved the environment.

Did this sort of thinking about the power that public opinion can have lie behind your setting up of the ecolabelling organisation, Green Seal?

We thought we already had their attention. We'd seen all these polls saying that people really wanted to buy green products but were deterred by so many companies' greenwashing claims. We thought that if we could create a clear, objective, third party that would provide a trusted certification akin to a laboratory seal of approval for the environment, then people would buy more of the certified products. At least that was the theory.

The theory?

A large number of Americans – many surveys say 20% or more – want to buy products that are truly superior from an environmental perspective, assuming that they are efficacious for the intended purpose and not too costly. A much larger number want to buy products that have at least some environmental attribute, preferably an obvious one, but will not pay any premium or accept even a trifling inconvenience.

Our slogan was: 'Vote with your wallet, not just your ballot.' Since the vast majority of people vote for green initiatives and candidates, we thought we could persuade them to buy very green products, too. By very green, I mean a product that, on a life-cycle basis – from the mine to the recycling bin – used less energy, produced no toxic by-products, disrupted no intact ecosystems, etc. So we initially tried to create a 'super' certification that could only be won by the best 20% of the products in any category, and would continue to evolve and improve over time.

We ran into multiple problems. I could go on for hours, but the most important problem was that ecolabelling developed a Gresham's Law. Other firms popped up that were willing to give their ecolabel for much lower standards – and even for no standards at all! One firm merely certified that whatever a manufacturer claimed was factual – even if the claim was humorously trivial. To get our Green Seal, you had to put your product through a detailed, expensive assessment to prove, on a full life-cycle basis, that your product was exemplary from an environmental standpoint. Our competitors would offer a big ecolabel, and the consumer would never know that they were merely certifying that – say – the product contained 3% recycled plastic.

For most people, anything with any sort of ecolabel was good enough. Shoppers don't want to take a graduate course on life-cycle assessment in order to buy some laundry detergent. They just want to get their clothes clean and hopefully do *something* good for the environment. So as soon as the market started filling with ecolabels that were – not to put too fine a point on it – fraudulent, we were in trouble. And when some major manufacturers started employing and advertising these deceptive ecolabels, our hopes of using the seal to promote a consumer revolution were destroyed.

This is before you even get to the fact that many socially responsible consumers worry about companies as well as about products. Well, bad companies often make good products, and good companies often make some bad products. If today's best light bulb is made by a company that previously created 100 toxic Superfund sites, should we deny the terrific product a seal? What is to be done if a small component in an electronics device depends on a mineral that was mined by destitute people for slave wages? What if an über-green kitchen appliance is made by a company that also makes land mines or nuclear weapons? It all gets very complicated.

Is Green Seal still around?

Absolutely! It's at www.greenseal.org. It has certified thousands of products: paints, oils, paper products, cleaning products, and so forth. One of its big growth areas has been certified green hotels, where a comprehensive approach has real advantages. It continues to be a strong voice for integrity and transparency regarding green products and services, and I admire the people there enormously. Alas, because of the abusive practices of some other firms, and the lack of a budget to help the public to distinguish between the real deal and the frauds, it hasn't become what I was hoping for: an almost universal green seal of approval.

It's such a difficult area, isn't it?

It may get better in an Obama administration, where the government might support such efforts instead of trying to kill them. It might also gain ground as a new generation of corporate leaders comes into power – leaders who embrace sustainability instead of merely greenwashing their old product line-up. Product certification has always been opposed by trade associations which, by their nature, work on behalf of the worst performer in their ranks.

Governmental regulations are a very important complement to certification programmes because they set a performance floor that products cannot fall beneath. The average refrigerator today uses only about 40 percent as much electricity as refrigerators 20 years ago. Today's devices keep your food just as cold; they come in the same sizes and the same decorator colours. But the government now has efficiency standards and it is illegal to sell inefficient refrigerators today. Green Seals should be awarded only to products that significantly exceed such regulatory requirements.

Current views

What is your vision for The Bullitt Foundation and how does it fit in with your current thinking?

My vision now is basically the same vision I had in Namibia: to apply principles of ecology to humans, to human settlements and to industries. In practice, that means that we are attempting to make the Pacific Northwest the leading edge in the United States in terms of embracing energy and climate policies that will move us rapidly away from dependence upon fossil fuels and fissile fuels and into sustainable energy sources.

In practice, that means that we are attempting to make the Pacific Northwest the leading edge in the United States in terms of embracing energy and climate policies that will move us rapidly away from dependence upon fossil fuels and fissile fuels and into sustainable energy sources.

We want to create a congenial environment for companies providing goods and services that are compatible with a sustainable future. Seattle – a medium-sized city – is home to Microsoft, Boeing, Amazon, Starbucks, Costco, Expedia, Nordstrom, Real Networks, Weyerhaeuser, REI, and other companies with a national and international presence. We want to move those firms in an increasingly sustainable direction and lure in others involved in photovoltaics, wind turbines, hybrid cars, smart meters, and the other components of a smart electrical grid.

We hope to test innovative policies that, if successful, will expand what other regions think of as possible. For example, climate policies nearly everywhere have been focused on how to reduce the CO_2 that is being emitted in any given year. Yet such cap-and-trade policies, which commonly involve offsets for things like forest preservation, might well lead to more CO_2 in the atmosphere in 2050 than if we'd taken a different approach in these early stages. Current policies that trade off forest carbon reduction for increased emissions from coal or oil risk undermining the pressure to make transformational investments in new technology. To meet the atmospheric carbon caps needed by 2050, we need soon to cover every southern wall with photovoltaics and build high-speed electrified rail to displace trucks and cars.

I was the founding co-chair of Ceres, a national network of investors, environmental organisations and other public interest groups working with companies and investors to address sustainability challenges such as global climate change. It has launched a global campaign to try to get industries to call for much more dramatic action in the climate arena. We're working to see if we can persuade big companies to come on board. The best companies are led by people who are smart enough to recognise that everyone has a stake in a sustainable future, and that not every corporate action needs to be rooted in competitive advantage. Sometimes CEOs will do things simply because they are the right things to do.

Can you give us an example of a regional role you've played?

There is a group in Portland, Oregon, called Central City Concern (CCC) that serves what's perceived of as the dregs of society: drug addicts and long-term alcoholics who want to pull themselves up, but who keep running into problems. CCC provides them with shelter, detoxification programmes and job training. CCC even gives them new wardrobes. The group tries to get its clients stabilised and ultimately out of CCC's facilities and back into mainstream life.

Years ago, CCC acquired several properties in Portland's former 'skid row'. That land has now become the hottest site for urban infill, where developers are building luxury condominiums and modern office buildings. So suddenly CCC found itself in possession of some valuable land *and* some money. And it doesn't want to be booted out of there and forced out to the suburbs. CCC is led by people who have themselves emerged from the programme, so they're really rugged, tough-looking, weather-beaten, authentic voices of the community that they're representing. They're also canny. They may not have MBAs, but they know what they're doing when they're negotiating leases and development contracts. You underestimate their business acumen at your peril.

CCC has to pay the energy bills and water bills of the residents in their programmes because, by definition, their residents have no money. Because those bills kept going up and up, CCC's leaders started wondering what they could do to put a cap on them. This led them to start thinking about green buildings. They talked to architects in local firms who were willing to work for them pro bono. First, they upgraded some buildings to LEED standards – a suite of standards for environmentally sustainable construction. Then they started thinking about designing a 'living building' – that is, a building that acts as an organism. Residents can pretty much get by on the water that falls on the building's roof and the sunlight that falls on its southern wall and its roof. The building is close to 'pea-patch' public gardens and has 100% recycling and composting of its trash.

It turns out, however, that it is against the law to capture the water that comes off of your roof in almost every western state in the US, because of a doctrine that says that somebody downstream from that water already has a right to it. So CCC tried to figure out how to get around this. We gave them a grant to address obstacles to constructing a 'living building', and they started talking to plumbers, to the state health officials, the state environmental officials, and local water officials to identify regulatory problems. Everybody kept pointing to somebody else as the ultimate obstacle. Finally, CCC pulled all the relevant officials into one room and said, 'OK, today let's enumerate everything that has to be changed in order to capture rainwater and see whether we can pull together a coalition to go to the state legislature and get whatever legislation we need.' After two hours of pounding around the room, it turned out that the people assembled had enough power to change the rules without going to the legislature.

As a result, in Oregon you can now use and recycle 100% of the rainwater that falls on your building. It's purely a result of a small grant to a group that tries to rescue drug addicts and alcoholics. This sort of initiative had never come from all the developers who are building green structures for wealthy baby boomers. It came from a group that was used to hearing 'no' and that had a tradition of not taking 'no' for an answer. We're constantly looking for that kind of opportunity.

What's your view on the role of business in the whole sustainability debate?

The best businesses operate in a way that allows them to take full advantage of all the opportunities they can find within whatever constraints society places around them. The smartest business leaders embrace policies that create a context where it is in every-body's interest to do the right thing and where people are penalised for doing the wrong thing. Companies can now dump unlimited quantities of greenhouse gases into the atmosphere without paying a price or a penalty. So rational businesses trying to maximise growth or profits look like villains. I don't view them as villains, however, unless they have been using their lobbying muscle and their political contributions to create and sustain this tragic misuse of government power. It is government's responsibility to establish the framework within which business operates.

Companies can now dump unlimited quantities of greenhouse gases into the atmosphere without paying a price or a penalty. So rational businesses trying to maximize growth or profits look like villains. I don't view them as villains, however, unless they have been using their lobbying muscle and their political contributions to create and sustain this tragic misuse of government power. It is government's responsibility to establish the framework within which business operates.

Today, the government gives its largest incentives to companies using coal, oil, and nuclear – not solar, wind, and geothermal. Forty years after oil production peaked out in the United States, and 20 years after global warming was accepted by the National Academy of Sciences as a serious problem, subsidising the wrong energy sources is just crazy. It's akin to the $80 000 tax break the government gave for many years to 'businesses' such as dentists and real estate agents who bought 8 mpg Hummers. When you pay people or companies to act against the public interest, you can't be shocked when they act against the public interest.

On the other hand, when the CEO of General Electric lobbies the government for tougher climate legislation, or the CEO of Applied Materials explains to Congress how public policy discriminates against solar energy, they are helping to align public policy with sustainability goals, and such corporate advocacy can be hugely powerful.

Do you think what's needed is more of a governmental regulatory approach?

Well, in some cases the best answer is an old-fashioned regulatory approach. Companies can't be allowed to spew poisons out of their smokestacks. For some toxic substances, the optimum release is zero.

However, in many cases the government can effectively use price signals. Our federal government is already doing so by giving gigantic subsidies to various kinds of industries – usually to the most politically powerful industries. We have dished out more than a trillion dollars to protect and preserve the most powerful institutions in the banking and insurance sectors – without demanding meaningful reforms as part of the deal. In the process, we are consolidating enormous power in a handful of companies, a result that I'm confident we will regret in the years ahead.

In the sustainability field, as in all other public-sector realms, we ought to demand that public policy be structured to internalise all the external costs and benefits, so that consumers see real-world prices. And in those cases where subsidies are viewed as necessary, they should be limited to behaviours that serve a public purpose.

Are you optimistic about our ability to solve these huge problems?

Like anybody who has spent four decades giving environmental talks, I can do a five-minute spiel that will make you feel suicidal. But my wife asked me one day: 'What, in Darwinian terms, is the competitive advantage of pessimism?' Her excellent point was that, if you have no hope, you are doomed to fail. Consequently, I have resolved to be an optimist.

Having said that, it's obviously too late to avoid some environmental tragedies that we could have easily avoided. Because we didn't follow through on the energy efficiency and renewable energy programmes begun under President Jimmy Carter, the world will lose some valuable beachfront, not to mention most of the rice-producing river deltas of East Asia. Because we didn't place a high priority on reining-in human population growth when the world had just a couple of billion people, the swelling number of humans will continue to drive much of the world's biodiversity into extinction. There are far more tigers today in zoos than there are tigers outside of zoos.

Here's an interesting fact that tends to shock anyone who cares about preserving wild things. Taken collectively, we humans and our domesticated animals weigh twice as much as all other vertebrates on the planet – on the land and in the sea – combined. In fact, humans alone weigh eight times as much as all the wild vertebrates on land. There is, of course, a relationship between weight and food consumption. A staggering percentage of the net biological productivity of the planet is being consumed by humans and by animals that we then eat.

Still, without optimism we are doomed. And in my principal area of work – renewable energy – there is abundant reason for optimism.

Getting more personal

What do you think have been some of the main influences on your work over the years?

I grew up in a small paper-milling community in the Columbia River gorge. It is one of the most stunningly beautiful little regions on the planet, but was being raped and pillaged by the industry my father worked for.

The logging industry?

Indirectly. He worked for the paper industry. Almost everyone in town worked at the paper mill. My high school athletic teams were called the 'Papermakers'. The Crown Zellerbach company was clear-cutting vast swathes of forest, losing all the topsoil, and filling the rivers with sediment. It was enough to make a responsible forester cry. At the same time, the paper mill was spewing out air pollution in the form of hydrogen sulfide and sulfur dioxide in breathtaking quantities, no pun intended. It rained almost every day, and the resulting acid pitted the paint on the cars so badly that everybody protested. The plant actually built a shower for cars so that you could work for eight hours and then drive out through a spray to scrub the sulfuric acid off of your car. But it didn't occur to anyone that if the air pollution was doing that to our cars' paint, it might be doing something worse to our lungs. Instead we took a sort of rough pride in the constant stench. We told ourselves that it was the 'smell of prosperity'.

Pretty much from birth, I had an awareness of that awesome natural beauty being torn apart by industrial processes. Everyone knew it was possible to harvest trees without creating a wasteland. Doing so, however, would reduce the profits. Everyone suspected that the mill could capture the sulfur before it went up the smokestack, but doing so would probably reduce the profits.

That sounds pretty seminal in terms of what you have done with your career.

I suspect my value framework, in a nutshell, came out of spending a lot of time in astonishingly beautiful natural areas while I was growing up, watching an unconstrained industry wreak utter destruction, and then being introduced to the biological sciences and to the idea of living with balance and harmony within the carrying capacity of an ecosystem.

I suspect my value framework, in a nutshell, came out of spending a lot of time in astonishingly beautiful natural areas while I was growing up, watching an unconstrained industry wreak utter destruction, and then being introduced to the biological sciences and to the idea of living with balance and harmony within the carrying capacity of an ecosystem.

Did education play a big role, considering that you kept going back to university to do further degrees?

Yes. My mother, in particular, had an almost Chinese value system when it came to getting an education. Neither of my parents graduated from high school, so education acquired the enormous value in their eyes that anything has to those to whom it has been denied. Mom always wanted me to be a physician, but that was simply her way of saying she wanted me to be well educated. In Camas, Washington, the best-educated man – and it was always a man – was the town doctor. I suppose I was motivated by both a genuine desire for knowledge and by a pragmatic desire for credentials. After Earth Day, it was important to me to be viewed as something more than an agitator or organiser. I wanted to be an organiser with enough knowledge and enough degrees that I would be taken seriously by serious people.

What is it about you as a person, do you think, that made you decide that it was important to disseminate your thinking to a wider audience?

I suppose it could all be seen as a rebellion against impotence. When I left on my three years of hitch hiking around the world, I was driven by the sense that the world was going to hell and I couldn't do anything meaningful about it. Earlier, when I'd been appalled by what my father's employer was doing to my local region, I saw myself as unable to do anything about it. Everyone worked for the mill, and there was a constant, nagging, background worry that one must not do anything to irritate the distant powers that issued everyone's bi-weekly pay cheques.

With some slight changes in my upbringing, I suppose all this could have led me to a desire to acquire great wealth and the power that can flow from that. Instead, it led me to decide to use the power of democratic politics to promote the public welfare.

What are you proudest of in terms of your work?

You know, it's funny because my dominant sense of my life is not pride but frustration. I'm intensely aware of all of the stuff that didn't get done. If I'd had four more years to drive energy efficiency and renewable energy forward under President Carter, I truly believe we could have changed the human prospect. Instead, President Reagan shut the programme down.

I'm now in my sixties and running out of time. My generation, which came of age in the 1960s, was absolutely convinced that we would turn over to our kids a world that was vastly better than the world we inherited from our parents. We've certainly made progress in a number of fields, but viewed as a *gestalt*, the world is in much worse shape today than when I was born.

By 1978, I had a clear idea of where America and the world needed to be moving to with regard to energy, and I'd written a popular book – *Rays of Hope: The Transition to a Post-Petroleum World* – that laid out the vision. Two years later, I worked with the SERI staff, other national labs, and brilliant university professors to prepare a detailed policy prescription – *A New Prosperity* – to lead us to the Carter goal of 20% of US energy from renewable sources by the year 2000. Since then, we've mostly gone the wrong direction. I sometimes feel I've lived the life of a modern Cassandra – describing a future that no one will believe.

To answer your actual question, however, I'm proudest of helping to give birth to a broad environmental consciousness with the first Earth Day in 1970. Before that, most people who cared about these issues – and there were a lot who cared about them – were in different, smaller groups. They might have been part of a group that was trying to fight a freeway through a city, or trying to get rid of lead paint in some tenement houses, or trying to ban DDT, or trying to save a wilderness area. What we did in 1970 was to say, 'You know, you guys are all operating from the same basic value system, and you'd be much more powerful if you could unite and work together as a united environmental movement instead of just thousands of disorganised small groups.'

In 1969, most Americans could not have defined what the word 'environment' meant. By the end of 1970, most Americans told pollsters that they considered themselves to be environmentalists. Today, most major universities have schools of environmental studies. There are environmental lawyers, environmental engineers, environmental architects. Every major project requires an environmental assessment. We've spent a couple of trillion dollars implementing laws that were passed between 1970 and 1973.

Perhaps most importantly, virtually everyone believes he or she has a *right* to a safe, healthy environment. This 'right' is much more widely held and deeply believed than many of the rights guaranteed to Americans in the founding Bill of Rights. I take some measure of real pride in that.

Do you think Earth Day has fulfilled its potential?

Earth Day vastly exceeded our expectations. We thought it would be a one-time event, and we hoped it would be pretty big. Instead it was enormous – the largest planned event in the nation's history. As it gathered steam, we decided to focus it on a legislative agenda, and over the next couple of years produced a tidal wave of legislation.

We've now taken Earth Day into a number of other countries and have had particular success in parts of the developing world and in places that are making a transition from totalitarian regimes to somewhat more democratic climates. For reasons that I can't begin to even guess at, governments that are completely intolerant of dissidents agitating for human rights, or religion, or democracy, are quite tolerant of groups that want to protest environmental abuses.

If you look at the people who were involved in the Velvet Revolution in Eastern Europe in 1989, a great many of them were involved with us in some early Earth Days. They were protesting dams, power plants, or a new nuclear facility, whereas if they'd tried to do the same sort of thing on some other more political issue they probably would have been crushed.

It's true in China too. If Chinese activists are talking about an environmental issue, the government gives them a lot of latitude. The Chinese governmental officials who are wrestling with environmental issues are, almost without exception, the most outspoken officials and the most willing to depart from the party line. I could make a similar case in India or Brazil. This tolerance for green troublemakers gives us an unparalleled ability to organise in those parts of the world.

But while we've had a fair amount of success in many countries wrestling with environmental problems within the context of the nation state, the big problems facing us in the future are mostly global issues. We have to create a global consciousness where people care not just about their community, but about everybody on the planet.

Nationalism is perhaps the last acceptable prejudice in the world. People who would never discriminate against someone on the basis of race, sex, or creed feel no compunctions about dismissing someone who happened to be born on the other side of an arbitrary border. However, environmental problems like global warming and acid rain and collapsing fisheries pay no attention to national boundaries. We have to solve the big global problems as a united human race.

It's my hope that Earth Day, which has become a huge secular holiday in more than 150 nations, can play some role in creating that global consciousness by taking advantage of ever cheaper, more powerful communications.

Finally, do you have what you would consider a defining moment in your life? Was it when you were in Africa?

Yes. That night in Namibia was when I decided what I wanted to do with my life, and the last 40 years flow directly from it. Actually, I refer to the whole thing with some reservations because I know it sounds a bit like the experience of an Old Testament prophet in the Middle East. In both regions you're really hot during the day; you're really cold during the night. You're all by yourself for a long period of time. You're hungry. I'm guessing that's when people tend to have visions. My vision just turned out to be rooted in ecology, and it led me into a very satisfying career.

7

....

Gary Hirshberg

Gary Hirshberg is president and chief executive officer (or CE-Yo) of Stonyfield Farm, the world's largest producer of organic yogurt. The New Hampshire company, which began as a small organic farming school, still abides by the original principals on which Gary and others founded it back in 1983: to make a quality product and earn a profit without harming the environment.

One of the company's five missions is 'to serve as a model that environmentally and socially responsible businesses can also be profitable'. For example, it was the first US processor to pay dairy-farm suppliers not to use artificial bovine growth hormone (rBGH). This hormone is not allowed per organic standards anyway, and since all of Stonyfield Farm's line is now organic, it is not simply a choice – it is required for certification. The company also promotes various social issues on its packaging.

Gary spent much of the 1970s pursuing his interest in ecology and the environment. He learned how to build windmills, harnessing wind power for energy, and worked as an environmental education specialist for the US government. For a time, he even ran environmental tours in China. By the early 1980s, he was the executive director of the New Alchemy Institute, a non-profit research centre in Cape Cod, Massachusetts, that published studies on organic farming, aquaculture, and renewable energy sources. He also became involved in a New Hampshire NGO called the Rural Education Center, founded in Wilton NH by former aerospace engineer Samuel Kaymen as an organic farming school.

In 1983, Samuel asked Gary, then a trustee of the Center, to become its director. The institute was struggling to stay afloat, and the pair came up with the idea of selling the organic yogurt Samuel was already making to bring in some revenue. They started with seven cows on the eighteenth-century farm Samuel leased, called Stonyfield, and the yogurt quickly gained a devoted local following. A 1987 plan to expand, via a partnership with a dairy in nearby Greenfield, Massachusetts, fell through when the dairy went into bank foreclosure, and Gary and Samuel went back to making the yogurt themselves.

They finally managed to grow their business by putting together a group of nearly 300 investors. Some were friends interested in socially-responsible businesses, while others were capitalists who believed that the US market for organic dairy products had terrific potential. After moving into a 20 000-square-foot plant in nearby Londonderry, Stonyfield Farm thrived during the 1990s, enjoying a growth rate of nearly 20% annually, and introduced new products such as frozen yogurt.

Eventually, Gary felt he should provide his loyal investors with a liquidity exit, and – now president and chief executive officer – struggled with the decision over whether or not Stonyfield should become a publicly-traded company. Gary and Samuel – board chair for the company – ultimately entered into a corporate part-nership with Groupe Danone. The French giant is the parent company of Dannon yogurt, and purchased an 80% stake in Stonyfield

The Danone deal allowed Gary and Samuel to pay off their original investors, and gave Stonyfield access to an impressive distribution network and marketing muscle. However, the company continues to rely on its own resources for market-ing, with the emphasis on community marketing rather that advertising, while access to the distribution network is also not the major benefit from the partnership with Danone. Furthermore, the deal was agreed only on certain conditions, including that Gary would remain in full control of the company as CE-Yo, and that Stony-field would be allowed to maintain its environmentally-conscious corporate policies.

He has received seven honorary doctorates. He serves on several corporate and non-profit boards including Applegate Farms, Honest Tea, and O'Naturals, a chain of natural fast food restaurants he co-founded. He co-chaired The Social Venture Network for five years and is the founder of the Social Venture Institute, a 'boot camp' for community-minded entrepreneurs.

He has also won numerous awards for corporate and environmental leadership, including the 1999 Global Green USA's Green Cross Millennium Award (inspired by Mikhail S. Gorbachev) for Corporate Environmental Leadership. He was named 'Business Leader of the Year' by Business NH Magazine *and New Hampshire's 1998 Small Business Person of the Year by the US Small Business Administration. His latest book is* Stirring it Up: How to Make Money and Save the World *(Hyperion, 2008).*

The professional journey

What, in your view, are you best known for?

I think that we're known for having been focused on sustainability and organics practically before anybody, at least in business. And for having proven that there really is no trade-off between a focus on sustainability and organics and profitability.

Can you give us some background?

To set a little context, we started the company in the early 1980s. But every-thing that we brought to bear in the founding of the company was a result of growing up in the 1960s and becoming activists in the 1970s. In other words, these were the times when the watchword was to question authority.

The late 1960s and early 1970s were also times when the first data was coming in on climate change, on depletion of clean air and clean water, on toxification, on the impacts of pesticides, of species loss and so on. Now, I was not a business person. In fact, I was trying at all costs to run away from business. But I did acquire a lot of insight into all this, because I had been attempting to raise money as director of several environmental NGOs. I was in the business of trying to get corporations and investors to donate from some of their profits, but it was clear that the charitable side of their activ-ities was very divorced from their actual enterprises. I saw that it was necessary to try to create some economic power on the solutions side of these issues. What I realised was that, unless business got deeply engaged with these really profound issues, we wouldn't even begin to work on solu-tions, let alone arrive at them.

How did you manage to raise money from companies?

Well, in my non-profit mode it was, in the end, I would say, largely emo-tional. My pitch was: what kind of legacy do you want to leave behind? And as I explain in my book, as I made the switch from the non-profit world to the for-profit world, I shifted into the whole Anita Roddick social respon-sibility rap of 'it's the responsible thing to do'.

But a few years ago – I had been chairing the Social Venture Network from 1993 to 1997 – I had this epiphany. It led me to step away from leadership of that organisation and to move much more aggressively towards interfacing with very, very large company decision-makers. Because I real-ised that, as long as we were leaning on the crutch of responsibility, it would always be a discretionary issue whether these corporate leaders could or would think in terms of ethics or the environment or future generations.

But I realised that this is not discretionary. We have a planetary emer-gency here. And nobody has the discretion or choice to ignore, as we have for 100 years, the impact of our economics on the planet. So I have shifted fully and forcefully into talking about the fact that this is a profitable agenda. It is a way to make more money, not something that's discretionary or ethical or even moral. Rather, this is very sound business.

Was it almost serendipity that you ended up with yogurt?

Well, I suppose it was serendipitous. We had a small NGO, an organic farming school called the Rural Education Center, which was struggling and I knew that I needed to move into the business theatre. My partner there, Samuel Kaymen, had some wonderful recipes for a variety of different products, including beer and pickles.

We have a planetary emergency here. And nobody has the discretion or choice to ignore, as we have for 100 years, the impact of our economics on the planet. So I have shifted fully and forcefully into talking about the fact that this is a profitable agenda. It is a way to make more money, not something that's discretionary or ethical or even moral. Rather, this is very sound business.

But at the same time, to be honest, I wasn't even sure I wanted to be in food or consumer products. My greatest hope was to be able to have an impact, from an agricultural point of view, on the supermarkets. I thought that perhaps technology might be the way to do that. But even more, I knew from my NGO background that organics really did work. It really did produce better tasting food that was better for people and better for the planet. So I felt it was really important to go directly at the forces that were undermining the credibility of organic. That's why a food product did make the most sense and the yogurt was simply delicious. That's certainly the serendipitous part.

What was your educational background?

I studied ecology and climate change in college. But my father and grandfather were in the shoe manufacturing industry.

That's interesting, because Jeff Swartz of Timberland, who is also interviewed in this book, has the same background.

As a matter of fact the Swartz's took over one of my family's factories from us. Our families have known each other for my whole life while Jeff and I are very close friends.

While I was growing up the planet wasn't even remotely a consideration for business people when it came to decision-making. As a young man that was very discouraging. I assumed it was the way business had to be, that the planet would be ignored and that's why I ran as far away from it as I possibly could. But eventually I figured out that actually that wasn't a necessary correlation and, as I say in the book, we've had this myth that the planet is a subsidiary of our businesses and really, our businesses are a subsidiary of the planet.

How did your parents react to your early career?

Well, that's a very interesting question. The Swartz family is one of the very, very few in the shoe business who have actually pulled through. And they did it by moving all their labour offshore. My father attempted to do that too, in Brazil in the early 1970s and then wound up in China in the early 1980s, but he just didn't have the financial staying power and so his business really went into a death spiral. Hundreds and hundreds of jobs disappeared when the business failed. So I had a front row seat to watch this really tragic story unfolding. By then my father was experimenting with real estate and he was still involved in shoes abroad. I think he was a bit discouraged about it because he had done everything he was supposed to do, but forces way out of his control led to the business's demise. So I suspect, though I don't know, that he probably thought my moving away from business was a good thing.

So your family has been a big influence on you?

My mother had five children, of whom I was the oldest. I think, just as quickly as she could, she turned her attention to the younger ones. One out of the house was a good thing. But I'd give my mom more credit for my evolution than my dad because she was really the original conscience in my life. She was the one who said, you've got to serve, you've got to give back. As a divorced mother who raised five kids and created a career at the same time, she was the one who said obstacles are nothing.

She was a senior buyer at the Disney Epcot Center in Florida. I remember we went to see this exhibition, the Land Pavilion, which was showing the future of farming and sponsored by Kraft. I made it plain that I thought that environmentally it was a disaster. I think she was horrified by my critique of it because Disney was a very, very good employer and she really enjoyed her time there. So to have this young 20-something coming out saying this is all wrong was probably a little disconcerting. At the same time, I realised that the Land Pavilion was getting 25 000 paying visitors *a day* vs the 25 000 visitors *a year* we had at the New Alchemy Institute. So that was eye-opening.

Apart from your family, what were the other major influences on your evolution?

Well, probably a very significant one was watching our local river catch on fire. My father's factory was on the banks of a river, and I used to love watching the coloured water – red, yellow, green – till it caught on fire. Rivers are not supposed to catch on fire!

Also, I was an active ski racer and I could see the pollution levels – a brown stain – rising in the sky. In college the first book I encountered that really shook me was the *Limits to Growth* study done in 1972 for the Club of Rome. It was the first model of what would happen if we humans continued our unconscious ways.

By the way, two very profound thinkers in this country, Helen and Scott Nearing, who wrote *Living the Good Life*, which came out in 1954, were an earlier influence. They were the original 'back to the land' folks. They were well into their 90s when I first met them, or Scott was. Helen was in her 80s. While their lifestyle was, of course, appealing to me as a very young person, over time I've come to understand that what was really most profound about their work was that they were advocating a very different relationship between people and nature, one that I don't think we still largely appreciate.

In that way they were two of the organic movement's original philosophers, even before Wendell Berry and some of the other more popular folks. So I think the combination of their advocacy for questioning authority and rethinking our relationship to nature, plus the *Limit to Growth* study which laid it out very plainly and numerically and bluntly, was very influential. Just seeing the general environmental deterioration was another big factor. And then in college I was surrounded by some truly magnificent scientists.

Where was that?

That was at Hampshire College in Massachusetts. It's a liberal arts college where students have a very unusual relationship with the faculty. There were no credits, no grades, no 'have to's'. You created your contracts with your advisers and would literally do their field research with them. One of my advisers, my geology professor, actually became my housemate because of his divorce. That kind of close intimate relationship made me very respectful of the discipline of science that is needed to validate assumptions.

When you first started to commit to sustainability, what did you find was the most effective way of actually spreading the word?

Visual or sensory impact. At the New Alchemy Institute, we would bring people in the middle of winter into a completely solar-powered green environment with bees and birds and butterflies and bananas and fish swimming. There would be two or three feet of snow outside. That would have an impact that no amount of words and speeches and books would.

And then, frankly, eating the food was quite something. My very first day at New Alchemy was one of their Saturdays when they were open to the public. It just so happened that there were a couple of *New York Times* writers there who were cooking tilapia. Eating healthy meant eating tilapia in those days! But this happened to be a very well-suited fish for this solar-powered aquaculture and not only was it delicious, but they were raving about it. They were just completely beside themselves with the taste of this fish which has now, of course, subsequently become much popularised. But right then is when light bulbs went off for me that, ah, yes, that's what this is about. This is about a better-tasting future. So I think visual and sensory is key. Obviously I've given my share of lectures and written my latest book and other books, but nothing impacts like people tasting, seeing and walking through a truly sustainable agricultural landscape.

You must have felt very, very motivated because a lot of people might think like this but haven't been very active in encouraging change. You've actually felt it was important to talk to people about it from the very beginning?

Yes. I think I was witnessing the literal and figurative bankruptcy of my father and grandfather's belief system. The business had failed and it wasn't just hundreds but thousands of people who worked for them who lost their jobs. The rivers were becoming polluted, with one catching on fire. All of the assumptions that had led them to make the right choices in business such as they made were turning out to be wrong. And so I think for me it was a matter of wanting to believe in something and, more importantly, to be able to validate the solutions by getting the scientific foundation to do it.

My thesis work was on the causes of alpine treelines: why trees were advancing at high altitudes. Mind you, this was in 1975 and 1976, so it was quite a while ago, but being able to see what I felt wasn't just the opinion of a bunch of raving crazy people with long hair, that this was clinically and statistically unassailable, was very powerful.

I'll tell you a very poignant thing that happened for me. I proved a methodology for ageing these trees that grow at treeline. They can be perhaps only 3 cm in diameter but they might be 100 years old. And for a lot of reasons nobody knew exactly how to age them. But I worked out a methodology with my adviser which did that. It's complicated and it's technical and I won't bore you with the details, but the point was that I was an undergraduate.

So the logical thing to do from there was to proceed with pursuing a doctorate and my adviser was doing what advisers do. He was contacting all of his colleagues and I was preparing for the graduate exams. Meanwhile I went to a lecture by one of the guys who would have been my mentor if I had gone on with that degree and he did a presentation on the probability of locating treelines based on environmental data. And, again, this is perhaps overly technical, but what he proved was that from a lifetime of work that he could predict with a 72% probability at what altitude trees would stop growing based on about 100 variables. And to get to 100% probability was going to take about 500 variables. And I realised that there was going to be a PhD thesis for every one of those variables and I would spend my lifetime proving through the treeline that the planet was warming – when I already knew the planet was warming.

And that's when I had this chilling moment. I'll never forget driving home from the lecture, asking myself – do I want to do that? The very next day I drove down to this New Alchemy Institute on Cape Cod just to check it out because I said, 'Well, I don't want to study the problem, I want to focus on the solution.' When I got there exactly what I've just described to you a moment ago happened to me. I saw these organic gardens, these greenhouses and these integrated systems where the waste from one system was the food for another and I thought: OK, what can I do?

What I realised was that, while I didn't know anything about these technologies, I knew I could bring my writing skills, which by then were quite polished. And, as it turns out, I also discovered I could bring my fundraising skills to help them. When you are in the business of fundraising and writing there's a certain degree of passion needed to really understand your subject. So the passion drove me there but it also became a necessary currency to make it a successful entity.

You've obviously brought a range of different attributes to your management style. Has that evolved over the years that you've been running the company?

Very much so. Well, first of all, it's important for me to confess that I had no knowledge of how to run a business when we started. I knew how to run a non-profit, but producing profit at the end of the month was very foreign to me and so I had a very steep learning curve in the first nine years. But I did the one thing that I'd say has been a constant from the beginning. I learned that, whatever you're doing, whether it's impossible, possible or probable, there's a direct correlation between your success and the passion you bring to it. I'd also like to believe I have been able to evolve and continue this philosophy. This applied to anything important, no matter how impossible it was, like launching Stonyfield. I'd go into the supermarket to talk about organic foods when no-one knew what it even meant. I always joked that we had no supply and no demand, but that otherwise we had a very good business!

And that means that, as we went from two of us to six of us to now 500 of us, I have always wanted everyone to feel that passion. Otherwise it just becomes a job, you're just pushing paper or yogurt pots and then you suffer, you become a commodity. So our compensation structure, our participatory structure, our management structure here has really tried to enable people to feel real pride and ownership in their positions.

What were the hardest problems or the biggest challenges in getting your beliefs over to possibly a sceptical audience?

Well, it has varied with the phases. In the early phase it was persuading anybody in a retail capacity that there was room on the shelf for a more expensive product that had this funny word 'organic' on it. But then the biggest challenge quickly became how to finance it and my first 14 years in business were completely dominated by my trying to find common ground with potential investors.

Because you were talking a language that they probably didn't understand?

Yes. They had seen Ben & Jerry's, they had seen other entrepreneurial businesses with a kind of an offbeat approach, but organic? That was a big question mark. Yogurt? Question mark. Climate change? Question mark. All I created were question marks. There were no periods, let alone exclamation marks. So I wound up with about 300 shareholders, all individuals who contributed in small amounts, some quite large by the end of it, but that's how we built it.

The other major challenge in the later phases – but also in the early ones, really – was convincing new people, potential colleagues and employees that all this sustainability stuff was not just a bunch of rhetoric from this child of the 1960s. I had to get over that it was genuine, and could be a true competitive advantage, but also that it was very, very important that they didn't have to buy into my belief system. They had to understand that to execute against this, with all the impossibilities and improbabilities that we faced, we were going to have to stay very, very loyal to that core green agenda. That meant questioning every decision in terms of its environmental impact. If we built a building we had to think about the materials. If we were dismantling something we had to think about the disposal of the materials. This was stuff that people were not trained to do.

You've formed a partnership with French consumer goods company Danone? When did you decide to do this?

We signed it in December of 2001 but we began the negotiations in 1999.

And why Danone?

Well, I had no desire to leave or sell at that point, but I did want to provide an exit for our shareholders. So I went out to seek an entity that would give my shareholders an excellent exit in terms of return on investment and at the same time leave me as independent as possible, if not completely so. In the end, Danone agreed to all of my terms. We talked to probably 20 major food corporations and it was the one willing to be intellectually and legally flexible enough to allow me to remain an independent entity, and that continues to this day.

Current views

How do you define sustainability generally, but also in terms of business, government and consumers? Because we gather that your big message, particularly in your book, is that business has to be in the lead here?

Absolutely. Well, I used the phrase earlier, a planetary emergency. I define sustainability now as survivability. I don't think sustainability is the best word. For 25 years I've been looking for a better one and haven't found it yet. But it doesn't really summarise what we're talking about here. We're talking about life on Earth as we know it. We're talking about a rate of evolution that is completely unnatural but also devastating for literally millions of species. And when I look not only at the rate of the various ecological trends that we're experiencing, but also at their synergistic effect, the combined effect … you know, everything I knew in the 1970s has been proven to be true now but for one thing – and that is that the rate of our ecological demise is happening faster. The rate of our climate change is happening faster than was predicted because we didn't understand the synergistic impacts as well back then. And so I see this all quite simply. There is no doubt now.

I don't think sustainability is the best word. For 25 years I've been looking for a better one and haven't found it yet. But it doesn't really summarise what we're talking about here. We're talking about life on Earth as we know it. We're talking about a rate of evolution that is completely unnatural but also devastating for literally millions of species.

When we set out it was with the aim of proving that it was possible to create a business that considers the environment in all that we do. We proved that one. That's over. We've moved beyond that. Now the principal mandate for the next 25 years is to evolve rapidly the solutions to show significant decision-makers the way and *how* we're going to deal with this stuff because it isn't a question of *whether*.

The planet is going to drive this agenda. If we think, with our Copernican worldview, that we're somehow driving the agenda – well, we're not. You see storms with the force of a Katrina, you see waves of species decline, water depletion, these hypoxias happening all over, where we're killing off estuaries. And how long it will take to reverse these trends? Let alone the fact that if we stop producing any CO_2 right this minute we would still continue to warm the atmosphere for 40 or 50 years. So when you look at the far-reaching impact of everything that we've done, the past choices, there is no doubt that we have to address them and I think the principal challenge at the moment is the lack of willpower.

Among whom?

Well, among everybody. The very tumultuous election we went through in the US has been not just an election, but an absolute paradigm shift and challenge. Do we continue to assert dominance over other people, other countries and our planet or do we shift into a mode of partnering? And change is scary to people. It's scary to everybody, not just decision-makers and politicians, but everybody.

And I think the vote of support for Bush was more about fear of change than anything else. There certainly wasn't a vision to embrace there. Instead it was the illusion that he would keep us safe, protected and keep the walls up. Obviously he was a failed formula and a failed presidency as far as I'm concerned. But what we need to do now is get people to recognise that change is inevitable. It can be profitable, as I explained in my book. But, more importantly, we are never, never lacking in our creative solutions. We just have to get focused. It's time for us as a species to grow up, that's for sure.

Can you point to any businesses you know that have bought into this message?

Sure. I have endless examples.

You mention a number in your book.

Sure. But let's just focus on one aspect for a moment. Let's just focus on organic. The largest food companies on earth all now have an organic portfolio or portfolios. The largest retailers on earth are now aggressively courting organic. If I had told you 10 years ago that this was going to happen, you would have thought that I had been smoking something. But, for example, I've given a keynote speech on sustainability to the senior executive team at Safeway, one of the largest retailers in America. It has its own organic brand called Safeway O, so my retailer has become a colleague. And, also, by the way, a competitor!

I could actually spend 100% of my time just giving speeches to major corporations. I've spoken at Google, I've spoken at Wal-Mart, I've spoken to the largest supermarket chain in Canada. I see the penetration and it's gone way beyond viewing organics and sustainability as a novelty. It's now a routine part of business and it's happened extremely fast.

Is it about creating a new business model and are companies which don't get this going to be in real trouble?

I think so, yes. I think an awful lot of people in business are seeking new ways because the paths they're on are obviously failing. For example, the dependence on non-renewable fuels has failed. Watching the US Open tennis on television I saw ads from Exxon talking about creating the technology for solar cells. Exxon in my lifetime has mostly scorned the idea of solar as a real solution and now it's using valuable, incredibly expensive television time to out-compete Shell and others who are betting on renewable energy.

But isn't the reaction among a lot of people just to get very sceptical and think, oh, they're just greenwashing?

Of course. And that's appropriate and will be one of the elements that may help to save our species: that we don't let these companies get away with just the rhetoric.

Is this initiative you have got going, Climate Counts, a way to make sure they don't get away with just rhetoric?

That's exactly what it is. Climate Counts provides a concrete, objective and unassailable numeric measure of companies' seriousness and sincerity about the planet, about climate, and that's what's needed. We have to be sceptical, but at the same time the entire discussion has moved from companies being sceptical of activists to activists now being sceptical of companies, which is great. It's real progress.

A lot of companies are struggling with this. What tips would you offer to anyone in a company trying to do this?

Well, I guess one tip I would offer is this phrase: $200 per barrel of oil. Any businessperson who understands the effect of $200 a barrel of oil understands that everything has got to change. There is not a single aspect of our economy that will not be profoundly affected by that. And so you can ignore it, you can close your eyes, you can close your ears, but as a CEO I see my role as living not in the present but in the future. I have to see what's around the corner, what's going to be affecting me and my colleagues down the road, not now. So if there's anybody out there who shares that perception – and I think most CEOs do – then that notion is very profound.

Any businessperson who understands the effect of $200 a barrel of oil understands that everything has got to change. There is not a single aspect of our economy that will not be profoundly affected by that. And so you can ignore it, you can close your eyes, you can close your ears, but as a CEO I see my role as living not in the present but in the future.

The way I describe it is that many, many, many things that used to make sense won't any longer. And many, many, many things that used to be completely nonsensical will now be thoroughly rational. There will be those who just shut it out and you know what? Their businesses are going to fail because, by not preparing, they're not going to be ready.

And are you relatively optimistic that solutions can be found?

I am optimistic, partly because as an entrepreneur I've seen the impossible come true many, many times. I wish I'd coined that Adidas phrase 'impossible is nothing' because I think it's right. But, more to the point, I've seen such amazing things happen in my lifetime. There were chlorofluorocarbons in the atmosphere and they are basically gone. Yet in 1990 that looked to be an even more immediate threat than even climate change. Getting rid of them was a result of human behaviour changes.

In the US there are now seatbelts laws, no smoking in restaurants and I'm watching the explosion of not only hybrid vehicles but also all the associated technologies of batteries, the chargers, the solar boosters and the catalytic converters. We are an entrepreneurial species and I think that if folks can just focus on the opportunities, it's very easy to see massive amounts of technological solutions.

That said, I do think we're too late to minimise, let alone reverse some trends. I think we're going to have a tremendous drop in biodiversity. I think we're going to have large parts of the globe become uninhabitable through sea level rise and toxification. I think we will see waves of immigrants in the multi-multimillions and I think we will probably see a great deal of human catastrophe. But, as I said before, I view this all as not just about sustainability but survivability and so in that context I do have hope. I do think that change will come and I think that we will get it right.

Do you think that change comes about as a result of pressure from consumers, pressure from business, pressure from government or cooperation between all three?

I think it's none of the three. I think economic and ecologic realities are driving it. We activists have played our part in interpreting those realities, while individuals in commerce and in roles that are relevant to government – but not in government – are buying into those interpretations. If I might clarify that last point: I don't believe government can lead on these issues because change is too fearful and if you advocate for it you're going to get thrown out of office. I think governments are there to preserve the status quo.

But there are those who've formerly been in government who see the bankruptcy of that notion. There are also folks who, in terms of manifesting real change – the tidal change that's necessary – recognise the limits of what government can actually do and who are in positions to be very useful. Al Gore is obviously a classic example, but there are plenty of other less well known people out there. I think what we're experiencing right now is a sort of societal evolution that is not being driven by any one segment.

Getting more personal

What is it about you as a person that made you decide that this was an important way to go? You're obviously someone who feels very passionately about things.

Well, I was the oldest of five in a house with a single mom, so I had to develop a lot of leadership skills early on, I guess. But you're asking about the passion side of it.

Well, about whatever you think it is that makes you tick.

Well, I think one of the things that happened to me early on was that my parents had a completely unsuccessful marriage. Yet while the divorce was certainly painful it was not as painful as the marriage. And I think that living in that environment I became very sensitive and protective of my siblings. I was also, I think, unconsciously very, very unhappy. And I wanted to be happy and I wanted other people around me to be happy. In adulthood that translated into a desire, when I saw pain and strife, challenge and difficulty, to try to be a problem solver.

What was the age range in your family?

They extended to seven years younger than me.

It sounds as though you're a nurturer, in a way, as well?

Well, I would leave that to someone else to judge. I don't know.

What are you proudest of in terms of your work?

Well, I'm proudest of the fact that my children who are teenagers and therefore constitutionally cynical are, in fact, genuinely very respectful and, I think, excited about the work I'm doing. My son decided to take a year off from college and of all the things he could do all over the world he chose to come here and work. I'm proud that this makes sense to him because you know how the pendulum swings? Kids wanting to be the exact opposite of their parents? And I'm proud that this apparently is sensible enough that it even makes sense to them.

Is there one defining moment you would single out that set you on this path?

I think there has been a whole stream of poignant moments. I think sitting on top of Mount Washington studying the treeline in 1972 or 1971 and looking up at this radiantly beautiful scene that I had loved my whole childhood and seeing this brown stain that was filling the sky all around me was really haunting. Because if there is any place on earth that I thought was clean it was the summit of Mount Washington and New Hampshire and it was clear that it wasn't. There was no escape. So I think that was a deep moment. Also, working in China.

> *Sitting on top of Mount Washington studying the treeline in 1972 or 1971 and looking up at this radiantly beautiful scene that I had loved my whole childhood and seeing this brown stain that was filling the sky all around me was really haunting.*

Tell us about that.

In the late 1970s and early 1980s I saw what I would have to say was the closest picture of hell on earth in terms of simply rampant pollution. It was absolutely despicable: horrifying amounts of chemicals being used on food, on agriculture and in incredible proximity to millions and millions of children. It shook me really deeply.

What were you doing in China?

I was leading tours to look at the ecological evolution of China and I was giving lectures all over as I was invited by a division of the Chinese Academy of Scientists to speak about what they called the soft path: solar, wind, organics, renewable energy and organics. So I did that over about seven years.

And is there any one thing in business that you would like to achieve?

Definitely. I want to see either Danone, or some of the other enormous companies that I'm associated with, put a major multi-multimillion dollar campaign behind an organic line. I think to see it be not a niche for them but a central focus. And I'm sure that's going to happen.

As the impact of oil is being felt in modern agriculture, organic – because it has a smaller carbon footprint and uses less soil in general – is going to make a whole lot of sense.

8

....

Tony Juniper

Tony Juniper is a British environmental campaigner, author and commentator, most recognised for his work as Executive Director of Friends of the Earth (FoE), England, Wales and Northern Ireland and Vice Chair of Friends of the Earth International from 2000 to 2008.

He was brought up in Oxford. In 1980 he went to Bristol University to study psychology and zoology before getting his first big environmental job at the International Council for Bird Preservation.

In the early 1990s he moved on to Friends of the Earth, where he stayed – in a range of capacities – until 2008. There, he oversaw the campaign that ensured the inclusion of a Climate Change Bill in the Queen's Speech 2006. This was supported by his successful 'Big Ask' Campaign throughout 2005 and 2006, when he worked with Radiohead frontman Thom Yorke. This led to the world's first national legislation on climate change, enacted in 2008.

During his time there he pioneered the use of celebrities to get his environmental message across, finding that often they proved more persuasive than demonstrations and placards. Yasmin Le Bon, for instance, helped to campaign against logging in Malaysia, and posed for photographs that were auctioned in aid of FoE. Others celebrities included Johnny Borrell from Razorlight, X-Files actress Gillian Anderson and Cold Feet's Helen Baxendale.

In the mid-1990s, Juniper and FoE were starting to win arguments with campaigns such as the one against the Newbury bypass in Berkshire, steering a fine line between civil disobedience and quiet persuasion. Even though the bypass was finally built, the campaign helped to end the Government's massive road-building programme. The battle against genetically-modified (GM) crops was a clearer success. There is still no commercial GM farming in Britain.

When he joined FoE, it had an annual budget of £4m, 85 staff and a mission to change the system, reform capitalism and switch to a pure green lifestyle. In March 2003, when he took over its running, the annual budget had risen to £11m and its 170 staff were professional, organised and focused.

Juniper now works in a variety of roles. Among others, he is a Special Adviser to the Prince of Wales' Rainforest Project and a Senior Associate with the Cambridge University Program for Industry. He sits on a number of advisory panels and continues to speak and write on environmental issues.

He has written a number of books, including the award-winning Parrots: A Guide to the Parrots of the World; Spix's Macaw: The Race to Save the World's Rarest Bird; How Many Lightbulbs Does it Take to Change a Planet? 95 Ways to Save Planet Earth; and Saving Planet Earth (a companion volume to the BBC series with same name). He has started work (2008) on a new book (called Harmony) with HRH The Prince of Wales.

The professional journey

What sparked your interest in environmentalism? Was it your family?

No. It's interesting. My father was quite a knowledgeable naturalist, although not particularly keen to go out in the field. And my mother had a fear, well, more a dislike, of most things with fur and feathers, never mind scales. But I kind of fed my own interest. I was also lucky enough to grow up on the edge of Oxford, with access to the River Thames and various bits of meadows and wetlands and woodlands that were wonderful places to learn about wildlife. So I spent my youth trundling around on a bicycle with a butterfly net and jam jar full of newts and became very familiar with natural history.

So you were self-taught?

I read avidly – great piles of books about birds and fish. I also had an aviary with a few budgies, canaries, parakeets and birds like that from the local pet shop. But mostly it was wild stuff. I was out there in the bush, if you can call it that. And I used to insist that my birthday presents were the things that scuttled in boxes rather than things that were inanimate. I spent nearly all of my meagre earnings on either acquiring birds or fishing tackle. Actually, that was another passion. I think most fishermen are naturalists. You go fishing to spend time with wildlife as much as anything else.

What was your first role at Friends of the Earth?

I was running its tropical rainforest campaign, which had several elements. One was to have some influence on the tropical timber industry – a major driver of deforestation – and that went from logging methods right through to what people were buying in the shops. We used our influence to help to establish the Forest Stewardship Council, a mechanism to help consumers choose good wood compared to destructively-produced wood.

We had a big focus on overseas development assistance and the different funds that were being spent by governments for poverty alleviation. Some of this was directly targeting tropical forests as a source of wealth and causing not only environmental damage, but also human rights abuses and, indeed, providing arguably only the smallest – if any – benefit for development. So we were working in that complicated area as well. And we were looking at the activities of corporations outside the forestry sector – for example, at companies involved in the production of tropical commodities, the mining sector and oil and gas companies – and the impact they were having.

At the time I think we had quite a major influence over a whole series of players involved with tropical forests in different ways. We raised awareness among consumers about the need to purchase more carefully. We changed the policies of some of the big development institutions. For example, we got the World Bank to say it would stop funding the logging of primary tropical rainforests, and many transnationals to engage with tropical forest issues in ways that continue today. So various roundtables, like the sustainable palm oil roundtable initiative, basically resulted from our campaigning.

Over what time period are we talking about?

This is starting in 1990 when I joined FoE. My interest in tropical forests really came from my background as a professional ornithologist and the work I was doing to try to stop the extinction of endangered parrots. I was really self-taught as a bird expert, although having a zoology degree of course helped. Because parrots are principally tropical forest birds I became very familiar with all of the issues concerning tropical deforestation. And then I took on different roles within the organisation, finishing up as director.

Rainforests are still one of the biggest issues, and it remains unresolved. Yet it is an appallingly unnecessary environmental disaster that is being perpetrated and it's not only going to be an environmental catastrophe, but it also has the potential to turn into a humanitarian calamity as severe environmental impacts start to feed back into the economy.

Would you say you're best known for your work with rainforests?

That, and more latterly climate change, though these two are inseparable really. They overlap. But rainforests are still one of the biggest issues, and it remains unresolved. Yet it is an appallingly unnecessary environmental disaster that is being perpetrated and it's not only going to be an environmental catastrophe, but it also has the potential to turn into a humanitarian calamity as severe environmental impacts start to feed back into the economy.

There are several ways of looking at this: the principal and most immediate is currently the global warming issue. About a fifth of the CO_2 emissions going into the atmosphere are now coming from deforestation and if we don't stop that we can't conceivably keep a lid on temperatures going above two degrees. And above two degrees we might start to get all sorts of unpleasant feedbacks occurring as a result of the warming. So it is at the core of the environmental challenge, but I think it is probably the most complicated task in history. You couldn't invent something more complicated.

Why is it so complicated?

You've got more than 40 different countries involved with more than 40 different governments, while the countries which own the rainforest themselves have many different cultures, many different languages and many different development contexts. Some of them are semi-industrialised countries, like Brazil. Others are very, very poor countries with little rule of law, like the Democratic Republic of the Congo. Some of them are bound into export markets and then that's all about world trade rules. Many of them are obviously suffering deforestation because of the behaviour of consumers in the Western countries who demand the soya and palm oil and timber – never mind minerals, the production of which is causing deforestation.

And you have all sorts of issues to do with ownership. Do the rainforests belong to the indigenous people who've been there for tens of thousands of years, or the governments who have taken office in recent decades? And at the end of the day who's got the right to tell who what to do about this? They can argue that the Western countries have deforested their nations centuries ago and now are saying that they shouldn't do it. So what's the deal in terms of the financial compensation that's going to have to go with this? Mix all that up, add half a dozen other things, then try to find a solution, and it isn't easy. But it's got to be done.

Do you think it will be the economic argument that really hits home?

Well, I've come to the conclusion that on these big environmental issues – and I put deforestation as one of the big ones up there with climate change and everything else – that there is no one single thing. And it's probably a foolish job to go to look for one thing that's going to be 'the answer'. But I think that a financial transaction, a business arrangement between the rich countries and the poor ones, lies at the core of what has to be done about tropical deforestation.

The way the Prince of Wales looks at this, and I think he's right, is to see the rainforests as a global utility – essentially a global air-conditioning system among other things – and so we need to pay for that. Everybody does. And the rich need to mobilise resources on the basis of their means and the poor countries and the developing countries have to absorb that on the basis of how much forest they possess. And that's the nature of the deal at the end. But the complexity that goes alongside that is absolutely huge. How much money, what institutions are going to control it, who's going to pay? How's it going to be spent on the ground and what's going to prevent it finishing up in Swiss bank accounts?

Given the complexity of these issues, what has proved the best way to raise awareness?

At times a placard-waving protest with people being carted off by the police can be very effective. At others you might want a much gentler approach, through a song delivered by a famous singer. Both of these are valid. And in between there are legal actions, research reports, public meetings, whatever. All of it is still necessary.

I think, however, we've just moved into a new phase where we do need to be a little bit more thoughtful about tactics. I would characterise the transition like this: for the last 30 years environmentalists have been very successful in making the case for technical changes to the law. Banning DDT, getting controls on the emissions causing acid rain, phasing out the chemicals depleting the ozone layer – all of these were famous victories, but they were delivered by a bunch of advocates, like me, talking to a bunch of politicians like the minister for the environment. That process affected a small group of people who happened to make a particular chemical or control a particular industrial process. That was fine and we've solved some enormous environmental problems by going down that route.

Now, though, we're into a new phase where the cutting edge of the environmental issue is not only that, but it's also rapid global warming, the pace of depletion of natural resources, and the consequent destruction of biodiversity. Now it's not simply a group of companies that need to be affected by a law – we have to change everything. We have to change the way people live. It's about aircraft, it's about the amount of stuff we use, it's about the kind of diet we have. It's about moving beyond technical regulations controlling particular industrial sectors, such as pesticides or power generation, and towards an agenda where everybody buys into a process of change. This is where you need a different approach, because now we've got to talk to a wide body of people, rather than the policy-makers.

What does this mean in terms of tactics?

This is actually quite new and I don't think environmentalists are either fully aware of the change or have yet thought through exactly how this is going to work. But we do need to. And this will require not only an understanding of policy and the necessary laws to control a particular chemical or limit certain emissions. It is also about the psychology of how people receive these messages. What do people feel when they are told they can't fly, that they should eat less meat or they have to use that particular stuff?

Presumably they rebel against it?

Exactly. So that's got to be something that's thought through very carefully.

Does the lead have to come from politicians?

There's a limit to what politicians can do now. It's very obvious in terms of blunt instruments like fuel duties and such that are taken by the public to be punitive. In a democracy there's evidently a limit and I think we've kind of reached it.

There's a limit to what politicians can do now. It's very obvious in terms of blunt instruments like fuel duties and such that are taken by the public to be punitive. In a democracy there's evidently a limit and I think we've kind of reached it.

One's often confronted with a dilemma in a democracy: whether you should swing with the apparent mood of the voters or have principles. Politicians are divided on this. Some of them get elected and then say: 'I'll do what I think is right.' Others spend a lot of time listening to those who elected them, thinking through what they might want. And both are right, of course. Navigating through that is the art of politics. But in terms of those who come in and say, 'I think the environment's really important, something must be done' – they're relatively few in number.

In the UK, Michael Meacher has to be the one who most environmentalists would hold up as a man who came in and stuck to his guns. He mastered his brief as well. He wasn't lazy and he didn't hold very fixed views about how things should be done. He just came in with a very strong personal passion for environmental issues and tried his best to do something about it. And he paid the ultimate price. Tony Blair sacked him in 2003. He lasted longer than anyone thought he would, though.

Current views

What have you found to be the best way to get business to take on board the different areas of sustainability?

Ironically, perhaps, given my campaigning background, since September 2008 one of the things I have been doing is working with the Cambridge University programme for industry. This was set up some 20 years ago to do exactly this – to engage with executives at a quite senior level to try to bring the sustainability issues as far as possible into the heart of companies. It's a complicated process, but essentially the arguments need to be pitched at two or three levels simultaneously. They focus on ethics, the practical implications, setting out the business issues. They set out the role of companies and a different kind of policy environment. And the programme asks: can you put all these things together? It adds up to the case for sustainability for companies.

There will always be different ways because the corporate sector is just so diverse. But in the end it is important to make some kind of a business case because those heads of corporations, though they're human and have children, are running businesses. So they have to be convinced of the need for change at a senior level. But it's also really important not to give the impression that these big problems can be solved by one or two companies picking up a little bit of a brand-led or business-oriented argument, like small change. We've got to cut emissions of carbon dioxide by at least 80% by 2050, to reduce drastically the amount of resources being used up, and to change the structure of agriculture. We've got six billion people now living well beyond the means of this planet. We're going to have nine billion by 2050 and a few companies making small changes to their core business is not going to cut it. We need all of them to make big strategic shifts – for example, out of fossil fuels and into clean energy.

We've got six billion people now living well beyond the means of this planet. We're going to have nine billion by 2050 and a few companies making small changes to their core business is not going to cut it. We need all of them to make big strategic shifts – for example, out of fossil fuels and into clean energy.

So what changes do companies need to take on board?

Changes to the system. And that's about them using their influence, which is considerable, in convincing governments to do things differently. One of the things I think is most interesting is how, over the last couple of years, quite a few of the big brands have moved into a position of public advocacy for big change and they're telling governments to do something.

At the end of 2007, 150 of the largest corporations published a joint statement called the Bali Communiqué. It sent a message to governments collectively negotiating in the UN to come forward with a climate change deal that reflects the latest science. A few years ago I was at the Kyoto Summit, and watched the business lobby there basically saying that the science is uncertain, don't do anything, leave us alone, and leave it to voluntary agreements. In 10 years we've gone from that to huge business lobbies saying, 'Sort this out please, with laws and regulations', and they're saying it to the heads of government in countries like the UK and the US. So I think that's a very significant shift, and I think that has to be part of the agenda for business.

Individually, yes, they can do bits and pieces. They can talk to their customers. They can enhance their brand with greener products and services. But until there's a collective shift where they all recognise that the fundamentals of the economy have got to alter we're not going to get very far.

Do you consider that oil companies have made giant strides in this direction?

It's a repositioning, it's not a stride. It was getting them to stop being a block. That was a significant shift. They were standing in the middle of the road. Stop, don't do anything. We're big oil, we're fundamental to the economy, the science is not proven, don't dare get on to our territory. They've now moved to the side. They say, OK, it's accepted, we've got to do something and that is important.

But, actually, it's very significant to see that what they've done voluntarily in terms of building up the renewables businesses. A number of them have downsized their renewables programmes and I think you could see this as being a lot to do with changes of leadership in those companies. And that's one of the underestimated factors I think in companies moving towards the green agenda: the importance of a charismatic figure at the top of the company.

So it is important for companies to be headed up by a visionary?

I disagreed with John Browne, long the head of BP, on almost everything to do with his business in terms of drilling for more oil and gas. But on global warming I would have to acknowledge him as one of the leaders, who pushed his company out in front and separated it from the rest of the pack, setting targets internally. You can see people who have repositioned their entire firm on the basis of the green agenda, but when they go it very often slips backwards. It is also a big danger, of course, relying on certain people, because when they go, so does their particular way of doing things. I think you can see this most clearly with BP.

What can sustainability offer business?

A future – because if we don't have sustainability, we won't have an economy. And without an economy we'll have no business. And one of the things that is potentially quite exciting about companies is the fact that they can take a long-term view.

Even though they're often driven by the City and its demand for short-term results?

Yes, they're driven by the quarterly figures and, yes, they're driven by shareholders, but can you think of any business which would say we don't want to be in business in 20 years? Or 30 years? You don't get a politician talking about being in office in 20 or 30 years. In the business world there is a unique opportunity to think strategically and long term. So sustainability really can and should be at the core of what companies are now planning, in terms of, for example, where markets will go and what will be some of the future risk factors. At that fundamental level sustainability, for a company, is about being able to continue in business.

Sustainability really can and should be at the core of what companies are now planning, in terms of, for example, where markets will go and what will be some of the future risk factors. At that fundamental level sustainability, for a company, is about being able to continue in business.

Do you think cost is a major factor in preventing them from taking a more sustainable approach? Or is it lack of education?

Cost evidently, competitive forces, a cut-throat free market and highly competitive sectors like oil, gas or even supermarkets. If one company moves too far, too quickly, its competitors – who are laggardly in terms of their sustainability behaviour – will probably be more in tune with their customers on cost. They'll seize market share and that will damage the real leaders. I think this is what did for the renewables businesses in BP and Shell up to a point. The soaring price of oil meant that it was possible suddenly to print money by sticking to the core business. So why waste money on renewables? It's this paradoxical signal.

What should companies be doing during the downturn?

High oil prices, which cause economic shock, don't mean that we have to look the other way on environmental issues; just engage with them much more quickly. Linked to that is the whole food issue. Food prices are, in part, going up because of the increased price of energy. They're also rising because of foolhardy attempts to try to deal with the oil crunch by growing biofuels. And you've got a direct correlation there. Not only has that led to an increase in fuel prices, it's led to an increase in carbon dioxide emission which, in turn, is going to cause economic shocks of the kind which are set out in the Stern Review.

So all this stuff is fundamentally now linked into a single agenda called sustainability. You can't say, in a downturn, the environment's for the good times. Now we're going to do the economy instead. It's becoming more obvious that you can't do that.

How often have you found that one group of companies talks to one section of government while another section of government goes and says something completely different?

Yes, there's a great deal of that goes on. An important cut-through moment took place, I think, in 2006, when a bunch of 12 of the biggest transnationals in this country went and saw the Prime Minister. These companies, from different sectors, went straight to the top and I thought that was a good moment. But you're right. What's going on behind that big set-piece event is all sorts of lobbying by different interest groups targeting different bits of government. One group of companies talks to the Department of Transport, another to the business and enterprise people, or the Treasury, or the housing people, or the environmental people. Some of them are talking to all of them.

And on top of all that, various trade associations representing particular sectors are sometimes saying the complete opposite to some of their members. At a sustainability course in Cambridge I challenged a group of executives. I said, look, you've all got good sustainability polices, that's why you're here. You've all got ambitions to build the environment and social issues into your businesses. I have a little bit of homework for you. Go back to your companies, find out all the trade associations you belong to and see if the policy they're advocating on your behalf actually matches your sustainability policy. And if they don't, work out what you're going to do about it. I think most of them saw the sense of this, although it appeared that few had done it.

What incentives do you think should be offered to both companies and people to change?

This is an utterly under-exploited piece of policy and thinking: how to create the incentives to get people to do things differently. Currently a lot of it is seen as punishment – and a lot actually is. A lot of the incentives are, of course, economic. Some of them are cultural and to do with fashion and how we can create a different kind of value set than that which society has lived by. So green living and sustainability are seen as what you want to do rather than enjoying conspicuous consumption.

That's quite a big psychological challenge, but on the economic side there are things which are more immediate and which can actually contribute to that process of cultural change as well. One is a feed-in tariff. This basically transforms the economics of renewable energy through governments establishing a law that says power generators which are feeding power into the grid will be paid at a certain level above the market rate for their green power, compared to non-renewable electricity. So if you then fit a solar array on your rooftop as a householder, government will fix the economics so that the payback time for that is 10 rather than 50 years. Suddenly you're stupid not to have a solar rooftop. The Germans brought about a big increase in the share of renewable energy they use through this measure.

Another thing you could do is change the vast amount of expenditure that is under government control to sustainable expenditure. About 40% of the British economy is under the control of government in terms of defence spending, health, education, police, buildings. Well, you could change a big bit of the economy immediately by government saying, we're only going to spend our money now on low-carbon products. Hospitals would have to be at the absolute cutting edge of sustainable technology. Many public vehicles could be hybrids with electric motors and the highest possible fuel economy. And by taking a more comprehensive and modern approach to the economy, and for example, thinking about energy prices in 20 years' time, this isn't actually a huge expenditure but an investment.

So it's about leading by example?

Exactly. But you create markets at the same time. So if the government says we're going to spend that 40% differently, all the people who were feeding those markets with heating equipment or double glazing or building design will suddenly think, we're going to supply that instead. Then extend this to research and development. If companies can meet certain criteria for the development of new products and services or technologies, corporation tax relief becomes a big part of the incentive. So the money you're spending in this stream of technological investment won't get taxed at all, while continuing to look for more oil and gas means you continue to pay tax above the standard rate. Those kinds of tools could also start to shift people's attention.

There are many difficulties. Some of them are short-term political ones. Others are now practical legal issues to do with how we've developed the global economy and the limits to what national governments can do because of world trade rules. We've kind of written ourselves into this process of integration and are now finding it very difficult to take control back again, but I think governments are going to have to do this.

One of the arguments of Prime Minister Gordon Brown has been that we have to find global solutions to global problems and the problems we're suffering at home are global. Basically he's saying there's no point in us doing anything because until everybody does it we're not going to do it. This is, in part, to do with his vision of growth and competitiveness being built around a global integration process. Many of us would say, actually, until you start doing this at home we're not going to get there.

So if we don't start good practice at home, nobody else will do it?

I think that's problematic. Part of it is to do with the institutions like the Word Trade Organisation saying that you can't protect your economy to help to innovate for sustainability because you have to be open to investment and must trade with other countries. Ten years ago we warned that this was a bad idea from the point of view of sustainability because you end up losing control of your own economy and having lowest common denominator policy-making. That's exactly what's happened. Now we're getting into this difficult phase, where the global issues are actually starting to bite on national economies and, as a result, countries are finding it quite difficult to cope. So that's a kind of a context which makes some of this very difficult for individual countries to do.

Is that going to be helped or hindered by an organisation like the European Union (EU)?

Well, the EU is geared up for more of this. It has got this agenda called Global Europe, which is basically a plan to lever access to markets and access to resources globally through accelerating the process of economic integration at the international level. Europe has failed to get its way in the World Trade Organisation but it's now pushing for various bilateral trade agreements with countries in Africa and the old colonial countries in the Pacific and the Caribbean in order to have these more liberalised economic relationships.

This is all about two things. First, it's about getting more access to resources and about investment opportunities for European transnationals in developing countries – taking over their airlines, health services, whatever else they want to liberalise. That's arguably an 'engine of growth', in a short-term sense, in Western Europe. But it's also a source of environmental destruction and indeed impoverishment in many developing countries as their local businesses are put out of business by much fitter, bigger global players.

Having said that, we look for crumbs of comfort around the table and on the climate change negotiations the Europeans are by far ahead of the other big players, the Americans, the Chinese, or the Indians, in terms of saying that we need caps, we need an orderly transition. So it's complicated.

How do you view greenwashing and green hyperbole?

There's a lot of that about and very often it's difficult to disentangle a genuine shift of policy or emphasis from a communications campaign. A lot of what some businesses are responding to, in terms of apparent engagement with the sustainability agenda, is a risk to their brand. So companies which happen to be in a vulnerable area, like chemicals, mining or whatever, engage in programmes of corporate social responsibility which actually aren't touching the core business in terms of the products that are being produced or the pollution controls that are put in place. You finish up with glossy reports, nice TV commercials, and programmes of CSR engagement involving seminars with people like me who are invited along to go and have a nice chat about what could be done and sustainability challenges.

There is a quite a bit of that around, but for your average punter it's really, really difficult to disentangle that from those people who arguably have taken the issues into quite a deep place and into how they run their businesses. And it drags everybody down. It's a real shame. Actually, I think some of the leading corporates should get together and set up a little unit which sniffs out greenwash and blows the whistle.

You think they should out 'greenwashers'?

The leading companies have a real interest in outing laggardly companies because they're investing real money, putting real business opportunities on the line, and they've got people who are trotting around, waving green flags with absolutely no intention of doing anything at all about it.

If you had to indulge in some crystal ball gazing, how do you see business, government and consumers adapting to the idea of sustainability in the future? Do you feel pessimistic, optimistic – or are you somewhere in the middle?

If one looks at all the evidence on the table at the moment you can sketch out, broadly speaking, two scenarios. Number one – you might call it the optimistic one – is that there is an awakening in the widest sense of the crisis that we're now facing at all levels in terms of the public, the corporates and governments. This will result in a national and global programme for an orchestrated and orderly transition to a sustainable society over the next 20 or 30 year or so. That could happen. And if you look at how quickly these issues became mainstream over the last decade, perhaps there is good reason to be optimistic, if that speed of change can be sustained.

Just as, or perhaps more, plausible, is that we will continue as we presently are with countries putting their short-term traditional interests to the fore of how they develop policy. So they'll continue to build new aircraft carriers in order to defend access to oil rather than cooperate with countries to invest in a programme geared towards renewable energy, say. They will invest large scale in biofuels, genetically modified crops and nuclear power programmes. These will further hasten greenhouse gas emissions and lead to insecurities as nuclear proliferation goes worldwide. And, of course, there are plenty of countries who we'd much rather had no nuclear weapons.

Then, in 20 or 30 years, as we begin to fight over agricultural land, fresh water, and the last few fish, there will be an exchange of weapons of mass destruction leading to a third world war. You can equally paint that as a plausible scenario of where we're heading and I think the choice that we have now is do we go for the planned transition to a sustainable way of living or do we allow these things to spiral out of control, potentially leading to deep tensions and conflict in a few decades' time?

The other thing, of course, which needs to be put across is that once the impact of climate change begins to kick in, particularly in developing countries, and as millions potentially die as a result of the failure of crops and changes to rainfall regimes, people in those countries will start putting two and two together. They'll work out that the Western countries had all the science required some 30 years before, yet didn't do anything about it. And that's not going to be a circumstance conducive to peace and under-standing in the world in the middle of this century.

Getting more personal

What set you off on the path to environmentalism?

The major influence comes from my childhood, I think. I had a fascination with nature that came from God knows where as a small child and it's stayed with me ever since. And I suppose the turning point was just after I finished my first degree at Bristol University in the early 1980s, when I thought to myself, I've got a choice. Do I go to the academic route and pursue my passion for natural history by spending my life in the forest with a pair of binoculars, writing theses, or do I apply myself to the conservation side of this and try to do something that we can hang on to, so that we can study it at all? Of course, I finished up going towards the conservation side!

Was there a seminal moment in your career?

In 1990 I travelled with Brazilian colleagues to north-east Brazil, and dis-covered the last wild Spix's Macaw. That made me decide that protecting birds was part of a bigger picture, that the world economy was impinging on the Spix's Macaw's plight, and that my role was to help tackle the underlying causes.

Given that it is now one of the most endangered birds in the world, I've been involved in efforts to save it ever since. It was on my return from that trip that I learned that I had got the job with Friends of the Earth.

What are you proudest of in terms of your work so far?

Looking back, I think I'm probably proudest of having played a role in making the environmental and sustainability agenda normal. I've helped to put it right at the centre of how people now think. It used to be an issue that could be dismissed as a fad, or the domain of a fringe. There are people who will still try to portray the sustainability challenge in that way, but I think if you look at how companies now talk about this, and the expectations of consumers – there is a high level of engagement there. And if you look at the party political competition in terms of who now is the greenest, it is part of the mainstream political process. So I think I'm proudest of having played a role in making that happen.

Probably the most profound thing that's happened in the last 10 years is that this issue is now at the centre of politics. We're in a downturn, it looks like difficult times are ahead, yet so far this has remained very high on the agenda. And there is, I think, an understanding that the food and fuel issues that we're presently experiencing are part of the economic stress and not different to climate change and sustainability issues. And if we've played any role in that, I think that's something to be proud of as well.

I'm probably proudest of having played a role in making the environmental and sustainability agenda normal. I've helped to put it right at the centre of how people now think. It used to be an issue that could be dismissed as a fad, or the domain of a fringe.

9

....

Professor Sir David King

Professor Sir David King is the Director of the Smith School of Enterprise and the Environment at the University of Oxford. Launched officially in October 2008, it is funded by a benefaction from the Martin Smith Foundation.

The Smith School of Enterprise and the Environment will conduct multidisciplinary research on private sector solutions to environmental problems, and promote environmental study as part of mainstream social science degree programmes. It will serve as a global hub, drawing together academics from different university departments to work with policy-makers and business leaders in developing practical solutions to the environmental challenges of the twenty-first century.

Sir David, who is also a senior scientific adviser to global financial services company UBS, is, however, probably better known as the former Chief Scientific Adviser to the UK Government and Head of the Government Office of Science (2000–2007). In that time, he raised the profile of the need for governments to act on climate change and was instrumental in creating the new £1 billion Energy Technologies Institute. In 2008 he co-authored The Hot Topic (Bloomsbury 2008) on this subject.

As Director of the Government's Foresight Programme, he created an in-depth horizon-scanning process which advised government on a wide range of long-term issues, from flooding to obesity. He also chaired the government's Global Science and Innovation Forum from its inception. He advised government on issues including: the foot-and-mouth disease epidemic 2001; post 9/11 risks to the UK; genetically-modified (GM) foods; energy provision; and innovation and wealth creation. In addition, he was heavily involved in the government's Science and Innovation Strategy 2004–2014.

Sir David appears in the film 'The Age of Stupid', talking about Hurricane Katrina.

He was born in South Africa and, after an early career at the University of Witwatersrand, Imperial College and the University of East Anglia, became the Brunner Professor of Physical Chemistry at the University of Liverpool in 1974. In 1988 he was appointed 1920 Professor of Physical Chemistry at the University of Cambridge and subsequently became Master of Downing College (1995–2000) and Head of the University Chemistry Department (1993–2000).

He has published over 450 papers on his research in chemical physics and on science and policy, and has received numerous prizes, fellowships and honorary degrees. He continues as Director of Research in the Department of Chemistry at Cambridge University, and is currently President of the British Association for the Advancement of Science.

The professional journey

Let's start with your current role at this new institution. What do you hope to achieve?

Basically there are two sides to the Smith School. One is the aspiration of the university that every student who comes up to study whatever major subject in their undergraduate course is exposed to the environmental challenges of the twenty-first century. So I'll be working with Department heads to appoint professors and lecturers in environmental law, economics, philosophy, physics, engineering and so on, from around the university. They will have a foot in the Smith School and a foot in their mainstream department. Although it's a very new topic for most of them, we are already finding very good people in those subjects moving towards areas such as environmental policy and environmental economics.

The second objective is that this School should be a global hub for seeking solutions to the twenty-first century environmental problems. And the idea of the global hub is that we work with governments and with the private sector and, of course, with academics. I'm setting up a partnership board and the partners will be heavily drawn from the private sector but will include governments and their agencies. As you can see, we're not short of ambition!

Were there any other institutions in the world that acted as a template for this?

No. We've created something unique. So I have been scoping what is already happening in Oxford and then appointing academic staff to associate membership of the Smith School from among those outstanding people who are already here working in environmental areas. In that way I can build a cohort of people who cover all disciplines and who can work in this space we are developing.

Where did the idea come from?

I'd been talking about this issue many times for many years, and the Smith family – Martin Smith and his family are the funders of the

School – certainly knew that. Once they came to Oxford University with a potential donation for an institution that focused on private sector solutions to environmental problems, the University got McKinsey to set out the vision for the School, which it did pro bono. In fact, the woman who led the project is now my strategy director on loan from McKinsey. The whole thing has been very carefully worked out.

Will you be a degree-awarding School?

Not undergraduate degrees. All the undergraduates will be connected to their mainstream departments. I don't believe in interdisciplinary under-graduate degrees. Everyone who comes to play in our School will bring their disciplinary knowledge to the table and then we will attempt to crack the big problems using these single disciplinary people working in a multidisci-plinary role.

The problem of getting academics and business people to work together for their mutual benefit has been one of the great debates in the UK. How will you breach what is often a big divide and get concrete results?

I have a very specific programme of work to manage that. It comes from my time in government, when I was parachuted into the foot-and-mouth disease epidemic in 2001 and was then working 24/7 on modelling the epidemic while trying to work out with experts from around the country what needed to be done. I took this to the Prime Minister, Tony Blair, and the Cabinet, who agreed to follow what I proposed and then I had to go helicoptering around the country to see that this was actually implemented.

In effect, I was moving directly from the theoretical analysis of what was happening, including taking input from the Ministry, and then actually persuading farmers that this was in the best interests of all. So I was thrown into the deep end and we delivered. The world's biggest foot-and-mouth disease epidemic was terminated in the shortest time after we'd implemented our plan.

This outcome set me thinking that I never wanted to be in that position again. In other words, I wanted to set up a professional horizon-scanning process so that we would be able to scan for opportunities and risks to the

UK. And having carried out that scanning process I then wanted to follow through with in-depth analyses of particular risks and opportunities. That was the beginning of the new Foresight process which I set up in government.

That's why what I've set up in the Smith School is something that might be a futures laboratory, in which we will manage a series of programmes of study. I'm establishing a partnership board and the partners are working with me on programmes of work we want to study. These are all related to environmental challenges where the outcome of the process will be of direct interest to our partners. Each programme of work then has a stakeholder board drawn from the partnership board. So each group of three, four or more partners would have a direct interest in the outcome.

So are they sponsoring it, in effect?

The partners are all sponsoring the futures programmes. They're putting money in and they expect to get something out. Each programme has upwards of 60 academics and others engaged in the programme of work, cutting across all disciplines and probably working for about two years, with the stakeholder board meeting perhaps every six months. They will oversee the outcomes, ensuring that the direction of the work is relevant to what they want. Those outcomes then go back to those stakeholders.

Imagine, if you will, that we have clusters of stakeholders. An energy cluster comprising the utilities, oil companies and engineering consultants would be an obvious one. Then there would be one related to retail business through producers and so on. And one related to insurance, reinsurance and banking. I'm aiming for a whole series of different clusters who will be represented on the partnership board and who will help me to decide how this is developed. That's a long answer to your question, but the answer is I'm fully aware that the School will come to nothing unless it's delivering solutions to a great number of the problems that industry faces and will face.

And you are confident that academics will be eager participants in this process?

What I've just described to you is very unusual for a university – focusing on seeking solutions. So the academics I'm appointing – and those who are associates in the School – will keep beavering away at the coal face of their study, pushing back the frontiers, but I'll also ask them out into the daylight to help me to seek solutions. My experience on the Foresight programmes in government, where I engaged with, I would think, about 1000 academics from around the UK and other countries, was that they were all terribly excited by this process.

Potentially, I suppose I could find that some academics and universities say that they shouldn't be about that. However, my experience in government indicates that it adds a real sense of purpose to the business of furthering knowledge.

Are you saying that, if they see that it's done intelligently and are comfortable that there's a sensible and rigorous framework, it will appeal?

That's absolutely right. When I was in government there were often sceptics. But the last report I initiated under the Foresight Programme on wellbeing had all the leading experts working on it. It has turned out to be an enormously important piece of work which will have an impact outside this country as well as inside. So I think what emerges is the ability to take all this knowledge base and turn it to good use for our society.

How will you get businesses which are also competitors signing up to work together?

A key part of this work, and it was true with the Foresight Programme, is that in order to engage the academics you have to guarantee that everything goes into the public domain. Every partner has to understand that there are no secrets here. So what is in it for the partners? What do they get? Because they are on the board, they see it before it sees daylight. The big advantage for them is that they're ahead of their competitors. In other words, if you're not on the board you're behind.

Let's turn to looking more generally at your career. This is a hard question, but what would you say you are best known for?

I'm hesitating before I answer because if you asked people in the American Chemical Society or whatever, then they'd respond that I'm a chemical physicist who has contributed to the science of solid surfaces and catalysis.

That's what I've been doing for 40 years, and not just at Cambridge. And I'm still doing it. So I think that those people might place me in the top four or five scientists in the world in that area. But those scientists might add, he's also involved in government. So there would be two separate views. And within that, by the way, there is an overlap in the sense that the work is related to environmental issues. At the Department of Chemistry at Cambridge, for instance, we are currently funded by Shell, by Johnson Matthey and BP and our work includes looking at improved car exhaust catalyst systems – improved catalytic systems for industry to create fuels which have a low carbon cycle.

When did you first identify the environment as an issue that you felt was important?

The answer to your question is that when I moved to Cambridge, in 1988, I was moving into a department with the country's – and possibly the world's – leading atmospheric chemists. There's a very interesting little story there. One of my predecessors won a Nobel Prize for his work on a very esoteric three-atom molecule. He had just studied this molecule to bits in the lab and his work on flash photolysis won him the Nobel Prize in Chemistry in 1967.

That was Ronald Norrish. And he didn't study this molecule for any other reason than that it was a good molecule to choose for studying. The molecule is called ozone. So when the importance of the small amount of ozone in the stratosphere was discovered, its ability to keep out ultraviolet radiation, and finally the fact that a hole was developing, particularly over the Antarctic, where we were losing ozone – well, it turned out that his successors in the department had all the knowledge that was required to study this.

The chemical reactions in the stratosphere – I think there are about 100 – had been studied in that group and they had modelled ozone in the stratosphere together with the applied mathematics department. That's how they became world leaders in modelling the development of the ozone hole and highlighting the role of chlorofluorocarbons (CFCs) in that. So I came into a department where the atmosphere was a big part of the engagement in terms of research. That's how, just by attending seminars and being exposed to all of that, I became aware that while the ozone hole was a problem, actually global warming was a far bigger one.

So when I came to government I was already answering the question when people said to me, what's your focus going to be? I said, climate change. That's quite simply the biggest problem that we're facing.

When I came to government I was already answering the question when people said to me, what's your focus going to be? I said, climate change. That's quite simply the biggest problem that we're facing.

Was it being part of that group that perhaps propelled you on to a more public platform?

Partly, but I don't think that was the major factor. I became Master of Downing College, so I was Head of Chemistry and Master of the College. And being Master certainly gave me a bit more visibility. But I also set up, with several other masters of colleges at Cambridge, something that has the strange acronym of CUGPOP, which stands for Cambridge University Government Policy Programme.

We decided that government really needed an insight into what the knowledge base emerging from research could do. So we set up this programme and wrote to the then-head of the Civil Service, saying: 'We'd like to invite 30 members of government to listen to our first discussion.' This was on therapeutic cloning, and we got two world experts on cloning to come, following through from the science to the applications of the science to the social consequences and then the political impacts. It was a one-day meeting, very well-focused. We'd set it up as a trial run but afterwards the head of the Civil Service wrote back and said, fantastic, can we have it twice a year?

But hadn't there been this connection between research and government before?

No. Not in this way. It makes for a very big gap.

Is this something that happens the world over, this big gap?

Absolutely.

So having done that, what difference has it made?

I would have said that no country is in a better position than Britain at the moment.

That's not something you often hear.

No, I know. So that programme was just wonderful. We tackled all the major issues, such as the global water supply, GM, animal diseases and human diseases. There you see the beginning of my Foresight Programme in government – the business of interdisciplinary groupings. It was new to the scientists, social scientists and economists who we were bringing together. And I think every one of us who attended those things was excited by it. Quite a few people from government never missed one, even though it's very unusual for such senior people to attend any session of this type.

How did you get your message about the importance of this scientist/government relationship across?

You're asking a very big question. You can move from a point where people say we'll go up to Cambridge and spend this wonderful day out in a lovely college. I'll get all this intellectual stimulation, I'll be entertained, it could be like going to the opera at Glyndebourne. But to what extent does this impinge on them to the point that they actually change their decision making? That is indeed a very, very big question.

I battled away on that for seven and a half years in government and, while I think I made an enormous amount of progress, it's going to take a generation to change. It's interesting, because I'm now advising the European Commission (EC). The European Commissioners do not have a scientific advisory system. So, for example, José Manuel Barroso, President of the European Commission, came to London to be briefed by me on climate change because he didn't have an adviser who could do that.

Isn't that a bit worrying?

No, it's fine. He can use what the major governments of Europe already have. But if you then look at where Europe has got to, for example on GM, there's no sense in which there is any advisory group within the Commission who can press for science to be heard at the top table. As chief scientific adviser to the Cabinet, my position was exceptional. I've lectured around the world, to people such as the Finnish Prime Minister and so on, who just ask me to explain what my job is because they're curious.

In fact the former Canadian Prime Minister, Paul Martin, after I spoke with his team, created an office of a chief scientific adviser. But all he did was set up an office with a chief scientific adviser plus a secretary. Whereas I had a private office of five people, 90 people outside my private office and a very large budget. You simply can't have an impact without having an office to back you.

Did you find that the skills set you needed to progress in academics was relevant to succeeding in government?

Totally relevant. I suspect that most people would think that my particular skill is the ability to explain very difficult topics to people with no science background. I might be explaining to Prime Minister Blair what fusion is, for example. I think he loved the fact that he could stop me and say, hey, what is fusion? And then I'd spend another 40 minutes explaining it to him and he would get it. He didn't have any scientific training, but he could understand it well enough so that he could then explain it to others. So I think that was an attribute that I brought to the job.

Perhaps you also brought a sense of mission?

And, of course, a sense of mission.

Could have just stayed in your academic department and carried on with your research?

Yes. But instead I stuck my neck out.

And we know what can happen to necks! Have you found, working in government, that it is hard for politicians to admit that they don't know something?

Yes, that's one part of it, but another much more difficult part is if the scientist comes along and says: here's a risk and this is how you should handle it. This is what the government knew I would always do: that I'd give it three months to ponder it and then I'd go out into the public domain and say what I had advised.

That sounds antidemocratic to a lot of people. And I was very sensitive about this, so I was very careful about every piece of advice I gave, but at the same time you can see that it puts the government in a difficult position. What are their choices? Very narrow actually. So you've got to be very careful not to appear arrogant and to be very, very careful that you are giving robust advice. But I felt strongly that my challenge as chief scientific adviser was to gain the trust of the public, which is why I could argue in government that I had to put my advice into the public domain.

Because then the public would trust you?

And because you would be seen to be open, honest and transparent. After all, there was all the suspicion about the BSE crisis, right before I came in. On the other hand, I had to retain the trust of the Cabinet and the people I was working with. That made for quite a difficult balancing act. So I had a number of, let us say, very fiery encounters.

But I also made some wonderful friends in the process. Paul Boateng, for example, defended me against the Deputy Prime Minister, John Prescott. We had come to a situation where I was heavily involved in the energy White Paper in 2003. This looked at how we could decarbonise our energy system. If you read that White Paper you can see that it doesn't quite add up because right until the end nuclear energy was in there as a big part of the process, including renewables and everything else. Because I knew that without nuclear we couldn't manage a 60% reduction by 2050.

But Prescott and Blair backed down at the last minute. I'd already gone out in the public domain saying we have to have nuclear. So at the end of the last meeting I had to say, well, you've made that decision, but if I'm asked on television or radio tomorrow, have I changed my mind? I would have to say no. My advice still remains that we need nuclear. And that created an explosion.

Then Paul Boateng stepped right in and said, Mr Deputy Prime Minister, we need the public to trust our chief scientific adviser. If he is seen to be changing his views according to a political decision-making process, that's the very reverse of what the public expect. So Paul understood it perfectly. And then the rest of the Cabinet backed him.

Current views

How do you actually define sustainability?

Well, I'd go with the Brundtland definition from the 1987 report. It's about leaving to successive generations a planet that is in as good a state for productivity as the one you inherited. And I think that sort of encapsulates the whole sustainable agenda which has become a massive challenge in the twenty-first century.

How important is the role of business generally in achieving that vision of sustainability compared with, say, consumers and government?

I think you're talking about a multidimensional problem and you shouldn't separate them. In other words, governments can only do so much in a democracy. In terms of leadership on an issue like this, they do need to be pushed by the population. Equally, companies need government regulations; they need government pricing policies on carbon dioxide or renewable obligations and so on. And they also need to take their consumer public with them. So it's all an interconnected issue. I wouldn't pull one out as more important than any other.

Governments can only do so much in a democracy. In terms of leadership on an issue like this, they do need to be pushed by the population. Equally, companies need government regulations; they need government pricing policies on carbon dioxide or renewable obligations and so on. And they also need to take their consumer public with them. So it's all an interconnected issue.

But it often seems that there are different forces going in different ways, doesn't it?

That's exactly why I've set up the Smith School of Enterprise and the Environment. We're working with governments, with the private sector and with academics.

Can the sort of change you hope to bring occur on a national scale? Or do there have to be global answers?

Oh, you can't work in isolation and that's why the Smith School is a global organisation. It's a global hub. There is no sense in which this is a problem that can be solved by any one nation. The reason why it's the biggest challenge our civilisation has ever had to face up to, in my view, is precisely that. It's a problem that can only be solved by all major nations working together. I've now spent seven years giving probably about 600 talks around the world precisely because it's a global problem. Once Tony Blair and the Cabinet were persuaded that this was a big issue the Prime Minister said to me, now you've got to get out there and persuade the other governments that it is, too.

Trying to change governmental minds is one thing, but how do you do the same with consumers – particularly in an economic downturn – when they're likely to be even more unhappy about green taxes?

I would like to see that we treat controlling inflation and reducing our carbon footprint as equal priorities as we move forward. And this means that the issue can't be marginalised so that when we have a period of low economic growth we suddenly say, well, now we can no longer afford that. It implies that it is an extra. It's not an extra. The government could very easily let inflation rip in order to get around our economic problems. But we all know that that just creates headaches for the future. It is exactly the same with carbon emissions.

What is your view on companies which pretend to be doing something but are really 'greenwashing'?

Greenwashing is a real problem. In talking to companies, the real test for me is whether the whole issue of decarbonising and energy saving, and so on, is embedded in the company or whether it's just a marginalised operation intended for public relations and nothing else. The PR side of a company's business is important, of course, because that is about companies being sensitive to consumers. But in order to take it to the next stage they then have to mainstream it.

Do you see much sign of this?

Well, in an article I wrote for a national newspaper in 2008 I gave DuPont as an example. It had said initially that it would reduce its greenhouse gas emissions by 5% – a target it failed to meet for three successive years. Greenpeace saw straight through it and publicly announced that the company hadn't reduced its emissions at all three years in a row. So DuPont introduced a system of awards and rewards in the company to hit its target and, once it did that, it achieved a 72% reduction.

It also saved the company money, didn't it?

That's what it discovered.

If they can see the financial benefits, the argument presumably is half won?

That's right. There's a big economic saving in reducing your energy usage. And the global economic downturn that we're in now has been driven by high prices of oil, and to a certain extent by food costs going up. That's what pushed our inflation up in 2008. High oil prices have then led to high prices on gas and coal. They just go up together. And here is an opportunity for us to emphasise the need to decarbonise our economies. But the way governments tend to respond is to consumer demand. The consumer says: I don't like what I'm paying at the pumps now. So the government turns round and says, we must increase the oil supply.

What I'm saying is that we should look at consumer demand and then, say, look for other means of travel. Rail travel needs to be made more attractive, as does public transport.

Are you an optimist about where we are headed in terms of climate change?

What you will see is the private sector suddenly realising that there is a very big opportunity here. Those companies that start gearing up to move into low-carbon technologies and reversing out of high-carbon technologies know that they're going to benefit. Moreover, every country is going to have to introduce regulation that will drive alternative technologies through. I think nuclear is a technology that is here today and that we need today.

There is fierce opposition to it, isn't there? Haven't you been challenged vigorously about your stance?

Yes, and I'd challenge them back. I'd ask them, don't you think that this is such a big problem that we've all got to think out of the box and think afresh? And they'd reply, absolutely. And I'd say, well, rethink your position on nuclear, because I had to rethink mine, though it was a challenge. So if you actually acknowledge the magnitude of the problem, of decarbonising the economy, then you have to take a really careful look at nuclear. I wouldn't be going down the nuclear route if I didn't think it could be done safely, and I do.

So the technology is there?

The most expensive energy technology in terms of lives cost is coal. The least expensive in terms of lives cost per kilowatt hour is nuclear. We just need to bear that in mind. And the reason is not because nuclear is safer, it's because everyone is so aware of the need for safety measures on nuclear.

Do you have any advice for companies struggling to find answers?

I've got plenty of advice for companies. You know I'm science adviser to the investment bank UBS now? The press made snarly comments about first Tony Blair and now me going into 'big money'. Actually, what I'm doing is advising its clients on its behalf on this issue of seeking opportunities around low carbon. The advice will be very company-specific because you can build clusters around different sectors.

In retail, for instance, you would ask how you deliver to consumers the choice that they'll want of low-carbon products. That means a vigorous regime of labelling, just as white goods are labelled. And I want simple labelling. So that unlike cars, where we say 179 grams per mile, I want just A, B, C, D, E so that a consumer's knee-jerk reaction – when going for something labelled A – produces the right response.

So there would need to be different approaches for different clusters?

Take a different one, like building contractors, builders or architects. How do you move towards very low-carbon buildings? That is new-build as well as refurbished old-build. The industry needs to be investing in research in areas such as ceramic, plastic and paint photovoltaics, so that whatever you put on the outside of the building generates the energy needed to run the building. That means that you're farming energy from the environment to the building.

A lot of these solutions are already here. Others, like plastic and paint and photovoltaics, still have to be developed. Another example is an area that I've worked in for many years, which is car exhaust catalysts. In the 1970s cities were getting clogged up, which meant that people were getting asthmatic and experiencing real problems from car exhaust. People who wanted to commit suicide knew that all you had to do was plug in the exhaust gas into the car and you could kill yourself from carbon monoxide fumes. Yet these cars were driving around pumping this pollution into the city.

So progressive car exhaust catalyst regulation was introduced. Manufacturers were told, successively, that in three years' time no car will be imported into this country, or built in this country, that doesn't meet the new standard. Of course, the car manufacturers scream blue murder every time a new regulation like this is introduced. It cannot be done, they say. How are we supposed to meet these regulations?

Yet they have met the new regulations every time. The single most expensive new part on a modern car since 1970 has been the car exhaust catalyst system. We all pay for it when we buy a new car, and the profits to the manufacturers go up every time. So I've never quite understood what the complaints were about.

Getting more personal

What do you think it was about you as a person that made you decide that it was so important to disseminate these concepts to a wider audience?

I only think about this when people like you ask me about it. But, if I do look back, I realise that from my childhood onwards I must have always had a bit of a social conscience.

I'm from South Africa, the country where I was born, bred and educated. I'm a very open person, and I was hauled up by the government's special branch for writing letters to the newspapers which were very critical of apartheid.

How old were you when you were writing these letters?

I was 22 and was doing a PhD.

And what was the reaction of your parents?

They were a bit unhappy about it. My family was on the other side.

That must have been very hard.

It was. I left home, though not of my own will. And then I left the country, again not of my own will. But I guess in a way the same pattern of behaviour repeats itself. When I go out and say global warming is more serious even than terrorism – and that didn't exactly create friends in Number 10 or in the White House – I just thought this job isn't worth hanging on to if I can't say things about it. And I sort of feel, well, you just get on with your life.

When I go out and say global warming is more serious even than terrorism – and that didn't exactly create friends in Number 10 or in the White House – I just thought this job isn't worth hanging on to if I can't say things about it. And I sort of feel, well, you just get on with your life.

You seem like someone who commits fully to whatever you've taken on. Do you agree?

I don't actually separate and compartmentalise my work life from the rest. I think, as a family, we all live our beliefs. It's part of our fabric. For example, my wife is currently in Zambia, where she's working on a VSO project. She was a partner in Eversheds, a litigation lawyer. She packed it all in and she's now managing a big project there for the Voluntary Service Overseas for a year and a half with HIV AIDS orphans. My daughter, meanwhile, is a civil and environmental engineer. She was working with Arup UK and has now joined Arup Africa, where she is working on sustainable building projects. So I think I can say I'm rather proud of what the family are doing.

What else are you proudest of, do you think?

I suppose it's got to be the run-up to Prime Minister Blair's decision to put climate change at the top of the G8 agenda at Gleneagles in 2005. Climate change was first and African development was second. What I felt was, yes, climate change is number one, but don't forget the impact on Africa. So I think that's probably what I'm most proud about.

Do you have what you would consider a defining moment in your life? One that set you on the path that you've eventually followed?

It's interesting because my family was traditional, living under apartheid and not questioning it. So why did I? We had a chef at home, as many South African white families did, who was black. He was from KwaZulu and was one of those people who had learnt to read and write when he was an older man. He had this remarkable memory for the history of his people, all of it oral. I suppose I was a bit unusual in the family for just sitting at his feet and asking him to tell me more stories.

He was a very big influence on my subsequent pattern of life because here was a man who others in the white community were treating as a second-class citizen, and that meant as less of a human being. Yet I realised that I was talking to an extremely intelligent person with a remarkably perceptive, but very different, take on the world. It was then I realised that there was something wrong with the general picture. I think that was quite important.

When did you finally go back?

The first time I went back was after Mandela was released, of course. I hadn't been allowed back before then. I arrived in Durban, where I was born, and the man who took my passport was of Indian descent. He opened it, read the details about my birthplace, then leant across, shook my hand and said, welcome home. I had tears running down my face. Here I was going back to this country with its terrible track record, and he made me welcome.

10

....

Amory B. Lovins

Amory B. Lovins, an American consultant physicist, 1993 MacArthur Fellow and 1997 Heinz Awardee, has been active in energy, resource, environmental and security policy in more than 50 countries for 30 years, including 14 years based in England. He has been called one of the Western world's most influential energy thinkers.

After two years at Harvard, he transferred to Oxford and two years later became a don there at 21, receiving an Oxford MA and, later, 10 honorary doctorates. He has been Regents' Lecturer at the University of California both in Energy and Resources and in Economics; Grauer Lecturer at the University of British Columbia; Luce Visiting Professor at the Dartmouth; Distinguished Visiting Professor at the University of Colorado; Oikos Visiting Professor at the Business School, University of St Gallen; an engineering visiting professor at Peking University; and MAP/Ming Professor at Stanford University.

During 1979–2002, he worked as a team with his wife (1979–99) L. Hunter Lovins – a lawyer, sociologist, political scientist and forester. They shared a 1982 Mitchell Prize, a 1983 Right Livelihood Award, often called the 'alternative Nobel Prize', the 1999 Lindbergh Award, and Time's 2000 Heroes for the Planet Award. In 1989 he won the Onassis Foundation's first DELPHI Prize, one of the world's top environmental awards, for his 'essential contribution towards finding alternative solutions to energy problems'. That contribution included the 'end-use/least-cost' redefinition of the energy problem (in Foreign Affairs in 1976) – asking what quantity, quality, scale and source of energy will do each task in the cheapest way.

In 1993 he received the Nissan Prize for inventing super-efficient ultralight hybrid cars, to which $10 billion was committed by industry, and in 1999, partly for that work, the World Technology Award (Environment). He also received the 2000 Happold Medal of the [UK] Construction Industry Council, the 2005 Benjamin Franklin Medal of the [UK] Royal Society of Arts, and in 2007, the Blue Planet and Volvo Prizes, honorary membership of the American Institute of Architects, Foreign Membership of the Royal Swedish Academy of Engineering Sciences, Time International's Hero of the Environment Award, Popular Mechanics' Breakthrough Leadership Award, and honorary Senior Fellowship of the Design Futures Council. In 2008, U.S. News & World Report and Harvard's Kennedy School named him one of America's 24 Best Leaders.

In 1982, the Lovinses co-founded Rocky Mountain Institute (RMI), an independent, entrepreneurial, non-profit think-and-do tank. He is now its Chairman and Chief Scientist. The 85 staff drive the efficient and restorative use of resources

to make the world secure, just, prosperous, and life-sustaining. (www.rmi.org/
images/PDFs/AboutRMI/RMI_2007-2008_Annual_Report.
pdf)

RMI's $13 million annual revenue is earned through a mix of private-sector
consultancy and grants and gifts. He also co-founded, led, spun off and in 1999
sold (to the Financial Times Group) E SOURCE, the premier source of information on advanced electric efficiency.

He led the energy design for RMI's headquarters, whose 99% savings in space-
and water-heating energy and 90% savings in home electricity paid back in 10
months in 1984. An $18 million utility experiment he co-founded and steered in
the 1990s validated his claim that very large energy savings could cost less than
small or no savings.

Until 2007 he founded and chaired RMI's fourth spin-off, the engineering firm
Fiberforge Corporation, and is RMI's lead practitioner – helping to redesign over
$30 billion worth of facilities in 29 sectors – in implementing for major firms the
tenets of natural capitalism, for which he shared the 2001 Shingo Prize (Research),
the 'Nobel Prize for Manufacturing'. In 2004, he led a Pentagon-co-sponsored
study on how to eliminate US oil use led by business for profit, and in 2004–06
served for the second time on a US Defence Science Board task force on military
energy efficiency and strategy.

His clients have included a range of blue-chip companies and organisations in
both the private and public sectors. He has briefed 19 heads of state, given expert
testimony in eight countries and 20-plus states, and published 29 books and several
hundred papers, as well as poetry, landscape photography, music (he is a pianist
and composer). He regularly addresses leading energy, business, security, environment and development groups.

The professional journey

What, in your view, do you think you're best known for?

That energy – and especially its efficient use – is a master key to unlock
most of the problems of resources, environment, development and security.
That advanced energy efficiency can save far more, and at far lower cost,
than normally assumed: indeed, it can save most of the energy we use far
more cheaply than supplying it even from existing facilities. That very large
energy savings can cost less than small or no savings, thanks to integrative

design. That an efficient world running on renewable energy would pay less for energy services than we do now. And that these transitions – which can solve such problems as climate change, oil dependence, energy insecurity and nuclear proliferation – can and will be led by business for profit rather than driven by governmental mandate.

When you started talking about these particular concepts, what was the trigger and what was the wider context politically, economically and socially?

Well, in the late 1960s I'd been reading books about the tangle of problems around energy, resources, environment, development and security. It was clear that the world was headed for serious trouble with all of those and that this was due to common causes with shared solutions. At the time I was an academic scientist, but realised, as American black activist Stokely Carmichael had remarked, that 'If you're not part of the solution you're part of the problem.'

And, meanwhile, I'd become involved with David Brower, the greatest conservationist of the twentieth century, producing a book of landscape photographs and essays about the Snowdonia National Park in North Wales.

So was this when you were over in the UK?

Yes, I lived in the UK for 14 years, so I became almost bilingual.

We like the 'almost'.

And this ended up helping to stop some large mining projects in the park by, ironically, a company I now work with, Rio Tinto – it was then Rio Tinto Zinc (RTZ) – which is now leading the greening of the world mining industry. But in 1981 I left academic life to work full time with David Brower and then ultimately to set up my own organisation, Rocky Mountain Institute (RMI), with my then wife Hunter Lovins, in 1982. At the time there was a widespread belief that technology would solve all these problems and it turned out that this belief was largely correct – but using a very different set of technologies than the cornucopians of the time supposed. A cornucopian, by the way, is a futurist who believes that continued material progress can be met indefinitely by continuing advances in technology that can overcome any obstacle. For doubting the efficacy and cost-effectiveness of their preferred technologies, I was accused of being a 'technological pessimist'. Now their descendants tend to accuse me of being a technological optimist!

It's nice that there's some consistency there.

Yes, but I suppose I could be fairly described as a neo-cornucopian. That's not to say the technological solutions are all that we need in every case or all that we should be doing, but they're extraordinarily powerful if combined with innovations in business strategy and in design – the translation of intention into effect.

Was it rather daunting setting up Rocky Mountain Institute? That must have been quite a leap to take from having a belief to actually doing something like that.

Well, I've always been a bit entrepreneurial and it didn't seem much of a leap at the time. Hunter and I hatched this plot while driving across the United States in a little pickup truck to go teach at Dartmouth in New Hampshire in the spring of 1982. At the time we couldn't think of another organisation, whether NGO, business or government, that we would care to work for.

So we looked at each other and Hunter suggested: 'Why don't we set up our own little not-for-profit?' I replied: 'Oh, horrors, administrivia,' and she said not to worry, because she had been running a group in California called Tree People, so she could handle that bit and I would be in charge of thought leadership and quality control. So we thought we'd gather together a handful of colleagues. It has lately been close to 100. Hunter left in 2002. We got a real CEO to succeed me in 2007, so now as chairman and chief scientist I can just focus on what I should be doing – thought leadership, special projects, strategic influence, mission stewardship and evolution, quality control, mentoring, rain-making and fund-raising.

Did you have quite firm principles for how RMI should work, or was it more – let's see how we go along?

Yes, we did have quite clear ideas about what it should and should not do and what it should and should not be. And those have served us very well, though they have evolved a bit.

Our mission is to foster the efficient and restorative use of resources to make the world secure, just, prosperous and life-sustaining. The short version is that we create abundance by design to bring about a world without waste, want or war, and in the spirit of applied hope. Applied hope, in brief, is very different from theoretical hope or glandular optimism We work hard to make the world better in the practical and grounded conviction that by starting with hope and acting out of hope we can cultivate a different kind of world worth being hopeful about.

> *Our mission is to foster the efficient and restorative use of resources to make the world secure, just, prosperous and life-sustaining. The short version is that we create abundance by design to bring about a world without waste, want or war, and in the spirit of applied hope.*

RMI is, first of all, unusual in structure. It's an entrepreneurial not-for-profit that has had 11 revenue models so far – 10 of them entrepreneurial and the eleventh is grants and donations. We've done five for-profit spin-offs, three from inside and two led by staff. And RMI is a public charity but uses the permission and encouragement of the American tax authorities in conducting programmatic enterprise. That is what would normally look like a for-profit activity but it supports our charitable mission. So we're an unusual sort of hybrid that has done a lot to invent the programmatic enterprise model as a 'think and do' tank.

So, over the years, 30% to 70% of our annual revenues, which are now about $13 million, have come from programmatic enterprise – chiefly consulting for the private sector to carry out our mission. And this has some unusual advantages. As we work with eager, skilful and highly-motivated partners/clients who have a real problem they need to solve, we both learn very rapidly by doing. This gives us the salutary discipline of market feedback and is rich in precious experience and insight from hands-on implementation.

It's also self-marketing because it builds credibility and buzz. It's faster and higher in both sales speed and success rate and lower in transaction costs than requesting grants from foundations. It leverages our grants and donations, in many years, two-to-one or more, and helps to make our innovation process more agile and self-directed. Most importantly it creates teachable case studies whose lessons we can spread, while it also engenders competitive pressure for emulation. In other words, we help early adopters to become so conspicuously successful at what we call 'natural capitalism' that their rivals are compelled by competitive pressure to follow suit or lose share.

Can you give us a flavour of the different activities you are involved in?

We do several main kinds of things. We do transdisciplinary syntheses that are built on deep original analysis. We do game-changing innovations that we sometimes open-source like the Hypercar. Two years after I'd invented it in 1991 we open-sourced it and thereby leveraged our $3 million R&D investment by over 3000-fold. We do a lot of targeted consultancy, as I've described. We do strategic influence, which the late Dana Meadows (senior author of *Limits to Growth*) defined as 'changing the mindset of the people who make the rules' – the most powerful intervention you can make in a complex system.

We do both targeted and, increasingly, some general public communications in old and new media, as well as a lot of network collaboration and some R&D consortia. Sometimes, just convening a timely conversation is what's needed. And besides the areas that we're currently noted for working in, there is a pretty diverse past list including things like water, community development, agriculture, forests, security and health. So it's an unusual portfolio.

Historically we've worked probably 90% with private sector because, in a tripolar world where the foci of power and influence are in business, civil society and government – typically in order of decreasing effectiveness – why would you spend all your time working with the least effective and most frustratingly gridlocked one when you can actually get things done? That's why we work mainly with the most dynamic sector, business, in its co-evolution with civil society. We do this mostly in North America and in other developed regions where we understand the culture better and feel we can be more effective, and we work with both civilian and military cultures, with a growing emphasis on pedagogy and design.

The people we look for to do all this are rather unusual, too. We hire not by discipline but by aptitude. That is, we look for all-round athletes who are literate, numerate, self-starting, fun, passionate about our mission, intensely curious, have a vision across boundaries and have a high tolerance of ambiguity. In consequence, we've been blessed with extraordinary people, many of whom have gone on to do very unusual things.

Let me end this explanation with one other thought. And that is that we've been able to be effective because of a toolkit of about a dozen methods that we've developed, refined and applied. I'd summarise it this way. We create abundance by design via 'end-use least-cost analysis', biomimetic inspiration (innovation inspired by nature, as in Janine Benyus's book *Biomimicry*), innovation-eliciting charrette processes, and whole-system integration of restorative technologies.

Then we implement the results in mindful markets. And that's where we have an even bigger toolkit based on the notion that the transition is led by business for profit. It's powered by natural capitalism, catalysed by institutional acupuncture, enabled by barrier-busting, lubricated by aikido politics, sped by innovative policies and business strategies, and scaled up by powerful partners.

What do you mean when you talk about natural capitalism?

If you go to natcap.org you'll find the short version of most of the arguments in a *Harvard Business Review* paper I wrote about natural capitalism in 1999. You can download free from the same site the English-language edition (there are about a dozen others) of our 1999 book with Paul Hawken, *Natural Capitalism: Creating the Next Industrial Revolution*.

Capitalism is the productive use of and reinvestment in capital; but what is capital? Conventional business dealt with only two types, money and goods: that is, financial and physical capital. But there are two other types – people and nature – that are even more vital and valuable, yet are normally either ignored or liquidated because they're not shown on the balance sheet. So a natural capitalist plays with a full deck, with all four types of capital, not just two, and therefore makes more money, has more fun and does more good.

Operationally, natural capitalism integrates four types of business innovations. The first and most familiar is radical resource productivity –

wringing far more work out of our energy and resources. We've figured out, and now demonstrated in 29 sectors, how to achieve expanding rather than diminishing returns to those investments in resource efficiency.

Second, production should be done the way nature produces – in closed loops with no waste and no toxicity. Third, both these shifts can be encouraged by a 'solutions economy' business model in which both the provider and the customer get rewarded for the same thing – doing more and better with less for longer. Typically, you do this by leasing the service that a product provides and that the customer wants, rather than simply selling the product. And then fourth, you make a lot of money with these shifts – in fact, you gain stunning competitive advantage – and then you should reinvest some of those profits in the type of capital that we're shortest of – nature – and also human capital, to achieve the fullest flowering of individual, community and culture.

So that's a rather commonsense set of shifts that many businesses are now making. As Edgar Woolard said when he led DuPont, those companies that take such opportunities seriously will do very well, while those that don't won't be a problem, because ultimately they won't be around. Of course, it's a slow shift but we see it rapidly accelerating.

Think about the industrial revolution in England. It came about when, to oversimplify a bit, there weren't enough weavers to make enough cloth for most people to afford. But if you'd come into Parliament around 1750 and said, don't worry, we'll make weavers a hundred times more productive, nobody would have understood this concept, let alone thought it possible. But that's what happened. Soon a Lancashire spinner could produce the cloth that previously had required 200 weavers. Such innovation quickly spread throughout the economy. It created purchasing power, a middle class, affordable mass goods, and all the artefacts that we see round us today as the hallmarks of an advanced industrial civilisation.

Well, a quarter-millennium later, here we are with the same impeccable logic: that you should economise on your scarcest resource – that's what economics teaches us to do – but with the opposite pattern of scarcity (as American economist Herman Daly points out). At the time of the first industrial revolution we had a relative scarcity of people to exploit seemingly boundless nature; yet today we have abundant people and scarce nature. So now we need to use nature, rather than people, far more productively.

How do others view RMI's vision of an entrepreneurial and yet not-for-profit model?

The tax authorities simply tell you how much you owe, but in the US they do happen to allow and encourage non-profit enterprise, so long as it's done properly (which requires care because this area of the law is complex and illogical). And during most of RMI's existence the rest of government has not been very interested in these matters. However, we're gratified that a great many environmental groups, and some groups of other flavours, have become very adept at engaging with commerce so that we don't view them as competitors, but rather as complementary or collaborative because we're all doing different things in the same complex ecosystem.

RMI's DNA also has some other distinctive elements worth mentioning. We have a hard-earned reputation for being utterly independent, saying exactly what we think and being fearless about what we say and what types of work we choose to do. We do our best to be honest. If we make a mistake we publish the correction and we try to do really solid scholarship and meticulously document where our conclusions come from. We've always been non-partisan, non-sectarian, trans-ideological and impossible to pigeonhole.

In a polarised society like the contemporary United States this is unusual, but it has served us well and it means that we're inclusive: we work with everybody. And part of that is also a non-adversarial style. We don't fight with opponents, we dance with partners. And we're actually not an environmental group. We are practitioners, not theorists. We do solutions, not problems. And we only do transformation, not incrementalism.

We take a long view. We tend to look ahead 50-plus years, but via practical steps to get there, and we view the world through a very wide-angle lens, albeit with a sharp focus. We insist on top quality. We're agile and opportunistic, but not reckless, in plunging into new things. And we have an unusual knowledge base, some in-house and some networked round the world with hundreds of associates whom we bring in on specific engagements as needed.

Our knowledge is both deep and broad. It's not deep everywhere, but it's deep in the areas where it has to be and we typically pick up a few new disciplines a year, but it's very broad and it's cyclic: the same topics and insights tend to come up like clockwork every 10 or 20 years which, I guess, means we didn't adequately communicate them the first time or, more commonly, we were too far ahead of our time for them to stick. I think what most distinguishes us is an integrative whole-systems approach – where you design the whole, not just the bits, and therefore get multiple benefits from single expenditures – and that's the key to the type of design that allows us to make very large energy and resource savings at small, no, or negative cost.

Looking back to when you set up Rocky Mountain Institute, did you find that there were certain audiences who were resistant to your message?

Well, the hardest mindset to penetrate, because it's hermetically sealed, is that of the theoretical economist who mistakes the map for the territory; who feels that behaviour can be influenced and interpreted only through price; and who believes that existing markets are nearly perfect or that market failures are immaterial. I think another sort of mindset that's hard to deal with is one that I was actually brought up in and have been trying to escape from ever since: namely that the world is essentially mechanistic, deterministic, linear and Newtonian. Of course, it's not like that at all.

Also, we were challenging some firmly-held beliefs in the traditional energy supply industries, which we did frontally in 1976 with an article in *Foreign Affairs* called 'Energy Strategy: The Road Not Taken'. This redefined the energy problem from 'how to supply more energy' to 'how to provide just the amount, type, and scale of energy that would do each task in the cheapest way'. I created the concept we call the 'soft energy path', combining very efficient use of energy with 'soft energy technologies' based on such resources as solar, windpower, bio-fuel, small hydro, and geothermal heat. This is opposite to the 'hard energy path' which depends on huge centralised fossil-fuel and nuclear power generation and other depletable, highly concentrated energy sources.

By 2000, my 1976 illustration of how much energy the US would use in a 'soft energy path' matched actual consumption within a few percent. But in 1976 it was intentionally controversial and I devoted about a year and a half to writing dozens of tedious responses to fatuous critiques. It's amusing to go back and see what we were arguing about then, because some of it has lately popped up again among those who have learnt nothing and forgotten nothing. But within a few years, after the dust had cleared, the smarter elements of the energy industry were pursuing a similar approach and getting duly rewarded for it.

Now within industry it's very widely understood that the energy efficiency potential is enormous and expanding, and that since it's cheaper to save fuel than to buy it, solving the climate problem is not costly but profitable. So the economic theorists simply got the signs wrong when talking about how much it would cost to protect the climate. It's a big number, but it's actually not a cost but a profit.

> *Now within industry it's very widely understood that the energy efficiency potential is enormous and expanding, and that since it's cheaper to save fuel than to buy it, solving the climate problem is not costly but profitable.*

From the look of your client list, this obviously resonates.

Yes, the problem really is that we can't answer the phone fast enough. We also need to become a good deal more disciplined in accepting only the most strategic opportunities and not get distracted by those projects that are tactically interesting but somewhat diversionary.

Do you recall the first big company which was receptive to your ideas?

Well, I think the first one of consequence would probably be Royal Dutch/ Shell Group. It called me in 1973 at the suggestion of the inventor of holography, Dennis Gabor. We helped Shell to develop scenarios anticipating the change in oil prices and the current furore over energy.

Current views

How do you define sustainability?

I don't.

Why not?

We don't use the word because it means so many different things to so many different people. We find it quite useless and confusing. For instance, we found people at the World Bank who thought sustainability meant that gross domestic product (GDP) grew at a constant rate.

So what do you call it?

Well, the vision part of our current mission statement, which we're about to restate even better, is to make the world secure, just, and prosperous and life-sustaining. And by 'secure', we mean free from fear of privation or attack – both parts of which can be greatly advanced by resource efficiency that turns scarcity into abundance.

So what about the phrase 'climate change'?

Well, I have no problem with that. And it's more accurate than global warming – although Hunter Lovins calls it global weirding, which more accurately captures what's happening in the global climate experiment. My first professional paper on climate change was 40 years ago, in 1968, and I've been following it with growing alarm and about every 10 years publishing a major analysis of how to solve the problem at a profit. In fact, we wrote a book in 1981 called *Least-Cost Energy: Solving the CO_2 Problem*.

As an early advocate of the idea that business could and should profit from dealing with climate change, were you somewhat of a voice in the wilderness?

Yes. And suddenly the wilderness has caught up. Clearly much of my work and that of my colleagues has been 10, 20, sometimes 30 years ahead of its time. If you look back, for example, at the summer 1980 *Foreign Affairs* you'll find a paper called 'Nuclear Power and Nuclear Bombs' in which we laid out a logical and rat-proof approach to stopping the spread of nuclear weapons. Had that been followed at the time we would not now be worrying about Iran and North Korea. But it was too far ahead, because in 1980 the world was dominated, just as it is now, by nuclear theology and we were unable to get it taken seriously in most policy circles.

But if we keep presenting the case ever more persuasively, as the evidence mounts up, ultimately I think the dripping effect does tend to erode resistance. There's a line in the *Tao Te Ching* about water. It says that 'that which is of all things most yielding can overcome that which is most hard' is a fact known by all but used by none: being substanceless, it can enter in even where there are no cracks. So with relentless patience we've been practising, if you like, the politics of water. We have been insidiously creeping in even where there are no cracks.

Typically, we use the data, logic, methods and objectives of those we need to convince, and eventually some of them say, wait a minute, this is an empirical question: I could try it and see if it works. After the initial hubbub over the 1976 *Foreign Affairs* paper I think the conclusion many reached was nicely captured by Dr David Sternlight, the chief economist of Atlantic Richfield, who said: 'I for one don't care if Lovins is only half right. That would be a better performance than I've seen from the rest of them.'

What's your view on companies who pretend to be green – who 'greenwash', if you like – but are only paying lip service to it?

Of course it exists and we're at pains never to be associated with it.

How do you deal with them?

Well, we haven't had to do so because we've not worked with any that have attempted to do that. We only engage with firms that have a deep and sincere desire to do what we're interested in. I've only had to sack one client and it wasn't for that reason.

How does Wall Street perceive you?

I think mostly very well. I keep getting profiled in the *Wall Street Journal*, *The Economist* and so on, although journalists are often at pains to quote some anonymous folks who think it's all rubbish.

There does seem to be a polarisation, with those at one end of the spectrum who really don't like business very much in the environmental movement and others who say: business can do this.

Well, it certainly helps if governments are steering – not rowing – in the right direction, but I think the rowing needs to be done by the private sector and civil society. I do tend nowadays to get criticised more from the left for associating with business or believing in the efficacy of markets. But that's not an unbounded belief. As you'll find in *Natural Capitalism*, I think markets make a splendid servant, a bad master, and a worse religion. They're very good at what they do and I use them a lot for that, but not to try to do what they were never meant to do or don't do well.

And do governments have a role?

Certainly in getting the rules right and rewarding what we want. In energy policy most countries try to pick winners, as the UK wants to do with nuclear power, even though it has died of an incurable attack of market forces: there isn't a penny of private capital put into it anywhere in the world, because there's no business case for it.

In the US, for example, despite subsidies upwards of 100% of cost, nuclear power is not attracting a penny of private investment. I'm currently updating a paper, called 'The Nuclear Illusion', summarised in a tenfold shorter version called 'Forget Nuclear', pointing out that if you put a dollar, a pound or a euro into a new nuclear plant you'll get about two to 11-plus times less carbon savings, 20 to 40 times more slowly, than if you put the same investment into what's winning in the market: namely, efficiency and micro-power. These have already captured upwards of half the world's market in new electrical services. Nuclear has 1% or 2%.

This sort of argument doesn't seem to be heard very often.

Well, no, and it's quite astonishing what you don't hear. Take China for example, which has the world's most ambitious nuclear programme. You hear a lot about that. What you don't hear is that by the end of 2006 China had seven times as much capacity installed in distributed renewables as in nuclear power, and the distributed renewables were growing seven times faster.

Do you have any tips for any business wondering where to start?

Well, it's easiest to start with the first principle of natural capitalism: radical resource efficiency. Just look for *muda*, that wonderful Japanese word that means waste, purposeless and futility. Look for any measurable input that produces no customer value, and set a goal of reducing it to zero. Don't benchmark how much *muda* you've got against how much your competitors have got. To hell with your competitors – go for zero *muda*. That's a tall star to steer by. A very good guide to doing that and the subsequent steps to take is Ray Anderson's *Mid-Course Correction*. Ray is a trustee of my Institute and very old friend and client, and some of our most fun engagements have been with him.

How does zero *muda* work in practice?

*Just look for **muda**, that wonderful Japanese word that means waste, purposeless and futility. Look for any measurable input that produces no customer value, and set a goal of reducing it to zero. Don't benchmark how much **muda** you've got against how much your competitors have got. To hell with your competitors – go for zero muda. That's a tall star to steer by.*

Well, for example, take the factory to which we brought some ideas about how to design pumping systems. We got a 92% saving in pumping energy, although we learnt later it should have been about 98%. And this was achieved just by using fat, short, straight pipes rather than thin, long, crooked pipes. It's not rocket science. It's good Victorian engineering rediscovered.

If you want to know, by the way, how to do radical resource efficiency and how to 'tunnel through the cost barrier' and make big savings cost less than small or no savings, go to rmi.org/stanford and you'll find 30 years condensed into seven hours of public lectures I did in Stanford Engineering School in 2007.

Getting more personal

What do you think set you on the path that you're on now? Were your parents a big influence?

Yes, in that they treated my sister and me as small adults. We were always included in the adult conversation round the dinner table about the big issues of the day and they also raised us to value public service, to try to help and learn, and to be good people.

But I was at risk, I think, of being seduced by academic life. I only managed to escape in 1971 because, fortunately, when I wanted to do a DPhil in energy, Oxford said: 'But it's not an academic subject, is it? We haven't a chair in it. Pick a real subject.' I thought it was important to do it anyway, so I resigned the fellowship at Merton College at Oxford, and went and did it. Oxford now has a chair in energy.

What is it about you as a person, do you think, that brought you to this point? Is it a deep curiosity about the way things work? Is it sheer doggedness?

All of the above. And I can't imagine anything to do that could be more fun and more rewarding and give me the privilege of working with such wonderful people as I'm working with now.

Are you someone who gets bored easily?

It's hard to get bored if you're working on and helping to solve most of the world's big problems. So that hasn't yet been an issue.

What would you say you were proudest of in terms of your work?

A few years ago I would have said redefining the energy problem. That is, the 'end-use/least-cost approach', which encourages people to ask what they are trying to do and with how much energy, at what quality and scale, from what source, can do the job in the cheapest way. That would probably have been the biggest idea that's likely to be noted in my legacy. Now, though, I think I'd say integration and integrative design, whether of technical systems or in social systems, where as I said before, you solve many problems at once without making new ones. Do you know our guiding parable about parachuting cats?

No.

OK. This is an essentially true story. A few of the minor details are still uncertain but not the key features. In the 1950s, the Dayak people in Borneo, particularly in the Kelabit highlands, had malaria and the World Health Organisation had a solution: they would spray DDT all over. They did so with generous enthusiasm, the mosquitoes died and the malaria declined. So far, so good. But there were side effects. For example, the roofs of the houses started to fall down on people's heads because the DDT had also killed tiny parasitic wasps that previously had controlled the thatch-eating caterpillars. The colonial government addressed this problem by giving people sheet-metal roofs, but then people were unable to sleep because of the noise of the tropical rain on the tin roofs at night.

Meanwhile the DDT-poisoned insects were being eaten by geckos which were then eaten by cats. The DDT built up in the food chain and killed the cats. Without the cats, the rats flourished and multiplied. Soon the World Health Organisation was threatened with potential outbreaks of typhus and sylvatic plague which it itself had created. It was thereby obliged to ring up RAF Singapore and ask them to come conduct Operation Cat Drop, parachuting large numbers of live cats into Borneo. By the way, I'm trying to trace it back through the RAF archives, which unfortunately are classified by date rather than operation name – you need to know the unit that did it in order to find it. I hope somebody will read this who has a grandfather who can shed more light on the logistics of parachuting cats: many intriguing possibilities come to mind.

Anyhow, the story shows nicely that if you don't understand how things are connected, quite often the cause of problems is the solution. And most of the world's problems are of this kind. We made them ourselves, while trying to do something else. So at RMI we try to solve or avoid a problem in a way that also solves or avoids many other problems without making new ones so that nobody has to parachute more cats.

Do you have a defining moment in your life?

Birth. Yes, it's been an interesting journey since then. I'll be 61 in a few weeks and hope I'll keep at this work a long time. My parents both made it to 97.

Churchill remarked that you can always count on the Americans to do the right thing – once they've exhausted all the other alternatives. We've been working our way well down the list, and by now we must be pretty near the bottom. There's a definite whiff of change in the air.

Churchill remarked that you can always count on the Americans to do the right thing – once they've exhausted all the other alternatives. We've been working our way well down the list, and by now we must be pretty near the bottom. There's a definite whiff of change in the air.

11

....

Professor Wangari Maathai

Wangari Muta Maathai was born in Nyeri, Kenya, in 1940. Professor Maathai obtained a degree in Biological Sciences from Mount St Scholastica College in Atchison, Kansas (1964). She subsequently earned a Master of Science degree from the University of Pittsburgh (1966) before pursuing doctoral studies in Germany and at the University of Nairobi. She obtained a PhD (1971) from the latter, where she also taught veterinary anatomy, becoming the first woman in East and Central Africa to earn a doctorate degree. She became chair of the Department of Veterinary Anatomy and an associate professor in 1976 and 1977 respectively. In both cases, she was the first woman to attain those positions in the region.

Professor Maathai was active in the National Council of Women of Kenya in 1976–87 and chaired it from 1981 to 1987. In 1976, while she was serving at the National Council of Women, she introduced the idea of community-based tree-planting. She continued to develop this idea into a broad-based grassroots organization whose main focus is poverty reduction and environmental conservation through tree-planting. What became known as the Green Belt Movement has assisted women in planting more than 40 million trees on private farms and community lands including farms, schools and church compounds. In 1986 the Green Belt Movement established a pan-African Green Belt Network that has exposed many organisations in other African countries to its unique approach.

Professor Maathai is internationally recognised for her persistent struggle for democracy, human rights and environmental conservation. She and the Green Belt Movement have received numerous awards, most notably the 2004 Nobel Peace Prize. Some of her other awards include the Woman of the Year Award (1983), Better World Society Award (1986), the Woman of the World (1989), Goldman Environmental prize (1991), UN's Africa Prize for Leadership (1991), Golden Ark Award (1994), Excellence Award from the Kenyan Community Abroad (2001), WANGO Environment Award (2003), J. Sterling Morton Award (2004), the Conservation Scientist Award (2004), the Petra Kelly Prize for Environment (2004), the Sophie Prize (2004), the Paul Harris Fellow (2005), and the Disney Conservation Award (2006).

In 2005, she was honoured by Time magazine as one of 100 most influential people in the world, and by Forbes magazine as one of 100 most powerful women in the world. Professor Maathai has also received honorary doctoral degrees from several institutions around the world: Williams College (1990), Hobart & William Smith Colleges (1994), University of Norway (1997), Yale University (2004), Willamette College (2005), University of California at Irvine (2006), and Morehouse College (2006).

The Green Belt Movement and Professor Maathai are featured in several publications including: Speak Truth to Power (Kerry Kennedy Cuomo, 2000) and Women Pioneers for the Environment (Mary Joy Breton, 1998), among others. She has also written two books of her own: an autobiography, Unbowed: One Woman's Story, which was published in 2006, and an explanation of her organizational method, The Green Belt Movement: Sharing the Approach and the Experience.

Professor Maathai serves on the boards of several organisations, including World Learning for International Development, Green Cross International, the Chirac Foundation, Discovery Channel's Planet Green, the Worldwide Network of Women in Environmental Work, the Global Crop Diversity Trust, Prince Albert II of Monaco Foundation, and the National Council of Women of Kenya.

In December 2002, Professor Maathai was elected to Kenya's parliament with an overwhelming 98% of the vote. Until 2007, she represented the Tetu constituency, Nyeri district in central Kenya (her home region). From 2003 to 2007 she served as Assistant Minister for Environment and Natural Resources in Kenya's ninth parliament.

In 2005 she was elected the Presiding Officer of the Economic, Social and Cultural Council (ECOSOCC) of the African Union based in Addis Ababa, Ethiopia. ECOSOCC was formed to advise the African Union on issues related to the African civil society. She was also honoured with an appointment as Goodwill Ambassador to the Congo Basin Forest Ecosystem, where she serves in an advocacy role for the region's conservation and protection.

In April 2006 the President of France, Jacques Chirac, honoured Professor Maathai with France's highest honour, Legion d'Honneur. She has also founded the Nobel Women's Initiative with her sister Nobel Peace Laureates Jody Williams, Shirin Ebadi, Rigoberta Menchú Tum, Betty Williams and Mairead Corrigan. In 2007 Professor Maathai was invited to be co-chair of the Congo Basin Fund, initiated by the UK government to help to protect the Congo Forests.

The professional journey

What would you say you are best known for? That's probably a difficult question, given your long and varied career.

I think that most people, when they hear my name, think of the environment and, more specifically, tree planting. Then, perhaps, they think about women's issues. Those are probably the first ideas that come to people's minds.

When you began to get involved in these areas, what was the context – whether politically, socially or economically?

Well, it actually started in the mid-1970s. I was, like many women at that time, involved in what was then the global women's movement. Back in Kenya we were preparing to go to the very first United Nations conference on women in Mexico in 1975, and it was while I was getting ready for that meeting that my mind was focused on what the women from the countryside were talking about – because they were talking about very basic things.

I had grown up in a place where many of the problems they were talking about did not exist, so it triggered my mind to the fact that something was happening to the environment. What they were talking about was lack of clean drinking water, lack of firewood, lack of adequate and nutritious foods, and poverty. Those were things that I did not know about when I was a child growing up in the highlands of Kenya.

So I almost immediately put aside the issues that had brought me to the conference, which were about women in the university, and started focusing on what the women from the countryside were talking about. I eventually linked up with them and suggested that we could rehabilitate the environment in which they were living by planting trees.

Who or what were the major influences on your work at the beginning, do you think?

I think that, quite often, when things like this happen it's partly because of the experiences you have had in the past. I was then in my mid-20s and I'd been to school. I had been to America and to Germany, and I had received my Masters degree in biological sciences. I was then working for my PhD. I was very much a product of the experiences that I had gone through. That is probably why I paid attention to what was happening to others rather than what was happening to me, because I recognised that I was a very privileged person at that point.

I had been one of the fortunate people chosen for the airlift set up by President Kennedy in the 1960s, in which the US gave scholarships to young people from Africa's emerging nations to study at US universities. So I think that the experiences in America, especially in the 1960s during Martin Luther King's campaigns for civil rights, affected me greatly.

I also spent some two years in Germany during the 1960s, and at that time there was a lot of student unrest. The Vietnam War was going on and there was a lot of movement for social justice. So we listened to the leaders of the time, like Martin Luther King and the Kennedys. We didn't hear much about people like Nelson Mandela, although they were already very much involved in their campaign. But in the course of my travels I also met women like Margaret Mead and Barbara Ward, who were already thinking about the environment. And women like the Indian Prime Minister Indira Gandhi were among those who really inspired us young women at that time. So all those ideas helped me to shape who I was and therefore the kind of issues to which I was paying attention.

What were the initial reactions to your ideas and the challenges you faced in getting those ideas across?

I think the biggest problem, which I must admit I'm still dealing with, is the fact that very many people do not see the environment as something that is integral to our daily lives. It tends to be seen as an outside issue, often associated with scientists and academics, but in fact it is very, very central to our lives. The air we breathe, the water we drink, the food we eat – all these are things that we cannot live without. So the fact that we weren't linking what was happening in the environment and our daily activities was a major issue for me then.

I think the biggest problem, which I must admit I'm still dealing with, is the fact that very many people do not see the environment as something that is integral to our daily lives. It tends to be seen as an outside issue, often associated with scientists and academics, but in fact it is very, very central to our lives. The air we breathe, the water we drink, the food we eat – all these are things that we cannot live without.

People were wondering why a highly educated person like me would waste my time with ordinary illiterate women in the rural areas, turning the soil, digging holes, and planting trees. After all, I was supposed to be enjoying the life of a successful academic woman in the university, teaching and preparing people to become professors. And in many ways I am not really sure why it suddenly became very clear to me. Maybe it's because I was born in the land, on the land, and maybe because I studied biological sciences. But something very early on showed me that these are issues that are very close to me.

At that time, as now, people wondered what all my activities had to do with the way they lived their lives, with politics, with economics, with spirituality. And I still hear people say: what have trees to do with the peace? What have trees to do with the economy? Yet the tree, for me, is a symbol of what we all can see in the environment, but it is also an entry point into understanding the link between the environment and all these other issues.

I still hear people say: what have trees to do with the peace? What have trees to do with the economy? Yet the tree, for me, is a symbol of what we all can see in the environment, but it is also an entry point into understanding the link between the environment and all these other issues.

What was your family's reaction to getting involved in these issues?

I came from a family which had received hardly any education, so I was the first generation to go to university and get a very serious education. My family were very happy for me and almost awed by the advances that I and my brothers and sisters made because we went way beyond even what our parents had dreamt of for us. Later on, though, especially when I had my own family, I think they were concerned that maybe I was paying too much attention to these issues.

Maybe, like others, they couldn't understand why I was spending so much time worrying about little things called tree seedlings, about women planting them and making sure that they survived, and looking for money so that I could give them an incentive to keep them planting these trees. So I think that the family later on might have thought: are you sure she's not a little bit crazy?

Fortunately for me, some friends did see that what I was dealing with was very important. You will remember that in 1972 the United Nations (UN) organised a conference in Stockholm which they called the United Nations

Conference on the Human Environment. It created an organisation called the United Nations Environment Programme (UNEP), which was headquartered in Nairobi. And some of those who came there – partly as NGOs to try to help to establish that organisation and to make sure it was responding to the mandate it got in Stockholm, and others who came to direct it – quickly became friends.

I remember in particular Dr Maurice Strong. He was Canadian and became the first executive director of UNEP. His wife, Hannah Strong, and I became very good friends and I would visit the headquarters occasionally and listen to him. In my autobiography, *Unbowed*, I discuss how I began having my ideas about planting trees and working with the women and with UNEP. And it was Hannah Strong who was very, very encouraging to me at that time.

Current views

How do you define the idea of sustainability – something that seems to mean different things to different people?

Well, I think it's still hard to improve on the statement coined by Gro Harlem Brundtland, the then Prime Minister of Norway, when she was leading the commission which produced a report called *Our Common Future*. This came up with this concept of sustainability, which is still my definition.

It recognises that we have limited resources on our planet and that these resources must sustain not just the current generation, but also the generations to come and that those generations have a right to be able to use those same resources and to meet what they feel are their needs. So as this generation uses current resources, it must be aware that it has to have a responsibility towards the one that follows. In short, sustainability is about our efforts, our ability, to utilise resources available to us sustainably. I'm using the word in such a way that we can meet what we feel are our needs but also make it possible for the future generations to do the same.

Essentially, what it must mean is that tomorrow, when you're not there, will your children be able to meet their felt needs? If they can't, then we have not used the resources in a sustainable way.

Are there examples of progress in this area in terms of sustainability which make you feel optimistic rather than pessimistic?

Human beings are very interesting. Sometimes they do things that almost appear to be self-destructive, but every so often they start doing things that are redemptive. Some years ago there were people who were very resistant to ideas about renewable sources of energy. I remember the first UN conference on renewable sources of energy held in Nairobi in 1981. The Green Belt Movement was one of the organisations which actually tried to share with the delegates the importance of planting trees and promoting renewable sources of energy such as wood, firewood or wood-based energies, wind, solar, oceans and so on.

At that time everybody was excited about these concepts, but then, because oil was cheap, and because technologies for producing other sources of energy were cheap, people kind of forgot them. But now, because there is a realisation that we are doing so much damage to our environment by emitting all these greenhouse gases into the atmosphere, that realisation and that understanding of science has really helped governments to start to take the issue of renewable sources of energy very seriously. That's why we had the conference in Poznan in December of 2008 on climate change, and in Copenhagen in 2009.

The world is now really keen to see if we can get away from sources of energy that also pollute our environment. So I'm encouraged because it does appear that, once people understand, especially governments, and they feel that their people are threatened, then they are very quick to commit the resources that are needed either to generate energy or to shift from the other sources of energy. So whether it is energy, food production, or simply the air we breathe, somehow the most important thing is for us to ensure that our leaders, those who make decisions on our behalf, understand the issues.

But I am optimistic. I'm always hoping that they will understand, even in Africa. This is our main focus: to try to make our leaders understand that the people are under threat and therefore they must make changes.

Do you feel that because we are now in an economic downturn, that it will be a harder message for governments to promote?

I don't think so. I think it would be a mistake if governments make the economic downturn an excuse not to take care of this issue. It's not as if the economy will improve if we don't take care of this issue. Indeed, things will only get worse and therefore it's in the interests of governments not to use that as an excuse. Because if we try to save the economy or save jobs but are killing ourselves at the same time – what good is that?

So I really hope that governments will not make that an excuse. I know they may, but we must tell them not to. The citizens of every country need to educate themselves about these issues so that they, too, can make the necessary sacrifices that will push our governments to make the right decisions about this.

It would be a mistake if governments make the economic downturn an excuse not to take care of this issue. It's not as if the economy will improve if we don't take care of this issue. Indeed, things will only get worse and therefore it's in the interests of governments not to use that as an excuse. Because if we try to save the economy or save jobs but are killing ourselves at the same time – what good is that?

How central do you think is the role of business in combating climate change?

Well, business is obviously a very strong driver because all of us are driven by businesses. After all, one of the reasons why businesses have got into trouble is because we stopped spending because we didn't have money in our pockets. So now they're trying to see how they can put money in our pockets so that we can spend and continue driving them. But I think what many businesses are also appreciating is the fact that, in an environment where the climate is threatened, the seas are rising, clean drinking water is not available, unemployment is rising, and the migration of millions of people is a real possibility, that all these factors are a potential threat to them. It doesn't matter whether their businesses are located in 'safe' places, or in those that will be completely under threat because of climate change. So I think there is greater understanding and many businesses are willing to do something to help to ease and reduce emissions.

What is not very clear is how this will happen. What can businesses do? For example, I'm trying to appeal to businesses to create green technology, to embrace it, and to create green jobs. We can engage in massive refor-estation programmes and massive protection of forests. We can engage in technologies that will make us more efficient in the way we use trees, the way we use wood and this would create more jobs. I think that businesses just need to explore and invest in research so that they can find other new areas of doing business. It doesn't have to always be oil or coal – we can change. People have changed all throughout history, so I think businesses just have to be brave and help us to move into new areas.

Is it a matter of their being prepared to take risks? Sustainability suggests taking a long-term view but many businesses are focused on the short-term quarterly results and their shareholders.

Well, it's not only the businesses that need to take a longer view. It is also the shareholders. We are all shareholders and it is we who must also help businesses to make that shift. Of course, businesses, especially in capitalism, are driven by profits and often they want profits yesterday. But we need to train ourselves to make that shift at times and allow ourselves to expect less profit and fewer consumer goods – although maybe we shouldn't expect less quality. As we have been saying for so many years, until we learn that the resources are limited we shall always experience shocks.

There is simply not enough for everybody who wants everything. But there can be enough for us to share. So I think that shareholders have to be willing not to make as much profits as they sometimes demand, because we should remember that sometimes when you make so much profit it is at the expense of other people.

There is simply not enough for everybody who wants everything. But there can be enough for us to share. So I think that shareholders have to be willing not to make as much profits as they sometimes demand, because we should remember that sometimes when you make so much profit it is at the expense of other people.

And do you think some businesses understand this?

Yes, I'm sure. Not every business wants to make a profit at any cost. There are very many responsible businesses and there are even ways of certifying companies which are green. I know many companies which are doing everything they can to make profits, yes, but not to make profit at the cost of destroying the planet. And so I have a lot of hope that many, many companies will change.

You can see many examples of companies which are willing to make sacrifices to make sure they don't go under. OK, you may be making $10 an hour. But maybe making $5 an hour is better than making none. So I think both companies and shareholders need to understand that we can't do business as usual, the way we used to, as if we did not understand what we were doing to our environment. We know that what we are doing has a cost to the environment and we must be willing to make the changes that are needed and the sacrifices that are needed in order for us to be able to benefit, but also to ensure that the future generations will do the same. That's what the concept of sustainability is all about.

Do you think it's better to offer a carrot or a stick as an incentive to companies and people to actually change?

Well, I guess both, actually. It's a matter of balance because, on the one hand, you have to give them incentives. For example, it's being suggested to some companies that they can cut emissions. But some of them will only be able to cut emissions up to a certain level. And they cannot cut to the level required by the regulations of the country at that particular time. So they're being told: OK, you don't have to do this. But what you can do is go and buy carbon offsets in some place like the Congo Basin Forest. I'm the Goodwill Ambassador of the Congo forest and I'm trying to say we should save forests like that because they help us to absorb a huge amount of carbon from the atmosphere and trap it.

If companies cannot cut all their emissions, they can go and try to invest in the protection of, say, the Congo forests, the Amazon forests, the South East Asia forests and other forests in other parts of the world. Those three particular blocks of forest, in fact, are the main lungs for the planet – so that's indeed a carrot for many businesses! Unfortunately they aren't doing this yet and I guess that part of the problem is the logistics of how to ensure that the carbon is actually trapped and that the trees remain standing. But there are very many businesses which are willing to not only follow the stick, the rules, at the national level, but also take advantage of the incentives to go out to other parts of the world and protect these resources that have been helping us to trap the greenhouse gases.

Do you think that there should be a more global approach to setting the regulations rather than doing it country by country?

That's why we have meetings such as those in Poznan and Copenhagen. The Kyoto Protocol does not aim to regulate these issues at a global level, because you still can't have one rule for every country. So what we will agree, hopefully, are some very broad guidelines which will then be applied at the national level so that every country will do its best. We are hoping to reduce the gases and improve the rate at which greenhouse gases are emitted. We are also trying to help populations to adapt, because global warming is already having an impact and some people are already suffering. Sometimes we talk as if it is a threat that is in the future, but in many countries it's a threat right now.

Do you think that the change in the US government with the election of Barack Obama will be a force for change for the good? You wrote a very moving piece in a British newspaper just after he won the election.

I think President Obama is a blessing to us all because he has broken barriers that many people thought could not be broken. He has helped us get on to the next level of consciousness, in much the same way that Martin Luther King did when he gave his 'I have a dream' speech in Washington DC. I think that one of the points I made, reflecting especially on Africa, is that so many of us here are not given the same opportunity that the US gave the President. But it is so important that we give our children an opportunity to realise their potential – because they do have potential.

And I challenged the African leaders: if President Obama had been raised in Africa would he have realised his potential in the same way that he did, because he grew up in a country where they believe in allowing people to realise their dreams? We know there are challenges but at least he is an example of the fact that, if given the opportunity, you can realise your dreams. And I said that in Africa we have so many children who are at war, who are hungry, who are growing up in poverty, not so much because there are no resources but because the leadership is failing them by not providing the environment in which they can realise their potential.

Getting more personal

What do you think it was about you as a person that made you decide it was so important to try to spread your views to a wider audience?

Well, as I said earlier, sometimes you really don't know why you do what you do. But you are guided and are enriched by the experiences you go through. Where I grew up in the countryside it was very green, very lush. I had a very protected, very happy childhood, and then I went to America in the 1960s. I think if I'd gone to America in the 1950s or maybe in the 1970s then I might have come out a very different person. So I think it is the experience and what you do with that experience. But I don't remember any particular thing that I can say, this is the reason why I turned out the way I did.

Were you a very determined child?

When you are a child you're just being a child! But I think I was lucky in having a wonderful mother who allowed me to dream and to do what I wanted. I don't remember being restricted or being confined. But then I was growing up in the countryside and there were very few things to confine me with. Also, I think I was endowed with a good mind. And my mother, bless her heart, sent me to school at a very early age.

At that time, the schools were all run by missionaries. The nuns at the first one were Italians, and then I moved to another run by Irish nuns. So I think those nuns also really helped me to shape up in the sense that they were also very encouraging; they nurtured my intellect, my curiosity and my desire to learn. They really nurtured it very, very wonderfully, when I look back. And so I was just a lucky child to have followed a path that was very positive and helped me to grow.

But you also had the ability to follow that path.

Yes, that's why I say I was endowed because I did well in school. I often say to young people, if you work hard and you do well in school, then you'll love school. Of course if you don't do well, partly because you are not working hard, then you'll hate school. I loved school, I just loved learning and I could never see me stopping learning. In a way that's why I ended up as a teacher in a university. And now I also love what I do, because I'm constantly reading, constantly exploring new things, constantly talking about new ideas with people. I think I'm just lucky that way – my mind just keeps learning. So I think that really helped me a lot in shaping who I became.

What are you proudest of in terms of your work?

That's a hard question, because there are so many things that one can say one is proud of: I'm very proud of my mother, my parents, very proud of the sacrifices they made, the decisions they made for me – I'm really very proud of them. They took decisions that nobody had before in their families and they did that for us. I'm very proud of my teachers, many of whom have now passed on, and I really feel like they are part of me. I see them every day in my life because they were such powerful figures and they really helped me to move forward.

I'm also very proud, for example, of the teachers of the school I went to in the United States, Mount St Scholastica College. It's now called Benedictine College, It was a small college in the American mid-West. It provided me with a haven at a time when there was so much turmoil there, and so much hatred and fighting during the civil rights movement. And it was largely a white college, a girls' college, almost all white. Yet they could not have been better. One of my best friends there was a young lady called Florence Conrad Salisbury, a white girl from near Wichita, Kansas. She made me feel so much at home. Every time we had a holiday – whether it was Thanksgiving, Easter or Christmas – I was on my way to Florence's home. I almost became part of their large family.

This was back in the 1960s, so I'm really very proud of people like that. Sometimes we tend to generalise about people, but you always find these golden angels in communities who are just wonderful people and who create an environment that you would have thought impossible in such circumstances. And then, of course, I'm very proud of all the wonderful people who inspired and encouraged me along the way. There are also my friends who stood with me sometimes when it was very, very difficult. I would have to write a book to mention all the people!

Was it exciting to receive your Nobel Prize?

Yes, it was very exciting. First of all it was very surprising because that was the first time that they had looked at the environment and recognised the link that we were making in our work between resources and the reason why people fight. We had suggested that, if we wanted to pre-empt many of the conflicts we have in the world, we needed to understand the linkage between competition and resources – especially when resources are degraded or diminished and there is competition for them. And so I was very, very excited and I knew that part of the reason why they were doing that was to emphasise that message and the linkage.

Is there a moment that you would consider that was the defining moment, the one that made you think, right, this is what I'm going to do from now on?

Well, I really don't have that moment because for me the whole journey has been a continuous one. Every so often I have had to make a choice about whether to go right or left. Like they say, you come to a crossroad and have to decide which road you travel. Sometimes you choose the one that has been travelled a lot, to quote Robert Frost, or sometimes you go to the one that has been less travelled, but you have no idea what lies ahead.

So I wouldn't really say, even to this day, that I knew that this is the way I will follow. I usually just follow where I feel my heart and my mind are moving and where I feel that the issues are important. That's the way I follow. But, up until now, I've always found myself right in the middle of this issue of environment that is so central to so many other issues. And sitting there I can almost touch every other issue, whether it be governance, peace, wars, conflicts or women's rights. Mention any one, and it will have something to do with what I am doing. And so I find myself extremely busy.

Up until now, I've always found myself right in the middle of this issue of environment that is so central to so many other issues. And sitting there I can almost touch every other issue, whether it be governance, peace, wars, conflicts or women's rights.

12

....

Ricardo Navarro

Ricardo Navarro is founder and director of the Salvadoran Centre for Appropriate Technology (CESTA), El Salvador's largest environmental NGO, which focuses on the country's critical environmental and social needs. The work of CESTA is essential in a country where the protracted civil war hurt the environment to such an extent that it is now the most degraded country in the Western Hemisphere after Haiti.

An engineer by training, Ricardo has worked in partnership with urban and rural communities to provide technical assistance for an array of projects. One project, Ecobici, teaches people how to make and use human-powered machines such as bicycle carts to collect rubbish, pedal-driven corn grinders, air compressors, and water pumps.

Bicycle power is one of his passions, and translates into wheelchairs made at the Centre's workshops for the impoverished victims of the civil conflicts that have gripped El Salvador. Another CESTA initiative, Econciencia, is an education-based initiative working with academics, community and church activists, trade unionists and students to promote what Ricardo calls 'rational thought' about sustainability.

He has served as president of Friends of the Earth International and won the prestigious Goldman prize, often described as the green equivalent of the Nobel Prize. He sees political struggle as entirely consistent with his other work, and received death threats for his activity during a campaign to preserve a forested district that secures the water supply for the capital San Salvador.

The plans of the developers were thwarted and Navarro was invited to run for election. He sat on the capital's council, when the Farabundo Martí National Liberation Front narrowly won the election. Previously he had served as an adviser to the Minister of Environment. He now devotes all his time to his environmental work.

The professional journey

Let's start by looking at your career. What have been the main highlights?

Although my basic training was in engineering in the United States, I have devoted 25 years of my life to environmental issues. Here at CESTA we promote projects such as sustainable management of solid waste, reforestation, bicycle use and so on. We also work on issues like sea turtle conservation and a lot of biodiversity projects.

During my education I found that one of the problems in science is that it is divided – split, I should say – into different compartments. As an engineer you look at some topics which, of course, helped my understanding of climate change greatly. But an engineer doesn't study the impact of social or environmental issues. We're not very concerned with poverty issues. Or with global warming. And I realised that we must look at the broader picture.

As an engineer you look at some topics which, of course, helped my understanding of climate change greatly. But an engineer doesn't study the impact of social or environmental issues. We're not very concerned with poverty issues. Or with global warming. And I realised that we must look at the broader picture.

It's when you look at what's happening in the world – with over-fishing, say, and its impact on the oceans – that you realise it is just a matter of time before we enter into a serious crisis. When you realise how much petroleum we're consuming, and the volume of greenhouse gases it's generating, then it's just a matter of time before that crisis really hits. Take the example of water in my country. I remember when I was teaching at university in 1984 and I became aware that the water table was going down by a metre a year.

The water level shouldn't go down. It should stay constant because we're always going to need it. The water companies, of course, faced with drops of this magnitude, kept opening wells that were deeper. As a matter of fact they opened up wells that were two metres deeper every two years! That's how they did things. But eventually, sooner or later, you're going to hit the bottom somewhere, you know?

What impact did this have on you?

Well, I started understanding more and more about these issues of sustainability and that they, of course, had a lot to do with environment, social issues, and economic issues and so on. When I was a lecturer in mechanical engineering on topics such as fluid mechanics and heat transfer I started a course on solar energy. The first semester I devoted to the basics and the second semester was on solar energy.

Also, while I was lecturing I started studying political science because I realised that scientists were speaking one language and politicians another. The motivating factor was that we need people who can translate technical things to political action. Then, after lecturing for seven years, I returned to the US, did a DSc in technology and human affairs and have been working on environmental issues as an environmental activist ever since.

Is that what you are best known for?

Yes, primarily as an environmental activist. Here in El Salvador we do a lot of work with the media, both national and international and have been holding a press conference every Monday for the last 20 or so years. But it's a constant struggle to convey big issues such as the fact that if we do not manage to live on a sustainable planet, or if things change dramatically, we're going to lose control of how much wealth we can generate. So that's why I have been devoted to the environment and that's what I'm best known for.

Haven't you also been involved in politics?

Well, I would consider myself more of an environmental politician or political environmentalist in the sense that we're always dealing with politicians. I started CESTA in 1980 to promote the use of bicycles. And I realised soon after that the problem was not that people didn't know how to fix bicycles or how to make solar collectors. The problem was more with the government. Politicians are the main obstacles when it comes to promoting all these things because they get the support of international and national economic interests to destroy a forest, for example, or build a shopping mall or widen roads or carry out mining. We're now struggling with mining activities in El Salvador.

However, three years ago the central government of El Salvador invited me to be adviser to the Minister of Environment, which I accepted because I thought that I could do something. But I found myself alone in the sense that, when I'd say to the Minister of Environment what I thought should be done, he would smile and things kept going on as usual. Then I was invited by the opposition party, the left party, to be a member of the city council. Ideologically, here in El Salvador, the left is better than the right, but environmentally there is not much difference. And again I found myself on my own when trying to convince people. It was as if I were speaking a different language.

So I decided that from then on I would devote 100% of my energies again to NGO activities. We can do much more from the outside because we can carry out more effective campaigns, and really exert pressure on politicians. And we have been successful many times in doing so. I was never a member of a political party but, of course, being part of a government you have some relationship with the political parties, and they tend to disappoint. I think it's better to do work from outside.

Wouldn't you be more effective being on the inside, so to speak?

Well, it depends. What happened is that they always offered me positions with no power. And without power, you are just an adviser. I didn't have a vote or anything. I couldn't do things myself. I couldn't order anything. I'd advise the minister not to approve that coal-fired power plant. And he'd go ahead and approve it. That kind of thing. Or, don't approve this mining project. And they'd say, well, we have to look at rural development, at this and that and this. So eventually you just feel worse than useless.

Being on the municipal city council, by contrast, was different. That was much better. I was one of 18 people voting. But, in the end, what it boils down to is that a bureaucracy doesn't move things. Unless you really have the power to say – you have to do this, you have to do that – then it's just a waste of time.

Have there been any people or events which have influenced you in your decision to devote yourself to this work?

Not really. I tend just to look at things and then extrapolate where they're going. I view the environment, for example, as an enterprise which has been losing $100 a week for the past few years. It may be a very big enterprise, and people may not be worried about this loss, but the very existence of this trend means that sooner or later this organisation is going to face a fierce crisis.

If you look back 30 years or more you can see that we haven't been headed in the right direction. CESTA was the first NGO in El Salvador, and when we started warning that we would be facing water shortages here the most common response was: 'Oh, that doesn't make any sense. We have plenty of water.' Now you read press reports every day about people protesting, going on marches and holding demonstrations, because there is not enough water in the communities. And the simple reason for that is that all the forests were being destroyed. A lot of water catchment areas were being ruined. So it was not hard to predict what would happen.

For instance, there is a big mountain range here called Cordillera el Balsamo. It is a very fragile area, yet they were destroying it. We pleaded with all concerned, saying please do not destroy this mountain range, it is of no use for housing, let it stay the way it is. We carried on trying to make our voice heard for eight years – until there was an earthquake; the mountain collapsed and killed 850 people. And then, of course, the government said: 'Oh, we shouldn't have done that.' It's always the same. Governments react when they see these big disasters, but don't act to prevent them. It doesn't take much analysis – if you look at the situation carefully – to predict when there's a disaster in the making. And this is what we have been saying about the environment for many years. Yet still such disasters occur.

How do you try to get your message across?

Well, as I said, we hold a press conference here every Monday and get, on average, eight different media attending from radio, newspapers and TV. So we're on the news almost every day. Radio is very important, because it has national coverage. Plus we do a lot of lobbying and hold demonstrations. But we also have an even stronger ally. And that stronger ally is the climate. For example, in 2005, when the rains came they continued for four days solidly and brought the whole country to a standstill.

There were mountain slides everywhere. It became dangerous to go out. But the thing is, since the disaster was predictable, all the government had to say was: 'We have to protect the mountains.' Unfortunately, in El Salvador, we usually have to wait until things happen – all because intelligence is not a very common commodity in political circles. Politicians see the impact of environmental disasters, and it produces a knee-jerk reaction. But we are making some progress, I believe.

What have been the big challenges in raising awareness?

Well, one of the challenges we have is that the big enterprises like construction firms view us as their enemies. How, they ask, can we be against houses if we live in one? Our argument is that we are against houses being built in areas that should remain as forests. There are a lot of areas that have already been deforested, and then used for housing because they're not attractive. Yet if they were to plant some trees and landscape it, it could become attractive again. But now the construction firms are destroying the last remaining forest and that will have a big impact on flooding.

We also have a lot of trouble with car battery recycling plants. They have caused so much pollution. We had some blood samples taken from about 500 children which showed levels of 15 micrograms of lead per litre of blood. One US agency claims that more than 7 micrograms can generate irreversible damage. It's really dramatic. We're fighting these plants, but the response is usually that we're just politically motivated. The government here in El Salvador is not very interested in trying to make some of these enterprises cease polluting, or destroying forests. In El Salvador we lack sufficient pertinent regulation.

Are all the businesses in your country generally hostile to your message?

No, not all. As a matter of fact, I have been having meetings with business people here who tell me that they would be happy to obey whatever regulations are introduced. But they want to see regulations for everybody because otherwise, they argue, their businesses will suffer. And they are right. But it is the very large businesses which don't want regulation. And they are the ones backing the government. They don't see the need to protect the resources for the middle and long term. They just look at the short term. That's why we're destroying our country.

It is the very large businesses which don't want regulation. And they are the ones backing the government. They don't see the need to protect the resources for the middle and long term. They just look at the short term. That's why we're destroying our country.

But as countries all around the world start introducing tougher regulations, won't that have some impact on the companies in your country? Particularly if they work internationally?

Well, yes, there should be international standards, but when it comes to countries in the Third World there usually isn't the technological capacity to investigate whether those standards are being met. So they're not. Think about petroleum accidents. They rarely occur in Denmark, but they happen a lot in Nigeria. They're rare in the UK, but there are many in Africa. Do you see what I mean? And it's the same companies. Why? They lower the standards in those places because technologically there is no capacity to investigate. And the politicians in those countries tend to have close ties with big business.

So what's going to break that cycle?

I have a strong confidence in awareness raising. Until we become aware of what is right and what is wrong things will continue the way they are. We work a lot on public issues in the hope that eventually more people will understand what's involved and things will change.

It's very hard to measure results, although with forestry we can count the number of trees. But to me the most important thing is to educate the public. It's very interesting because sometimes people will come up to me in the street and complain that whatever is happening is because of 'climate change' or 'ozone depletion'. It does look like people are becoming more and more aware. It's a bit like slavery. Until people became aware that all human beings have equal rights, apartheid found a ready audience. These are the kind of things that I am hoping for. I don't know if we have enough time, but at least we have to try.

Current views

How would you define sustainability in general and, more specifically, in terms of business and government and consumers?

Well, sustainability is the ability to sustain. The question is: what do you want to sustain? That is the question that should be asked. Of course I want to sustain my house, my community, my country, my continent, my planet. I wish the best for other planets and all that but primarily we want to sustain our societies because that's what we are part of.

Think of society and development in terms of a boat and its engine. The boat is society and the engine is development. Of course we need the engine to move the boat from place to place. Of course we need development to generate light, say, or to transport water, to produce shoes, televisions and all that. But think back to the boat and its engine. If a boat is approaching an iceberg, powered by its engine, then we'd say: stop the engine and we would put it in reverse.

That's the point. Society has, until now, experienced development based on consumption of fossil fuels but when we see the iceberg of climate change on the horizon we have to stop it. We have to stop and say, wait a moment. If we continue unchanged, we'll destroy ourselves. We must make the society sustainable, not the development. Yes, we need development but perhaps there comes a time when we should say: stop it. Not any more – at least for 10 years – until we understand what's going on.

And in order to make a society sustainable we need a least four things.

Which are ...?

One is at the environmental level. We cannot have a sustainable society if we are destroying our water resources, over-fishing our lakes and sea, or putting much more CO_2 in the atmosphere than it is capable of processing. So we need to handle the environment carefully, to ensure that our relationship with the atmosphere, with nature, is based on protecting it, not destroying it. So there should be a limit on what we do to the environment.

Second, there is also a social element to sustainability. There are 6.6 billion of us on the planet, so we might just as well try to get along. Because if we don't we will destroy ourselves. We have the weapons to do it. So we have to respect each other, we have to recognise that every human being has a right to housing, to education, to health, to freedom – all these kind of human rights. It's very important to achieve that if we want to have a sustainable society.

Third, economics. We have to aim for economic efficiency. We shouldn't be so wasteful. But there is a fourth one which is not usually written about in textbooks and that's political. Political means that we must have a democratic world if we want a sustainable society. Big corporations have too much power. It's not democratic. When US president George W. Bush didn't go to the Earth Summit in 2002 in South Africa it was because 15 large transnational corporations advised him not to. Is that democracy? If we don't have a democratic world we will not have a sustainable world.

You obviously feel strongly that politicians are too focused on economic concerns.

One of the main problems facing the world is that economic forces have become political forces. That is wrong. Because political forces are the ones that decide what to do in the world and it's wrong if they make decisions based only on economic criteria. We have to abide by environmental criteria because we're part of that environment. For example, water has to be protected no matter what. We should not let the climate get hotter and hotter because that will destroy us. So everyone has to focus on environmental concerns.

What this means is that, instead of having a political-economic system prevailing, we should have a political-environmental system prevailing. We should have a social objective, because we're the same species and we should be concerned about each other and respect human rights. And we should let the market operate within limits. That's very important.

For example, business people are the ones who make fishing happen and, if it weren't for them, I wouldn't have fish in my house, right? I need fish, and I need enterprising people to go fishing. But you need to approach a body of water, a lake or the sea, and calculate how many pounds of fish you can remove safely every week. If the answer is 100 tons then, OK, that's the limit. It's as simple as that.

We're part of nature, so we should respect it and not modify it in a way that would damage us. That should be like a commandment that everybody should follow. And once we understand that, and the importance of the social objective, we should let the business people do what they are good at doing. And I believe business people are needed to make the transition to a sustainable planet. But the main decisions cannot be taken purely on the basis of economic criteria.

Can you give us any examples?

A lot of businesses are producing solar collectors. These cells are expensive. They need to be cheaper and we should help those people to produce more solar cells until, like computers, they become cheaper and cheaper every day. Good architects are tackling similar problems. If a house should only consume so much energy, what will it take to generate this amount? It requires solar cells on the roof, shade from trees, and adequate ventilation. But how do you achieve this?

Here in our Centre, for example, when we tried to build a second floor the civil engineers said, oh, you have to put in air conditioning. I said, no way. Since I was teaching solar energy at the university I took my books in and I showed them the solution. So we don't need ventilation, or air conditioning. We just have what we call solar passive housing. And that is so simple.

Are there any businesses that you'd point to that are already following these principles?

Well, there are some – like bicycle manufacturers – that I like a lot. The bicycle is probably the best piece of technology that has ever been devised. I could say the same for solar collectors. There are a lot of people who produce organic medicine, while companies which have tackled issues like low energy consumption, for example, are good. Yet it's much easier to point out the bad ones like the mining industry.

What do you see as the role of bodies like the World Bank? Can you see them playing a role in establishing some sort of international framework for regulation?

The danger with the World Bank and other large institutions is that they get involved with projects that later prove damaging. I remember, for example, all these stories about the World Bank's involvement with dams. But they didn't bring all the benefits that they promised. The trouble is that the criteria have been more economic than environmental or social. And this is the problem with many of the big institutions.

I remember trying to convey this to James Wolfensohn, the former President of the World Bank. He agreed, but admitted that if he were to say so in public everybody in the World Bank would be against him!

Do you think that you can make profits, and still follow a sustainable agenda?

Oh, certainly. As a matter of fact, it's very important to make profit. The problem is not profit as such, it's when – in order to make profit – you destroy whatever is in your path. Profit should be allowed. I believe profit is normal. People have a right to profit – but, as I said, within limits.

When I go to a restaurant and people sell me a dish, I am sure they are making profit. And that's OK, because I want that dish. It's the same when I buy a shirt. People are making a profit from selling one to me. That's OK too provided the shirt is not made with this or that chemical, or has destroyed this or that forest. Profits are fine as long as they do not become the main driving force, and that is the major problem around the world.

What will be the impetus for more companies to rethink how they operate?

This will require strong political institutions – but the problem is that we don't have them. In the United States, for example, I believe that neither the Republicans nor the Democrats have the potential to be an important political force. There are a lot of good parties around with a lot of good people, but to me the main difference between the Republicans and the Democrats is that the Republicans are supported by Pepsi-Cola and the Democrats by Coca-Cola!

The point is that the world requires a strong political force right now. It should be able to say, on climate change, for example, that in 10 years' time no vehicle manufacturers will be allowed to make cars unless they're run by solar energy. But how can any politician say that? How will the oil firms react? How will the car firms react? So I believe the fact that strong economic interests are very much entrenched is a major obstacle.

Do you think that NGOs in general, and your NGO in particular, have made progress over the last 10 to 15 years?

Some things have changed. At least awareness has grown, so people are more concerned. My concern is that I don't know if we have enough time, particularly with climate change. We're not acting fast enough. Look at the Kyoto Protocol, for example. It looked for a reduction of CO_2 levels by 5.2% from 1990 to 2012, but instead, by 2007 humanity had increased emissions by some 38%. Now I don't know if any country has been capable of reducing emissions, although some European countries like Germany are claiming that they might achieve their national target of 8%. But people in Germany are producing less CO_2 now only because they are buying the goods in China. So we've just moved the problem elsewhere.

We're not acting fast enough. Look at the Kyoto Protocol, for example. It looked for a reduction of CO_2 levels by 5.2% from 1990 to 2012, but instead, by 2007 humanity had increased emissions by some 38%. Now I don't know if any country has been capable of reducing emissions, although some European countries like Germany are claiming that they might achieve their national target of 8%. But people in Germany are producing less CO_2 now only because they are buying the goods in China. So we've just moved the problem elsewhere.

China is becoming the big emitter of CO_2. But we have to realise that we need a commitment from everyone. And my concern is that I don't know if we have enough time. Things are getting really bad in the short term. We have to move faster and I believe we need the support of business people and also religious people. I think the Pope should declare it a sin to emit more pollution than you are allowed to, according to the carrying capacity of the planet.

Are there any examples of people trying to make a difference that make you feel optimistic?

Definitely. There are examples in small communities in different cultural settings everywhere, from Colombia to the United Kingdom. Take Denmark, where I have seen people trying to close roads to cars and restricting them to bicycles. There are many good signs everywhere in the world: people are using solar energy, wind power, bicycles, hydro ecology, organic farming. There are also examples in Southern countries where local and indigenous communities are trying to stop the opening of new oil wells. There are millions of examples – but they are very small and usually the economic forces around them do not support them.

What would you like to see happen?

There are two things that we have to do now as we face the impact of climate change in the near future. One is to see how we can reduce emissions of fossil fuel to the atmosphere. The other is to work out how to avoid the destruction that ensues. We need to keep the forests that are still around intact since they help to stabilise the temperature of the planet. So those are two objectives for the short term.

It would help if we were to try to organise our cities for more bicycle use. A lot of politicians will say that we have a bicycle infrastructure. They're right; we do have a bicycle infrastructure everywhere. The only problem is that it's being used by cars. Draw a line down these roads and we'll have enough infrastructures for bicycles. I think it's very important to promote these issues of renewable energy. We should try not to consume more than we need. It's also better if we are able to plant food locally, and process our waste locally. Industries that generate a lot of pollution should be discouraged.

We must try to find a way to get rid of armies across the world, because we're spending over $3000 million a day on the defence industry. Then we could redeploy the personnel, so that they could be on standby for natural disasters, like flooding, where they could go and help those in need. I'm not saying we have to get rid of these people. No. Let's make these good jobs, let's increase their salaries. And all the money saved from military spending could be used to repair or equip houses so as to reduce their consumption of heating fuel, for example. We have to learn to live in peace.

Because if we don't adapt, the planet will force us to. That will happen because the atmosphere is changing dramatically: there will be more hurricanes, they will go on for longer and God knows how the chemistry of the atmosphere is going to change. It's very important to realise that we cannot get away from nature. It's not a matter of wanting or not wanting.

I could, for example, travel to the UK and not pay taxes. I'd hide from the police and maybe they'd never catch me – but in nature I cannot do that. In nature if I pollute the air I still have to breathe it. So I have to realise that I should not pollute the air, period, because sooner or later it will impact on me. If I destroy the forest or pollute the water I will be damaged. Sooner or later we have to understand this. If we don't do it consciously, and try to follow nature's laws, then nature will force us to change.

One final aspect is that climate change is a sign of the grave injustice that is taking place in the world, because the problem has been generated by people who consume – the richer people – and it has been the most vulnerable people, mostly impoverished people, who suffer the consequences. So the most important commitments of reducing emissions have to be taken by people living in countries with high levels of consumption.

Getting more personal

What was it about you as a person that made you decide it was so important to take these concepts to a wider audience?

Well, first I realised that we could have a very nice life in any country – whether in El Salvador, Finland or wherever – but to achieve this needs collective action. I cannot do it by myself. So it is very important to decide, with other people, what will benefit us all. Personally, I believe that solidarity should be the main social currency: solidarity among all for the benefit of all. Furthermore, I think it would be good to be able to provide future generations with an environment where they can live comfortably.

Have you ever had a defining moment where you realised, this is what I want to do?

Well, 30 years ago or so I started realising that the world was not moving in the right direction, even though I can't remember any major crises then. But when I was 24, and began to examine the statistics, I knew that things would have to change. It was not anything dramatic – more like something that developed gradually.

Do you feel very passionate about everything that you do?

Oh, certainly. You have to look at things with passion. Passion is good in every sense. Yes, I am passionate and I'm also optimistic in that, if I lose a battle, it's a case of OK, on to the next fight. I never get disappointed. That's very important.

Has your family been an influence in what you do?

I come from a family with four brothers, although one of them was killed during the war here. The other three are very concerned about things and are involved here and there, but I am the one who is 100% committed. And I now stay away from politics – although I obviously talk to politicians all over the world – because I want to devote all my time to the environmental struggle. For the simple reason that it's worth it and it's what most inspires me. If I had $5 million, $10 million or $20 million, whether in gold or currency, it would just end up in a bank. But if I were able to transform something that is dying into something that is living, that would be worth so much more. And that's why I am so keen to devote my life to this environmental struggle.

If I had $5 million, $10 million or $20 million, whether in gold or currency, it would just end up in a bank. But if I were able to transform something that is dying into something that is living, that would be worth so much more. And that's why I am so keen to devote my life to this environmental struggle.

What are you proudest of, in terms of what you've achieved to date?

We've achieved many things here in El Salvador. We managed, for example, to get a Ministry of the Environment that we didn't have before. We've been able to stop many forests from being destroyed although we have lost others that have been destroyed.

It's a bit like being a boxer. A good boxer wins a lot of the time and sometimes loses, but he keeps fighting. If you were to ask a boxer, what has been your best fight, he'd be hard put to pick one because each fight has something special. So I feel very satisfied and happy about the work I'm doing.

13

....

Dr Vandana Shiva

Dr Vandana Shiva is a physicist, environmental activist and author. Born in the valley of Dehradun, Dr Shiva trained as a physicist and received her PhD in physics at the University of Western Ontario in 1978. She later went on to do interdisciplinary research in science, technology and environmental policy at the Indian Institute of Science and the Indian Institute of Management in Bangalore.

Dr Shiva participated in the non-violent Chipko movement during the 1970s. The movement, whose main participants were women, adopted the tactic of hugging trees to prevent their felling. In 1982, she founded the Research Foundation for Science, Technology and Ecology, which led to the creation of Navdanya. This is a biodiversity conservation programme she founded to support local farmers, rescue and conserve crops and plants that are in danger of becoming extinct and make them available through direct marketing. It has its own seed bank and organic farm spread in northern India.

Her book, Staying Alive, *published in 1988, helped to redefine perceptions of third world women. Dr Shiva has also served as an adviser to governments in India and abroad as well as non-governmental organisations, including the Women's Environment and Development Organisation and the Third World Network. She is one of the leaders of the International Forum on Globalisation, and a figure of the global solidarity movement known as the alter-globalisation movement.*

Throughout her career Dr Shiva has fought for changes in the practice and paradigms of agriculture and food. Intellectual property rights, biodiversity, biotechnology, bioethics and genetic engineering are among the fields where she has contributed intellectually and through activist campaigns. She has assisted grassroots organisations of the Green movement in Africa, Asia, Latin America, Ireland, Switzerland and Austria with campaigns against genetic engineering.

She has been featured in a number of documentaries, including 'Blue Gold: World Water Wars' by Sam Bozzo, Irena Salina's documentary 'Flow: For Love of Water' which was screened at the 2008 Sundance Film Festival and 'The Corporation', protesting against large corporations as a seed activist. She is also featured in the documentary 'Fed up! Genetic Engineering, Industrial Agriculture and Sustainable Alternatives', as well as in 'The world according to Monsanto', a film made by French independent journalist Marie-Monique Robin. The documentary showcases the disastrous results of genetically-modified organisms (GMO).

She has received many awards for her work. For example, in 1993, Dr Shiva received the Right Livelihood Award (also known as the Alternative Nobel Prize) '... For placing women and ecology at the heart of modern development discourse.' Other awards received include the Global 500 Award of the United Nations Environment Programme (UNEP) in 1993, and the Earth Day International Award of the United Nations (UN) for her dedicated commitment to the preservation of the planet as demonstrated by her actions, her leadership and by setting an example for the rest of the world.

She is the author of numerous books and has written over 300 papers for leading scientific and technical journals. Her latest book is Soil Not Oil *(2008).*

The professional journey

Given the richness of your career, do you feel there's anything specific that you feel is linked with your name?

Saving seeds and biodiversity.

Can you elaborate on that?

Well, 20 years ago I started this movement called Navdanya, dedicated to the protection of biodiversity and saving of seeds. And, I would imagine, if we count the number of farmers who were involved, the seed keepers and the number of varieties we have saved, we are probably one of the biggest seed saving movements in the world. So I'll just give you an example: 3000 rice varieties, of which 400 are grown on our farm in Dehradun, another 500 in Orissa and 250 in Bengal. We also have 150 kinds of kidney beans, 50 kinds of wheat and nine kinds of mustard.

What was your motivation to do this?

Well, it was really a two-step process that educated me as to the value of the seeds and biodiversity. The first was in 1984 when India went through extremely violent extremism and terrorism in the Punjab. And the Punjab was the land of what was called the Green Revolution. A central figure in the Green Revolution, Norman Borlaug, had been given a Nobel Peace Prize and as this violence grew I kept asking myself: this was supposed to be about peace. Why is there such violence, why is Punjab at war? I'm trained as a quantum physicist, so I guess being so much on the outside I could ask these questions.

If I'd been an agronomist I'd never have questioned it, I'd have just kept doing the breeding. But being on the outside of this field and also being part of society I could ask this very basic question. The 'father' of the Green Revolution gets the Nobel Peace Prize, but why are there are 30 000 people killed in Punjab – which is six times those killed on 9/11?

Then, in June of that year our prime minister, Indira Ghandi, sent troops to invade the Sikh's most sacred shrine, the Golden Temple, where the leader of the separatist Sikh militant group, Jamail Singh Bhindranwale, was hiding and he was killed. By November, Indira had been assassinated. So this vicious cycle of violence was increasing and increasing and I'm asking myself, why are people taking to the gun when they should have been prosperous, according to the narrative and the story? And then by December we get another tragedy which is the Bhopal disaster. And that killed 3000 people in one night, and has also killed more than 30 000 since then and crippled hundreds of thousands for life.

So I look at 1984, interestingly, as an Orwellian year in every sense. All these people had died because of the tools that we had shaped for agriculture. And I was asking myself, what's going on? I started studying the system a little more closely and realised that a lot of it had to do with creating monocultures.

I look at 1984, interestingly, as an Orwellian year in every sense. All these people had died because of the tools that we had shaped for agriculture. And I was asking myself, what's going on? I started studying the system a little more closely and realised that a lot of it had to do with creating monocultures.

Could you explain what you mean?

This was about breeding the new seeds that needed chemicals which got the farmers into debt, so when they were supposed to be getting prosperous they were actually becoming indebted.

Who was behind this move to monocultures? Was it the big chemical companies?

Very much so. The companies which had grown out of the Second World War selling chemicals to kill, then moved the chemicals into agriculture, but agriculture didn't need these chemicals so they had to adapt plants in order to respond to them, which was the whole basis of the breeding movement of the Green Revolution. The miracle varieties of the Green Revolution were based on transforming the plants to adapt them to the chemicals.

And so by the end of that year I'd started to ask these questions. By 1987, three years later, and partly because by then I'd done my book, which is called *The Violence of the Green Revolution*, I was invited to Geneva for a meeting on biotechnology. I wrote back to the organiser and said: 'I don't do this sort of work, you know. Yes, I've studied the Green Revolution impacts, but I am not a biotechnologist.'

And they said, 'No, this meeting is to take stock of this emerging technology.' And the meeting was a very interesting mix of people. The corporations were there, the scientists were there. They weren't just the scientists involved in genetic engineering, either. The meeting included other scientists like me who were involved in the impact of technologies on the environment and people. There were people from health and from trade unions as well.

Also at this meeting was the biotechnology industry (the old chemical industry, which had become the biotech industry and then taken over the seed industry). It was now one industry. It was also the pharmaceutical industry. It's one industry. So we're talking about tremendous power. And they said, we are too small for the future. By the turn of the century we'll be five and it's only the five who survive who will control the market. So they needed the tools to control the market, which included owning the intellectual property on seeds and plants and living material created through genetic engineering. They laid this out as a business plan.

What was your reaction?

By the time this discussion was over I said that this sounds like a dictatorship over life! I just felt the urge to keep spaces free for nature, evolution, biodiversity and the species as well as for the farmers because, once you have intellectual property rights, then the farmer saving seed is treated like a thief. Once you have genetically-engineered seeds there is also the contamination issue, which was so predictable.

So I just took inspiration from Gandhi. Back in the 1920s and 1930s the British Empire had taken over textile production entirely. India supplied cotton and indigo, the plant for dyeing, but then we had to buy finished textiles from Britain, when we had been the biggest textile manufacturer of the world. Gandhi dealt with this by pulling out a spinning wheel and saying that the only way to free ourselves from this was to spin our own cloth. In my heart and mind I was thinking, what would be the spinning wheel of today to deal with this complete totalitarianism of an industry that interestingly had assigned itself the name the life sciences industry? And I just thought OK, if it's about life then it's about the seed.

Did this idea come after you had thought long and hard about it, or did it just sort of pop into your mind?

It popped into my mind after a few chilling moments when I heard that corporate dream of total monopoly.

So you then decided, this is what I'm going to do?

At that time I was helping the Bhopal movement and also the movements around dams like the Narmada. So I literally went back from this meeting and said to the people of Bhopal, this is what we must do. There was an urgency about it. If we waited there would be no seeds left to save. And that's how I started out.

You mentioned Gandhi. Were there others who were influenced you?

Oh, yes. A tremendous teacher, a scientist called Dr R.H. Richaria. He was very interesting. He, in fact, had come to Britain as part of the Civil Service because in those days they used to train the civil servants. You had to be very smart to qualify. So he came here, but his heart was not in administration. He left the Civil Service training and joined Cambridge University to do rice research, which is where his heart was. He ended up being India's top rice researcher.

He is the one who counted the varieties, went back to the tribals and saved the seeds. He is the one who taught me that India used to have 200 000 rice varieties. He is the one who taught me that, in fact, native varieties can have higher production rates. It's just that scientists have never looked at this tremendous richness. And, of course, when I decided I was going to save seed, he is the one I turned to.

Did he ever say, well, you're a quantum physicist, stick with that and save the world another way?

No, no, because Dr Richaria was an amazing scientist. As I said, he was the top scientist of that time in rice. But he always recognised that the tribals had a real knowledge. And so he didn't have this idea of expertise as locked into someone who has gone through a particular kind of high level of education. Having worked with the tribals he knew that knowledge can exist in other ways, other forms, and he was in fact thrilled that someone like me was turning to this as my life's mission.

Was there anyone else in the world doing this sort of thing at the time, apart from you and the doctor?

Well, there were people who were thinking about seed, but not doing the same thing. There were two people who worked together at that time in an organisation called RAFI, the Rural Advancement Fund International, in the US. This was a sharecroppers association and the two people I met as part of the search were Pat Mooney and Cary Fowler. Now, Pat has continued to play a tremendous role in this area through his organisation the ETC Group – the Action Group on Erosion, Technology and Concentration. And the other one, Cary, is the brains behind the Nordic vault – Norway has created a vault in the Arctic to preserve a wide variety of plant seeds from around the world in an underground cavern.

But I realised that it wasn't enough for me to research and analyse. I decided that I had to work on the ground at the community level by going from village to village.

What were the challenges you faced? After all, you were going to be dealing both at a higher level, but also – literally – at the ground level.

Well, even though I'm neither a biologist nor an agronomist I'm fortunate enough to have had parents who were very highly educated and enlightened.

My father was a conservator of forests and my mother ended up farming. Both parents were very close to the first agriculture minister of India, K.M. Munshi, who was very creative. And our libraries were full of books of the plants of India or gazetteers of the Himalaya.

So, although I'd chosen the life of a physicist, there was, I suppose, a naturalness in the move, in the transition. What I did was pick up these old books, these ancient books in my parents' library and I started to go to the villages because there had been so much erosion. I would go to the villagers and say, do you remember growing this crop? And show them the pictures. Because English and local names are totally different. Not only that, but in every place the name is even different for the same thing! So the images of the plants were really important to have.

I'll give you a very interesting example. It comes back to the British again. Because the British had not been vegetarians like us, they had never really had a diet which was dependent on plant proteins because their proteins came from meat. So when the British came we were eating our chana, which you call chick pea, and a dahl called tur, which is pigeon pea. And something else was called cowpea. And something else was called horse gram.

And I realised when I was doing this work on seed that the English name was only related to treating the most precious of our foods as animal feed and chicken feed because the British didn't know how to use them elsewhere. So when you take that English name people just imagine this is not a human food.

Of course, since the foods had already been degraded by their being seen as horse and cow feed, there was no respect for the diversity. There was no interest in finding out that there are 500 varieties of pigeon pea. And 80 varieties of mung bean. That was a big issue: naming and identifying.

The second issue in terms of identification was the fact that the scientists in universities only knew the major crops. They knew the rice, they knew the wheat, but they didn't know the native varieties because the science community that deals with plant genetic resource conservation is quite separate from the one involved with plant breeding. But it's the breeder who interacts with the farmer. And the breeding community is ignorant of biodiversity. And the people in plant genetic resource conservation had no interaction in the dissemination of those seeds – they just collect them. What the farmer gets in return for diversity is uniformity. So the scientists didn't have the knowledge as a community and I also found that, by and large, neither did the men.

The men?

The men in the villages, because the women are the seed keepers. And so it ended up that my best teachers in all of this were women. Grandmothers would say: 'Yes, I used to grow this really big. I have a little bag with a few seeds lying in the corner of my store, a seed bag.' And they would go out and bring it to me and share it with me. And that's how we built up our seed collections.

What about the people at a higher level? Did you find, in the early stages, that they'd listen to you, or was it a challenge?

In the first few years I went from village to village, walking on my own. I went round with what money I earned from teaching and writing. I could support two or three people to do the work and as I got involved I realised the erosion was very fast and we needed to do this on a much bigger scale to make a difference. So I had to start thinking about doing project-based work. I got my first support from the food and agriculture organisation of the United Nations. But those in charge in the Indian government – the officials, the bureaucrats – tried to prevent my starting the seed saving by saying that only the state can deal with seeds.

Who was it who was trying to stop you?

Officials in the agriculture ministry. So I went all the way to the agriculture minister. I said, you know, your officials are blocking this. And I told him what was happening, why I was starting the work. He happened to be from an agricultural background.

When are we talking about here?

We're talking about the late 1980s, early 1990s. And he understood. So he overruled all the bureaucratic obstruction and said this is national work, it's in the public interest and it has to be supported.

But did you find resistance in other areas? Particularly from, say, the big seed companies?

Of course.

Do you think they saw you as 'the enemy'?

Oh, yes. In fact, at the World Summit on Sustainable Development in Johannesburg in 2002 I was given the Bullshit Award for Sustaining Poverty by the Liberty Institute of New Delhi, a business-oriented think tank. I said to them, you're calling it bullshit, but for me it's cow dung and we hold it sacred. It's wonderful compost! Two Swedish film makers then made a documentary called 'Bullshit' about this in 2005 which followed me over a two-year period, from my organic farm at the foot of the Himalaya to institutions of power all over the world – for example, my battle with Monsanto to stop it patenting an ancient Indian strain of wheat.

Did you face any other opposition?

Well, the Green Revolution had left this assumption of miracle varieties and miracle chemicals. And that brainwashing is very deep. Farmers would say, well, we can't grow with these old seeds because they won't give us enough production. And I could say, but I have grown this wheat and it's giving me six tons per hectare, which is double the Green Revolution yields.

So you could prove it?

We could prove it. But, of course, that took time. Initially I just went round like a seed pilgrim, you know? Just travelling and giving seeds to farmers and letting them save them. But I realised that there were so many people who doubted the possibilities. That's when I started a farm where we could do the seed saving. I wanted to show the wheat crop, and that it was possible to have high productivity with biodiversity. Show that the trade-off was not between food security and diversity. That, in fact, the more diversity you have, the more food you have from your acre. And better food security.

Look at what monocultures have given us. We are now destroying the Amazon. I wrote another book in 1993 called *Monocultures of the Mind* which is about how, by maximising certain kinds of production, we are systematically 'weeding out' other kinds of life and making entire spaces disappear, where trees are seen as nothing more than timber and crop yield is the only measure for economic value of cereals. But in traditional societies, trees have multiple purposes, from food, water reservoir and shelter to nutrients of the soil around them. Timber value is only one small part of the whole.

Look at the fact that this non-sustainable system of agriculture and farming has created a new level of violence. Two hundred thousand Indian farmers have committed suicide – most of them since the new seed companies have entered India. Most of them have been farmers growing cotton from genetically-modified seed. So I started a seeds of hope programme right in the heart of the suicide belt.

Look at the fact that this non-sustainable system of agriculture and farming has created a new level of violence. Two hundred thousand Indian farmers have committed suicide – most of them since the new seed companies have entered India. Most of them have been farmers growing cotton from genetically-modified seed. So I started a seeds of hope programme right in the heart of the suicide belt.

Do you sometimes feel that you're a voice in the wilderness, given the billions these companies have to spread their message?

I definitely feel I'm a voice in the wilderness. The only difference is that I feel the wilderness is so rich!

Current views

How do you actually define sustainability?

Well, for me sustainability is ecological and social. Ecologically it means that the biodiversity in a particular ecosystem should continue to be there for the next generation and the future, and that the water flowing downstream should continue to flow in the same quantity and the same quality. It means that the air should stay as clean as when human beings entered the breathing world. For me the measure of sustainability, ecological sustainability, is nature. Are we allowing nature to perform ecological functions?

For social sustainability my first measure is, are people able to make a living? Is there sustenance for people? Social sustainability is sustenance for people. Are we generating enough security in society in the ways we live to ensure wellbeing, joy and happiness, which to me are vital elements of social sustainability? I remember reading a newspaper article that said that most children in UK are unhappy. I think that's a violation of social sustainability. Unhappiness is not a normal human state.

I know what difference being happy makes and what difference being unhappy makes. The point is that being unhappy changes you biologically. Unhappiness is not just a state of mind; it becomes a state of body. Too much of the Western world is on Prozac. I think it's wrong that Indian farmers are committing suicide. That's a violation of social sustainability. And all these are indicators that we are not reproducing ourselves as a society with health and wholesomeness.

What role should business play in this?

I think business has to be part of the yardstick of nature in society. The emphasis on the bottom line, on maximising returns on profits has caused business to become disconnected from nature's sustainability and society's sustainability, from nature's wellbeing and society's wellbeing. So definitely I think we do need a reorientation in business models.

In what way?

Well, I'll give you a very simple example. I think part of what the World Trade Organisation's rules have done is reward the worst predators. So if you see who's climbing fastest in terms of the richest people in the world they are the most unjust. They are the ones who grab their way and we literally now have a rewarding of greed and irresponsibility. The ones who are doing the worst business are being rewarded the most as businesses. And I really feel this has become like a cancer on the planet and there's a huge challenge, including for business itself. Because I don't think the majority of businesses want to be part of the destruction of the planet.

The Bible says do unto others as you would have them do unto you. I'm sure many people who work for the big agri-businesses go home and buy and eat organic food. This is about not leaving your ethics on the doorstep when you enter the company. It's a difficult challenge.

There are companies which have taken a far more sustainable route and doing very well. So it doesn't have to mean that you're going to be uncompetitive, does it?

No, it doesn't mean that, but you have to be doubly ingenious and innovative. Anita Roddick and her work at Body Shop is one example of how you have to do things so differently that you carve out a whole new space.

What about governments?

For governments, what does sustainability mean? I think this whole measure of growth, the gross domestic product, the gross national product, has become too much the religion and reason of the state. The only measurement. The Indian government jumps up and down with excitement about 9% growth. Wow. And I keep counting the number of farmers' suicides. I keep counting the number of children going hungry. Two-thirds of India's children in this last decade have become malnourished. One-third of the hungry children of the world are today in India. We have been pushed into chasing a false illusion of growth.

So I think governments have to get away from this single-minded chasing of a mis-measure of the state of society and economy: growth.

Isn't that a tall order?

It's a tall order, but frankly if you look at the fact that we have managed to treat food not as something that nourishes our body, not as something that gives livelihoods to half of humanity, but we've actually redefined it as a commodity – now look at where we are getting. Food prices have doubled in a year. I can predict they're going to go up fivefold in the next two years. We will create situations that will be unmanageable. So when I say we need this change I'm saying it as a scientist with the full awareness that the present trajectory cannot sustain itself politically, ecologically or economically.

Is your message getting across, do you think?

Well, I've addressed Prince Charles's business and industry forum many times. And I have just done lots of training for Indian industry on climate change. The interesting thing is that they listen when they're thinking as citizens and human beings.

However, the minute they have a vested interest in that field they switch off, and try to ridicule me. But I have lived a long, long life. I don't live by the kind of judgements I get from around me. I live by my conscience. And that's why I've managed to keep going.

Do you think that publicly-quoted businesses can take too short-term a view because they are measured on quarterly results?

The businesses look at the next quarter, but these days business employees are being judged on a daily basis. So the overall institution is quarterly, but the whole performance system is daily. I'll give you a very simple, very tragic example of this.

Delhi used to have a public transport system, a publicly-owned bus service. But the World Bank, which is very good at advising privatisation as a solution to any ill, told us we must privatise our transport system. The public system was dismantled and private buses were put on the road. The private buses pay the driver and conductor according to how many routes they travel, how fast and how many tickets they sell. What is it doing? Every day two to three people are being run over in Delhi. You know? That target culture. So what I'm basically saying is it's not even a quarter, it's every minute of your life that you're being driven.

What's your view on the danger of 'greenwashing'? Does anyone ever try to associate with you in order to use your reputation to prove their 'green' credentials?

I think there is a lot of greenwashing going on. I personally don't make myself available to it. I take it on myself that if someone has actually invited me then I work on a long-term responsibility plan.

So you show them just why this is the right path to take?

Yes. And how doing it any other way will be so costly overall. My way of working is really to inspire the higher aspects of our humanity and ecological responsibility. That's why I talk about democracy: to basically make everyone feel they're citizens of this earth. And that's another dimension of sustainability for me in terms of your identity politics. Who are you? An investment banker? Not only.

But if you're a big company with, say, thousands of employees and have been doing things the same way for so many years, where do you start?

Well, I think the first place you start is in not making the problem worse. That's part of the tragedy. A big food company doesn't have to go and cut down the rainforest for palm oil in Indonesia. It needs to stop that. That's a new aggression. A commodities business doesn't have to go into the Amazon and cut down the rainforest. So, yes, we know you have inertia. In physics we know the higher the mass, the higher the inertia. Corporations have higher mass, therefore higher inertia. It can be hard to change your trajectory, to change your structures. But at least do not create new momentum. Do not grab control over policies and laws to make it better for you to be a predator on the planet. So I think you can begin with that and the rest will follow.

In physics we know the higher the mass, the higher the inertia. Corporations have higher mass, therefore higher inertia. It can be hard to change your trajectory, to change your structures. But at least do not create new momentum. Do not grab control over policies and laws to make it better for you to be a predator on the planet. So I think you can begin with that and the rest will follow.

Doesn't the direction have to come from the top of the company?

No, it has to come from both top and bottom. I think we've passed the stage where easy top-down solutions will work. Because at the top it can be greenwash. At the top, corporate social responsibility can be the glossy ad in *Time* magazine. And stop there. You have to be in Nigeria to really judge whether Shell is changing its performance.

Have you seen any examples of businesses that have really seen the light, that have got the message – particularly when it comes to your area of seeds?

The tragedy is that today there are two groups of businesses that are just becoming worse by the day. One is the genetic engineering biotechnology seed industry. The second is the property and real estate industry. These two are going further and further away from their responsibilities to the earth and their responsibilities to society.

Isn't one of the problems that when people start hearing about 'climate change' you can see their eyes glaze over and they think, oh, God, not again?

That's true, but I think there we have to prevent significant phenomena being reduced to empty words. And we must always maintain the content. And content only comes with concreteness. So we have to take something like climate change and give it concrete meaning in our lives. What does it mean in terms of the way we heat our houses? What does it mean in terms of the vehicles we drive? What does it mean in terms of the kind of food we eat, where it comes from, how it is grown? I think the minute you make it concrete you get authentic choices to make.

What would you say to someone in business wondering where to start?

I think if you have a child, look at the world through your child's eyes.

Are consumers also forcing change by telling companies what they feel is important?

Yes. Exactly. I mean, why did genetic engineering not spread in Europe? Because the consumers organised as a major force. Wendell Berry, the American writer, poet and farmer, is a dear friend of mine. And he produced a very beautiful phrase: eating is an agricultural act. So in the area of agriculture and food it's so clear that when you're eating you're already shaping the agriculture you want. It's an agricultural act.

Do you see consumers, then, shifting away from chemically processed foods to more organic options?

There's a huge shift. For instance, I built the organic movement in India. How? Starting from seed, I obviously had then to go to production. When the farmers then grew these wonderful crops organically such as an amaranth or a particular millet, they said we've no place to sell it. And I didn't want 'museumised' conservation and I didn't want black-hole conservation.

'Museumised' means that you do a little bit and everyone comes to look at it. And 'black-hole' means that you keep sinking money into it to maintain it and the day the money dries up the conservation goes. For me the issue of seeds and biodiversity was too vital. So I said, how does it become an element of the way people live? Which is why we brought it into the production systems of farmers. And once it was in the production systems of farmers, they were the ones who said, now we need marketing arrangements. So we said, OK, let's organise direct marketing. And in the process we built this huge organic movement. Some 300 000 farmers are members of Navdanya.

And I want to take it to half a million within the next two or three years. I also do lots of seed pilgrimages throughout the country. I just travel with colleagues and go through five states at a time so that we reach new areas beyond where we work intensively. But awareness of food is growing tremendously because the degradation of food is growing tremendously.

What is happening in the United States, with its powerful agricultural industry?

Now the interesting thing is that I probably have given talks in every part of the United States to major organic movements. The farmers there are like the farmers of Europe and the farmers of India in terms of wanting to live right and do the right thing.

Also, my books are read a lot in the universities and I therefore get invited to do a convocation address or an annual address regularly. Interestingly, I think the youth in the States are the most advanced. Even more than the

European youth, if you ask me. Definitely much more than Indian youth who are busy right now joining call centres.

For instance, about five years ago I was invited by the students of the California university system and we did a retreat and then they organised themselves as California students for sustainability. And then they asked: what can we do? Since I work so much on food, agriculture, biodiversity, I said make your kitchens and your dining room halls local and organic. You know, these kids actually got it going. They worked to get their administrations to cancel contracts with the monopoly running these university and institutional kitchens. And then they started writing contracts with local farmers.

So are you optimistic?

No, let me put it this way. In my capacity as someone who acts and works with networks of people who are taking responsibility I'm hugely optimistic in terms of the power of people to make change. But as a scientist I look at the trends and see that, of course, it's a very, very pessimistic situation. So I would say I'm a scientific pessimist and a political optimist.

Getting more personal

What do you think it is about you as a person that has made you so passionate about this? When you were a child, for example, were you very outgoing?

No, I was a recluse. I was a total recluse and I'll give you just a few examples of that. The two reasons I picked physics are one, because I loved the world of nature and understanding natural law and physics was the way to understand at most fundamental levels. Einstein was my big inspiration. The second reason I loved it is you could sit with your paper and pen and solve equations. I just loved that quietness and tranquillity of a life of the mind. And that's a personality that I was most comfortable with.

But it's life that has taught me to become more able to speak out. I went to a convent, a Catholic convent, and they made me the head girl and as a head girl I had to run the assembly. And I said to the Reverend Mother, I hate to speak, I don't want to speak. Don't put me up on the stage. Allow me to do any other work from the background.

That's interesting, because you seem very assured when you speak in public.

Well, I wasn't, I can tell you. When I was a senior in high school it's the last thing I wanted to do. And now here I am. I spend half my life speaking. But I think part of it is because I speak from my deepest truth and I see it from my deepest conscience and I speak from my deepest heart that I've overcome that shyness because the larger concerns become so important.

Have you had to learn to be forceful to get your message across?

No. No. I was always a tough one, that way.

What are you proudest of do you think?

Being a mother. I have a beautiful boy who is now in his 20s.

And is he following in your footsteps at all?

He has become a creative photographer. At least he's not an investment banker! He did try for three months to pull my leg and said, mum, I'm going to be a biotechnologist. So I said, well go ahead. Then he realised how boring it is because it's a life of pipettes and Petri dishes.

Is there a defining moment in your life? Was it when you were in Geneva and decided to save seeds?

No, before that I had another defining moment. I was born and grew up in the Himalaya. Dehradun is my home town, where I returned to create these institutions I have set up. It's a valley in the mountains and was very beautiful until recent urbanisation. I protected the valley because I was asked by the Ministry of Environment to do a major study way back in 1982 and that study led to the banning of mining and the first environmental case in the

Supreme Court of India that said when commerce harms life, commerce must stop because life must carry on.

It's a very beautiful valley. It has got the Ganges, the Yamuna River, the Himalaya on one side and the Shivalik Range on the other. Hence my name: Shivalik means the locks of Shiva. The forests are treated as Shiva's locks.

So having been born in the Himalaya, and having walked these forests where my father was forest conservator, by the mid-1970s I was feeling very concerned about their disappearance. And a movement was started by local women called Chipko. And it was my watershed. I became a volunteer.

'Chipko' means to hug, to embrace. And the concept was we hug the trees and prevent them from being logged. We give our lives but we protect the tree. That's where the whole idea of tree-hugging began. And working with these women, my world opened up. Because, as a daughter of a forest conservator, I knew the forest and I also knew the trees as pure, natural systems. And I realised that this is the basis of sustenance. It's nature providing life to humans. I did it every holiday. Even when I was doing my doctorate in Canada I would fly back to the Himalaya.

'Chipko' means to hug, to embrace. And the concept was we hug the trees and prevent them from being logged. We give our lives but we protect the tree. That's where the whole idea of tree-hugging began. And working with these women, my world opened up. Because, as a daughter of a forest conservator, I knew the forest and I also knew the trees as pure, natural systems. And I realised that this is the basis of sustenance.

You sound like someone who quite enjoys your life.

I'm happy. I enjoy my life.

Do you have to travel a lot?

Yes, I travel a lot. I should travel a little less.

But I suppose to get your message across you have to?

And it's not just getting my message across, it's also about meeting the growing networks which are bringing about change. I'm now vice president of Slow Food, this other movement on food issues. I'm on the executive board of the new movement called the World Future Council, being the voice of the future. Of course, I could live a wonderfully peaceful life, build our farm, our local networks, but I think because we're in a globalised world and the economy is globalised, the sustainability movement has to be globalised too and it's just in the nature of what has to be done.

Because everything everyone does affects everyone else?

Yes. And I'm working very hard at making sure there is another generation to carry on. Every minute of my life I'm aware that none of this can happen if too much is carried by one individual. That's not sustainable.

14

....

Jeffrey Swartz

Jeff is the third generation of the Swartz family to lead Timberland. His grand-father Nathan started the predecessor company to Timberland in 1952. Jeff's father, Sidney, and his uncle, Herman, launched the Timberland® brand in the early 1970s. Jeff was promoted to President and CEO in 1998, after working in virtually every functional area of the company since 1986.

Under Jeff's leadership, Timberland has grown rapidly, from $156 million in 1989 to $1.4 billion in 2008. Timberland today competes in countries around the world, designing, manufacturing and marketing footwear, apparel and accessories for men, women and children.

Jeff leads an organisation that believes that doing well and doing good are inextricably linked. Timberland struggles every working day to demonstrate that the business of business is to deliver results for shareholders, employees, customers, suppliers and consumers world wide while demonstrating best practices, measurable impact and sustainable programmes. At the centre of this commitment to be accountable to all stakeholders is Timberland's commitment to reducing global warming and preserving the outdoor environment.

In 2006 Timberland introduced an industry-first 'nutrition label' on all of its footwear boxes in an effort to provide consumers with greater transparency about the company's environmental and community footprint. A year later, the company launched its Green Index™ rating system, which provides a measure of the environmental impact of specific products they buy and the company that provides them.

A commitment to active citizenship through initiatives like environmental stewardship, global human rights and community involvement is not new to Timberland. In 1988, Timberland launched a ground-breaking private/public partnership with City Year, a national youth service organisation. Jeff joined City Year's board in 1989 and was the national Chair from 1994 until 2003. As a national founding sponsor, Timberland has invested to fuel City Year's growth and impact, including provision of clothing such as Timberland's signature yellow boots and outwear.

Recognising that there was a passion within Timberland for voluntary service, Jeff initiated The Path of Service™ programme in 1992. The programme gives all Timberland employees 40 hours of paid leave each year for community service during the work week. Service sabbaticals – which provide up to six months of paid time leave for employees to serve in capacity-building roles in social justice organisations – is the latest evolution of the Path of Service™ programme.

Being accountable to a whole range of stakeholders, from shareholders to community activists, has made Timberland a better company. Timberland has appeared on *Fortune* magazine's *100 Best Companies To Work For in America for 10 consecutive years and has also been named one of the Best Places to Work by* Working Mother *magazine. It has been listed on Business Ethics list of 100 Best Corporate Citizens and in 2002, Timberland received the Ron Brown Award, a Presidential award recognising outstanding corporate leadership in social responsibility.*

Jeff was one of 19 founding CEOs selected for President George W. Bush's task force on national service called Business Strengthening America. He is on the board of directors for the Climate Group, Share Our Strength, Honest Tea, City Year, the Harlem Children's Zone and Limited Brands, Inc. In addition, Jeff is a regular member of the World Economic Forum and the Two/Ten Foundation, an organisation providing charitable funds and services to individuals in the footwear industry. In 2002, he received the Two/Ten Foundation's T. Kenyon Holly Memorial Award for Humanitarian Achievement.

Jeff received an MBA from Dartmouth in 1984, and a BA in Comparative Literature from Brown in 1982.

The professional journey

Why is sustainability so important to Timberland?

We operate our business around the notion that commerce and justice don't need to be antithetical notions. We think we can make high-quality products and delight our shareholders, we also think we can make consumers realise that this is a really great company with really great products and can create a context where people are really proud to come to work and feel dignified in the work they do. And we can do that in a way that's accountable in terms of running a for-profit business environmentally, socially and in terms of human rights. As a steward

We operate our business around the notion that commerce and justice don't need to be antithetical notions. We think we can make high-quality products and delight our shareholders, we also think we can make consumers realise that this is a really great company with really great products and can create a context where people are really proud to come to work and feel dignified in the work they do. And we can do that in a way that's accountable in terms of running a for-profit business environmentally, socially and in terms of human rights.

of the third generation, I know that if there wasn't a mission at the heart of what we do it would be hard to sustain what we do.

What sort of challenges do you face when you talk about this to others?

There are two kinds of challenges in general. Challenge number one is: 'I believe, but I can't do what you can do. Because in my organisation the CEO doesn't care as you care.'

And the corollary to that question is: 'Can you give me the math that says your investment in sustainable business practice pays off in the short term?' But that assumes that every investment you make has to pay off in a year or two years. So if you buy that assumption you're trapped.

It's like justifying your marketing budget. As the old marketing adage says, I know that 50% of every marketing dollar we spend is wasted. If I only knew which 50% I would cut my marketing budget in half, but I don't know and I do know that if I don't market then I will lose brand headway. So I've got to market.

When it comes to sustainability, yes, there are some obvious ones like change the light bulbs. That's what I always tell people when they get into the frame of mind that says 'But the sky is so big and the stars are so far away and how can we do sustainability?' Change the light bulb!

I can't bring the stars down and I can't make the sky small. And so I don't know if you can optimise the business model from a sustainable perspective to the point of perfection but I do know that if your CFO is on the ball and he or she is paying attention, then you explain to me why your lighting fixtures wear out and aren't generating cost savings. And I'll tell you what – it's not the same thing as saying we all have to move back into a cave, and everything will be OK. This is straightforward: change the light bulbs. The payout is clear and yet people don't.

They say, well, it's only a light bulb and so therefore I'll do nothing. And I think, wait – do something. And by the way, if everyone changed the light bulb, you know what will happen? We'll solve the problem we have now that when the light bulb fails, you have to dispose of the mercury in it. Even better, the cost will come down because the market mechanism will force it to come down.

And, by the way, the core of the outcome of everybody changing the light bulb is unpredictable in terms of its substance but clear in terms of its impact. Because if all of a sudden there's a buck to be made in low-energy lights, then there will be people thinking, OK, maybe I've missed the light bulb thing but maybe I can get in early into something else. And then the market mechanism will create eco-systemic change. Someone's got to go first. And someone's got to be buying it. That takes faith and not intellect.

Can you elaborate on that a bit?

Take the solar array on my house in the suburbs. It added so much cost to the house that somebody without my resources couldn't do it. It would be irrational to do it. I told my kids we're going to do it even though it's irrational, because we can afford it and some day it will be rational. But I don't say to everybody, you should have solar energy inside your house. The only way it will be rational is if the market starts to engage. And I don't argue with rational.

Then you read that retailers in America are putting solar arrays on their roof. Wal-Mart, Home Depot, Best Buy and Macy's are all talking about a programme that is, from our perspective, relatively old news, but they're doing it, OK?

This also shows what governments can do. None of them, including Timberland, would have done it without an incentive from the government. In California, where we built a huge solar array on our distribution centre, it was in large part because the State of California said we'll partner with you – meaning we'll help to defray the cost. It will still be irrational, Timberland, but we can make it palatably irrational.

As a CEO I get to make a choice about and be accountable for how many palatably irrational choices I make. If the sum of my choices is not palatably irrational, I get fired. Whereas if you make a palatably irrational choice about the solar array in California and then you make a palatably irrational choice to be less eco-friendly in another dimension, then you balance it out. So you can say: perfect we're not but good we are, and better we will be. It's about transparency all along the way so no one can think it's greenwashing. So we still have polyvinylchloride – PVC – in some of our boots. It's a terrible chemical. Yes, there is a way to take it out. But we can't afford to do it right now.

So those are the two big challenges I get. One is 'prove it'. That's a math point. The other is about 'the perfect is the enemy of the good' – in other words, pursuing the 'best' solution may end up doing less actual good than accepting a solution that, while not perfect, is effective. With the latter, I raise the question by saying at the start: to be clear, we are a ravager and a pillager of the physical environment. We make boots and shoes and clothes for a living. We take rubber which is a natural extract from a tree and we turn it into a sole. It doesn't happen without noise and light and energy and sweat and our value chain encompasses the environment and the developing world. So we have human rights concerns. We have physical environmental concerns. We have energy and chemicals. It's all a fundamental part of making boots and shoes and clothes. Period. And so let me start from the point that it's not perfect and never will be.

But we'll also never relent in our drive to be better. Judge us on that basis and we can have a dialogue. Don't throw a brick through my window. I hope instead what you'll do, when you want a pair of shoes, is to see an array of choices in front of you and partially discriminate between the choices on the basis of Timberland's commitment to be better. That you will make an independent judgement based on real information about which company's doing enough and which one's not doing enough.

So you have to be careful about not promising more than you are actually doing?

Yes. That's why transparency is a big deal to us. I believe, and we've been acting on it for years, that a consumer with an efficient access to transparent information will make better choices.

I believe, and we've been acting on it for years, that a consumer with an efficient access to transparent information will make better choices.

Where it really becomes powerful is when the consumer says that's interesting to me, the information is accessible to me and I'm going to act on that information. You can see it in the organic food industry. The consumer says: here are two apples. One, according to the nutrition label, has this kind of pesticide and herbicide and this kind of carbon footprint. The other organic one has a very different profile.

They both look like apples. And they're both here in the store. You know what? I need or want an apple and I prefer the organic one. That's revolutionary stuff.

Now, what is lacking in the footwear, apparel and fashion industry is access to that data. So what's going to be the point of difference? Nobody goes into a store in the brown shoe business and says, I need a Timberland boat shoe. They come in and they say, I need a boat shoe and then they look at price, aesthetic and availability.

So we put a nutrition label on the shoe box that talks about renewable energy content, that talks about the absence of child labour, that talks about the number of trees we've planted as an enterprise respectful of carbon sink as opposed to carbon exhaling and I'll tell you this. If even one in every three consumers says, why doesn't the other guy have a label on the shoe box, there will be labels. And when there are labels, labels reveal information and the information puts pressure on the CEO and the value chain will respond. They say we will lower our carbon footprint, we'll do a better job respecting workers' rights. The result is they have to do this because being good enough simply isn't good enough.

It sounds like a delicate balancing act.

It's interesting. When you say to consumers does country of origin matter? They say, absolutely. How important is 'made in the USA'? It's central, they say. But then you ask, so where are those shoes made? And they'll reply that they don't have the time to think about that. So it does matter to them but they don't necessarily *act* on the basis of that. If you make a shoe in the United States at the same price as the exact same shoe, they would prefer it. But they won't seek it out. What they say is that if you do your job well, they will prefer it.

To me that's the key to the kingdom. So if you say to the consumer, do you care about the environmental impact? And they say, yes. Then you say, well, then why are you buying XYZ brand? Did you know there's lead in that? Or that it was made by child labour? They say, don't tell me that because it will make me feel bad about myself which will really annoy me. Whereas if you say to the consumer in an affirmative way, see this beautiful shoe for $19.99 that fits your foot? It was made in a way that respected the human rights of all the people in the value chain. And it has got minimal packaging and it's actually disassembleable and recyclable – not that you'll have to do that. And it's made with a lace that's made out of soda bottles.

They say, that's nice. But if I don't like it I'm not going to wear it. Now, to me that's the beauty of the market mechanism. The market sets the rules. And so you can't make a $19.99 boat shoe for $29.99 and say look, mine is greener. They say, sure, but it's $10 too much.

So this has been the guiding philosophy the company was founded upon?

The company that my grandfather first started was called the Abington Shoe Company and it was a shell for ambition and passion – a shoe factory that my family poured their guts into. When they finally got to make the bold decision about branding the company they chose an abstraction, an evocative name, Timberland, which is consistent with the product and with the New England heritage that our family name wouldn't have been. It was a great marketing decision.

When you think about the family businesses that are a large part of our industry, many of them are eponymous in the sense of a company like Ralph Lauren. Even though that's not really his name, it is a stage name, and it's important to him. For us, however, from when my grandfather started the company, he didn't want either a stage name or to have our own name as synonymous with what we stood for – our principles and practice.

But why?

Let me answer that by first explaining something. When people decide to leave Timberland I always ask them: are you leaving here or are you going there? There's a very big difference. If you're *leaving* here that could mean that you are running from something and it's easy to convince yourself that the grass is greener on the other side. Whereas if you're *going* there because it's a compelling proposition and it suits you in your heart, then great – go for it.

So whether you're running *from* something or you're running *to* something, it's either an affirmative model or a fear-based model. My grandfather was an immigrant to this country. And his leaving the land of his birth was in a large part a fear-based model. He felt he wasn't safe there. 'This is my country, this is my language and this is my culture but I'm not welcome.'

What that meant – and you can see it in my dad, you can see it in me too – is that we are 'hiders in plain sight'. We are transparent about our principles and our values, but it's not supposed to be about the personality of the individuals. And it isn't.

For example, it's a hugely important religious principle to me that the investments in social capital that I make as a private citizen are always done anonymously. I believe as a principle that associating your name is less important. It's actually the wrong thing for me to do – not for others, just for me. This notion of anonymity is important to me. It's a religious principle and it's of real consequence.

Now that's tricky if you make your whole living in the brand world, right? And so you need a construct that will allow you to have a conversation with consumers. Timberland becomes that vehicle and explains on some levels why we try so hard to tell the story of Boot–Brand–Belief–our slogan–as opposed to boot *or* brand *or* belief. We want to tell the whole three-dimensional story of what we are passionate about, what we hope for and we do it through this metaphor called Timberland.

But aren't companies often an embodiment of the people who run them?

True.

So you are both Mr Timberland but you're also your private self. How do you deal with that?

What I don't want when I speak is that people conflate the personality of the speaker and the rhetorical flourish of the speaker with a message. And our central message is that commerce and justice are not antithetical notions.

I remember when I gave a speech at the Annual Tomorrow's Company conference in London in 2005. I was asked a question by someone quite senior in the Church of England. He actually questioned the assumption that we have to accept the marketplace. And I said, very respectfully, that that was a hard question. I just didn't know.

But if you do take the market as a given, then I've got to struggle to make the case that commerce and justice are not only not antithetical but more than causally related. I accept the framing question that says maybe the market cannot be. But my view is that I think we have to have a market mechanism. I don't know another system that would serve humankind better.

What I want, when they call the roll at the dawn of time, at the time of ultimate accountability, is to be marked present against this message. It's a tricky point. It's not really about me, but about Timberland being not only marked as present, but also being so marked forcefully and actively leading this notion that commerce and justice are not antithetical.

Are you saying that, as the person who has to front up the company, you have to speak a lot to spread the message, but it's the message, not you as a personality, that should be getting the attention?

Right.

What have been the main influences on your work?

I guess there's a big family part of this. In our family the boys make the boots and the women determine moral compasses.

My grandfather was a shoe guy. I remember as a little kid being in my grandparents' tiny kitchen with a little table in it. My grandfather would came home from work on the subway because he worked in the South End of Boston and they lived 20 minutes away in the suburbs. And my grandmother was always in her dress because he was coming home for lunch. He would come in and there was this incredibly beautiful ballet because it was a tiny kitchen and so you had to have the moves choreographed, right?

After he had a thimbleful of rye, which he always said was good for his blood, he would sit down probably with the same lunch every day and it started at this minute and ended at that minute. They talked about things in a certain order and he left, back to work. And then she was visibly less animated for a nanosecond because there goes the light of her life but I was still there and the light turned back on because I was the first grandson.

But, as tough as my grandfather was, and he was the toughest guy I ever knew – missing fingers where the machine chopped the fingers off, no problem, no sympathy, don't want it – as tough as he was, she was tougher. She was sweet and anything she baked was sweet and everything was fine unless there was strife. Because if there was strife she was the toughest person in the world. Her belief was, we've only got family. There was no other belief beyond that. The accident of biology is the determinant of all that's good and bad in the world. That's a family member and that one's not. That was a belief that you couldn't avoid with my grandmother.

Along comes the next generation and I have the same impression of my dad washing the grease off his fingers every day, performing the same ballet at dinner. He'd come home and walk to the sink and wash his hands. We were all at the table waiting and dinner was ready. Then the conversation began and my mother spoke first and my dad spoke second. It wasn't formal as if there was rules, it was just the way it was.

It's very interesting when so many family companies by the third generation either are sold or disappear. But Timberland has flourished and remained true to its mission. Were you always determined to be in the business?

I was not particularly interested in the business part *per se* except as a connection to my father and my grandfather. In fact, I was told to go the other way by my grandfather. He said, you will not work in the shoe business. It's dirty, smelly and dangerous.

Were you the oldest?

I'm the first grandson and it's a relatively small family. I have a younger brother and a younger sister. My father has one brother, who has two children. My grandfather said you may choose to be a doctor or a lawyer or a certified public accountant because those are professions that don't put you at the whim of the buyer, the machines aren't noisy, it's not scary and it's portable. I remember this phrase ... it's portable. What did that mean? He said, if you get chased out of this city, you can pick it up somewhere else. And I thought, why would you get chased out of this city? I didn't know what he was talking about. I now know what he was talking about. He was thinking, when he left his country, that I have skills, I can make shoes. I can do it in America because they need shoes there too.

So I had that choice and I chose to be a doctor. I had already applied and been accepted and was very keen to do that. And then my grandfather died the summer I graduated from high school, killed by a drunk driver.

And so after we observed seven days of mourning my father did what the men in my family did: he went back to work. What else can you do? Because I was the oldest non-busy grandchild of the five grandchildren, I went with him.

And I'll never forget that first day back. It was a Proustian experience of smelling the factory – suddenly very, very clearly I smelled familiar smells that I associated with a deep overlay of loss. And I decided I wanted to be connected. I didn't want to lose that. I wanted to keep that smell in my nostrils.

How old were you?

I was 18 and I didn't want to lose that connection. My grandfather and I had an active, wonderful, very special relationship. I knew what I had with him and then he was gone. And as I began to learn more about the factory, I started to see that there was what you do and how you do it. He always talked about that. Not in that language. He talked about it with deeds, not in words because he wasn't a words guy. But as a little baby duckling you get imprinted, right? I actually knew a lot more about the belief agenda from my grandfather than I would have any other way.

He ran the business based on strong principles?

Absolutely. You cannot get up from the land of your birth and walk across a continent and get into the belly of a boat the first day you've ever seen the ocean without courage. And courage has to be on the basis of principles.

Current views

How do you define sustainability? Because one of the things we've found fascinating about all these interviews is that there are different definitions of the same word.

I think about optimising within constraint. It's a hard, hard, hard thing for a Western-trained problem-solver. A Western-trained problem-solver wants the answer. Sustainable means striving to goal. Sustainable means the perpetual motion machine.

And the hardest thing I've had to struggle with when it comes to this notion of commerce and justice is the embracing of optimising within constraint – meaning you will chase the rabbit and you will never catch it. You won't catch it, but you can get a heck of a lot closer. There is a Yankee notion in New England which is 'imperfect but better', which is also a continuous improvement in the Japanese sense. I can either be despairing or sage and I'd rather try to be sage, which is to say I think that imperfection is part of the market circumstance, and I don't accept that as an excuse for mediocrity but I accept it as a condition. So the reason that that's important is if you don't you can be paralysed. That's why people don't change the light bulbs. They say, I changed the light bulb but the world didn't get transformed.

Who do you think should be leading the charge? Business? Governments? Consumers?

I think of the model of leadership for complex social problems as an intricate dance at an intersection between animals of different species. Again, that to me is not the acceptance of imperfection but of the need to optimise, as opposed to *getting* it right. And so I think there isn't a paradigmatic solution for complex problems except to the extent to say here is a roundtable with a social and business problem at the centre of the table. There is a creative way to deal with it if we listen to the activists, if we talk to the citizen, if the investor's voice is heard, if the business person's voice is heard and so on. We can come up with a better solution that solves problems with the profit we owe our shareholders and the minimising of negative impacts and the maximising of positive social impacts.

It's about getting the smallest group of self-interested people who will yield leadership to the person whose ideas should be leading at any given moment. When you have interested parties at the table the question is not, who's in charge of the committee? The right question is: what particulas problem are we trying to solve this minute?

Does this have to be done country by country or globally?

I think the right construct is not nationalist because in our business if you want to optimise the value chain you are talking to suppliers in China, talking to transportation companies that go across the globe, talking about retailers – in our case in 85 countries – and manufacturing entities and so forth.

Let's take a look at a shoe. The value chain is a really tricky monster. It starts with a cow and ends with a customer. The cow is in one place and the cow has nutritional issues and manure issues and animal husbandry issues and then there is transportation and how the meat is processed and the leather is processed and how it is transformed. If you follow as if you had a camera lens you see that the value chain cuts across nation state boundaries and different regulatory environments. Which means that no one can be in charge from a government perspective.

It also cuts across industries where there are both large and really small players. I can bring influence to bear on the large player. But how do I get attention from some of the other really tiny players? If you really wanted to optimise the supply chain/value chain and make it truly optimised around the dimensions of commerce and justice, do you realise how many people would need to be in the room?

Now – that's no excuse for not trying. It's just fair and honest to say out loud that with all the progress we've made we haven't begun to see the kind of progress we need to make.

If you really wanted to optimise the supply chain/value chain and make it truly optimised around the dimensions of commerce and justice, do you realise how many people would need to be in the room? Now – that's no excuse for not trying. It's just fair and honest to say out loud that with all the progress we've made we haven't begun to see the kind of progress we need to make.

So this sort of collaboration is hard, and I do believe that the forcing mechanism is the marketplace. I won't say business, but it's the marketplace. So, for example, the German government has taken a strong stance on packaging which environmentally is a leadership view relative to the French government, for instance. I think the advantage of being a global company is that we see the legislation in different countries, and if you are thinking about this goal called sustainability you can go one of several ways. You can think we'll solve that problem in one country but not bother where it doesn't apply. Or you can say, why don't we apply that standard in the US where there's no such regulation?

The solution has to be dynamic and multidimensional. It isn't just government and business. The church has a point of view about this, as do the NGOs; there are consumers swirling in and out of this and there are other industry competitors and collaborators.

Many investors take a very short-term view. What's your take on that?

The only thing short-term investors want to hear is return on investment capital. They say, you promised this, you'd better deliver that. And so our narrative includes a conversation about how we do it. They are score keepers. They want us to look backwards and forwards.

They say ... tell me what you're going to do in the third quarter. And then you tell them. And then they tell people, this is what we think Timberland's going to do in the third quarter. If we do better they say, good for you, but if we do worse they say, we told you they were idiots and so on. You get to tell the score in the future. I don't think that's very helpful. I don't think it's valuable to investors.

But you have to do it, don't you?

We understand what the rules are. So at that intersection we comply.

Can you see that ever changing?

That's a very good question. I think the answer is maybe – meaning it will require an invention of language which hasn't happened yet. So you could have a conversation with a lot of people and you could keep it to acronyms. What's the earnings before interest, taxes, depreciation and amortisation (EBITDA) in the last trimester? You could use EBITDA and return on equity (ROE) and return on investment (ROI) and people know exactly what you're talking about. And if you say that the ROE of Timberland is 35% which is top peer quartile performance, people know what they need to know. If you said that Timberland's greenhouse gas emissions have reduced by 25% – even if I told you that – it doesn't mean anything because you don't know from what level, compared to whom, done how and for what cost.

There's no language. And so there needs to be a language, which I believe must be done because what you measure is what gets looked at. There needs to be a quantitative measure of good versus bad. That's why we created the Green Index. People like numbers.

The Green Index, which the company first produced in 2007, measures the environmental impact of your products based on climate impact, chemicals used and resource consumption. Could this index become a basis for new measurement framework?

We've been looking for four years to give it away to our competitors. And we deliberately called it the Green Index rather than the Timberland Index because do you think a company like Nike's going to use the Timberland Index? The Green Index is as banal a framing brandwise that we could come up with – with the express notion that we give it away.

And has anyone signed up?

We have had lots of conversation but no takers so far.

Generally, how worried are you about the future? Do you think your children, for instance, are going to live in a world where they can breathe the air?

The answer's definitively yes. We're going to solve these problems and we're going to solve the next batch of problems after that because we are this infinitely curious and deeply optimistic race called human beings. The sweep of time matters. There's no chance, none, zero, that my grand-

We're going to solve these problems and we're going to solve the next batch of problems after that because we are this infinitely curious and deeply optimistic race called human beings. The sweep of time matters.

father in all his imagination could have imagined today. And so I am decidedly and determinedly optimistic – not in an intellectual sense because I can always make the case that the sky is falling. But I've got to believe that that's a fake assertion because it's in our hands.

That's very encouraging.

Microcosmically I absolutely believe it. I see too much evidence backing up my point. If there's a will, which is back to the leadership model, then yes, there's nothing we haven't been able to do in the 5700 years since creation or however you date your calendar.

Getting more personal

What is it about you as a person, do you think, that makes you so passionate about everything you do?

I have a reflex arc – everybody does, right? You hit them on the knee and their foot jumps. I operate from the not-good-enough perspective. I don't know where that comes from. I don't say that's a good thing. I just know that what I have in common with my friends who are fellow travellers in this struggle is that we operate from the not-good-enough mode. I'm not good enough. I can do more. More is expected of me.

What would you say you are proudest of?

The only answer I can come up with is that I don't think much about that. And that's the truth. I like the line by singer/songwriter Warren Zevon which says, 'I'll sleep when I'm dead.' There'll be infinite time to think about it. Having said that, my suspicion is if there's thinking in the grave that's not what I'd be thinking about. I'll be thinking I could have or I should have and didn't.

So even though you run a company that's so successful on so many fronts, and inspire others, you shy away from the word proud?

What do I take joy from may be another way to say it. I take joy from the accomplishments of others. But it's about them, not me.

15

....

Sir Crispin Tickell

Sir Crispin Tickell has had a long and distinguished career as a diplomat, academic and environmentalist. As author of the influential Climatic Change and World Affairs, *he explored the relationship between climate change and international politics in the 1970s. He has many interests, including climate change, population issues, conservation of biodiversity and the early history of the Earth.*

He was educated at Westminster School as a King's Scholar, and Christ Church, Oxford, graduating in 1952 with first-class honours in Modern History. He went on to do his national service in the Coldstream Guards as a second lieutenant (1952–1954).

On leaving the Guards he joined the British diplomatic service, where he was at the Foreign and Commonwealth Office in London until 1955, and then at the British embassies in The Hague, Mexico and Paris. He later became Chef de Cabinet to the President of the European Commission (1977–1981), British Ambassador to Mexico (1981–1983), Permanent Secretary of the Overseas Development Administration (now Department for International Development) (1984–1987) and British Ambassador to the United Nations and Permanent Representative on the UN Security Council (1987–1990).

He was appointed MVO in 1958 and later knighted as a KCVO in 1983 on the Royal Yacht Britannia, to mark the conclusion of Queen Elizabeth's official visit to Mexico. He was appointed GCMG for his work at the UN in 1988.

Sir Crispin helped to write Prime Minister Margaret Thatcher's seminal speech on global climate change to the Royal Society in 1988. He chaired the Government Panel on Sustainable Development (1994–2000), and was a member of two government task forces: one on Urban Regeneration, chaired by Sir Richard – now Lord – Rogers (1998–1999), and one on Potentially Hazardous Near-Earth Objects (2000).

His academic career is as impressive as his diplomatic one. For example, he was President of the Royal Geographical Society (1990–1993) and Warden of Green College, Oxford (1990–1997). From 1996 until August 2006 he was Chancellor of the University of Kent.

He is currently Director of the Policy Foresight Programme at the James Martin 21st Century School at the University of Oxford (formerly the Green College Centre for Environmental Policy and Understanding), Chairman Emeritus of the Climate Institute in Washington DC, Chairman of the Trustees of the St Andrew's Prize for the Environment since 1998 and has been Adviser at Large to the President of Arizona State University since 2004.

In addition, he is the president of the UK charity TREE AID, which enables communities in Africa's dry lands to fight poverty and become self-reliant, while improving the environment. He is also a patron of the Optimum Population Trust.

Apart from his book, Climatic Change and World Affairs, *he has contributed to many other books and publications, as well as speaking regularly on radio and television. A full list of his career highlights can be seen at www.crispintickell.com*

The professional journey

What would you say you are best known for? That's probably a difficult question, given your career.

The trouble is I'm known by different groups of people for different things. When I was Ambassador to the United Nations I had a lot of public attention because I was giving press conferences at what was quite an interesting time since it was at the end of the Cold War. So I have a certain notoriety on account of that. After that I became an academic and then, I think, I'm probably better known as an environmentalist and an expert on climate change nowadays than anything else.

Is that now your main field of interest?

I think it's the main activity, yes. But I also give lectures on the UN and international governance. And, of course, international governance and environmental issues are not unconnected.

In a way, then, would you say you are dealing with sustainability in its widest sense? Whether it's in the political sense, economic ...

... Or anything else. I quite agree with you. I remember I did actually raise environmental issues once in the Security Council in the late 1980s. I didn't get a very sympathetic hearing – remember, the Security Council is concerned with issues of peace and war. But I did point out that if, for example, somebody ran short of water and dammed a river, then people downstream would have good cause for getting extremely concerned. So those are the sorts of parallels I would draw.

That's interesting. Why did you bring that up then?

Well, I thought it was important because we were having a discussion about the whole range of issues connected with river basins.

However, perhaps I should really begin by saying that any particular contribution I have made, I think, has been to help to build the bridge between aspects of environmentalism and science on one side, and public policy-making and public understanding of the issues on the other. That's really what I became involved in when I went to Harvard for my sabbatical as a Fellow at the Center of International Affairs in August 1975, even though my contribution in the beginning was regarded as very eccentric.

Why eccentric?

Well, there were some at Harvard who thought it was all very eccentric because the prevailing scientific judgement in the 1970s was that climate change was a very slow process and thereby would not affect politics directly. There were others who said that this is the kind of thing we leave to the Massachusetts Institute of Technology!

I was saying, on the contrary, it can happen very quickly. And anyone who studies the history of changing climate becomes aware of the fact that it can take place very quickly indeed. That is now the generally accepted view and it is the critical point because if you believe it's very slow, then it hasn't got much relationship to current politics or diplomacy. But if, on the other hand, you think it can happen very quickly then it does. Although this point was gradually being accepted, it didn't gain public acceptance for another 15 years.

Anyone who studies the history of changing climate becomes aware of the fact that it can take place very quickly indeed. That is now the generally accepted view and it is the critical point because if you believe it's very slow, then it hasn't got much relationship to current politics or diplomacy. But if, on the other hand, you think it can happen very quickly then it does.

How did your stint at Harvard come about?

I'd been working on European, NATO and military/defence issues as head of the department at the Foreign and Commonwealth Office dealing with

East/West relations and, in particular, the Conference on Security and Cooperation in Europe. When I finished, I wanted to take up something completely different. I searched around and considered two propositions. One was to look into the impact of climate change and world affairs, which I did, and wrote a book about, based on lectures that I gave at Harvard and MIT. My other option was to look at whether elites in societies had a genetic background.

I decided that the first option was the more fruitful. The Foreign Office wasn't terribly keen on it, and neither was Harvard, but I did it just the same. I then did a course in meteorology at MIT and was able to master the essentials of the subject within two months or so. And I read all the books on the subject that existed within three months. Now it would take 300 years, there are so many.

And what did you do after Harvard?

By 1977 I was the Chef de Cabinet to the President of the European Com-mission. As such I was, as it is called in the jargon, a Sherpa. That is someone who helps to prepare the texts for heads of state attending what were then the G7 meetings. The point was to make the meetings as unbureaucratic as possible. I represented the European Union on matters where there was Community competence, which means those areas where those present from the Community had to defer to the common view. I circulated a paper on climate change to the G7 in something like 1978 or 1979, and so brought it on to the agenda – although admittedly not many people bothered with it at that time.

Were you very much a lone voice in the wilderness, do you think?

Well, no, there were people in the academic world, such as Steve Schneider and others who had written books about climate change. And, of course, it came up at the Stockholm meeting on the environment in 1972 and it was from there that a whole range of international institutions were set up. So it's not as if it wasn't on the world's agenda. But what I found so interesting was the relationship between that and politics and economics and actually making an impact on current affairs.

Who were the main influences on your thinking?

Before Steve Schneider, there was Hubert Lamb at the University of East Anglia, who in many respects was my mentor. He wrote a very famous book called *Climate, History and the Modern World*. He was a real pioneer because he showed the importance of climate in history. How, for example, the downturn at the beginning of the fourteenth century may have affected the population's vulnerability to the Black Death.

Because. ...?

The medieval warm period, when the population increased greatly, lasted till about 1310. Then came harsher winters and reduced harvests, which resulted in famine. You then began to get several years of cold and wet winters. So the Black Death met a rather vulnerable population, accounting for the loss of about a third of Europe's population.

You are well known as having been instrumental in encouraging Prime Minister Margaret Thatcher to become an advocate of the need to take environmental issues seriously. How did that come about?

Well, I could claim that I was among those who persuaded her to do so.

Please go on.

I knew her slightly from my days at the European Commission. But in 1983 I was Under Secretary of State for Economic Affairs in the Foreign Office and accompanied her on a visit to Paris to call on the French President Mitterrand. In the aeroplane, on the way back, her private secretary asked: 'Has anyone here got any ideas for the G7 summit of 1984?' So I put up my hand and said, yes. He said: 'Are you brave enough to explain it all to the Prime Minister.' And I said, yes. So along I went to the front, sat down and talked to her about it. The following day I was summoned back to No. 10 Downing Street to explain it all in more detail.

As an indirect consequence of all this, one of the first times that environmental issues generally came up in a G7 meeting was that when environment ministers were sent off to go and write a paper about it. And climate change was one of the central themes.

What arguments did you use?

Well, I made the point that every wise politician has to take into account that climate is changing. By 1983, of course, the evidence was getting much stronger and there had been a lot of work done on a number of levels which hadn't actually penetrated to the political world.

Later on, not only did I help her to write an important speech in 1988 for the Royal Society on the subject, but I also persuaded her to hold a Cabinet meeting on climate change. Indeed, I even came over from New York where I was then living to speak at it.

I remember that I accompanied her to one of her last acts as Prime Minister to the International Conference on Climate Change in Geneva in 1990. She was one of only four heads of state in government who spoke there. This was just before she had her misfortunes and left office. John Major took over and he inherited the positive attitude of the British government towards all these issues, which is why he asked me to run the Government Panel on Sustainability. I used to concentrate on about four issues a year and, with the help of the government, try to get action.

Looking at politicians generally, have you found that when it comes to difficult and long-term issues like climate change, they espouse the cause when they're in opposition, but very few do so when they get into power?

It raises a whole lot of very difficult issues in which you have to balance the short term against the long term. In the case of Margaret Thatcher there were two very important points: she was a woman in a man's world, who wasn't going to be pushed around by a lot of men. Secondly, she was the only scientist in the Cabinet at the time. So when people started to talk to her about this she felt that she had a strong advantage. That's why I think she took an interest in spite of the efforts of one or two people to discourage her from pursuing this any further.

What was the general reaction to these arguments at the time?

Many people at the beginning were very sceptical about the whole thing because it didn't seem to be well aligned with the aspirations of business communities. But after successive reports of the Inter-Governmental Panel on Climate Change, people began to realise that the problem was real and important. When I chaired the Government Panel on Sustainable Development, for example, we looked into the business implications and it was quite obvious that there were some big ones.

Interestingly, in the 1980s the United States was in some respects very sympathetic to all this kind of thing – at a certain level. I remember once talking to George Bush Senior at a series of meetings at which the top people in the US government were reasonably open to it. And I sat on a panel at the US National Academy of Scientists when I was in New York at the end of the 1980s to look into some of the implications. So it was a relatively neutral subject, though there was a certain amount of pressure, with people saying don't confuse us with facts. It's rather sad what happened in the United States with the administration of George W. Bush. They were got at by a lot of very naked vested interests.

Having said that, you'll find very few genuine scientists in the United States who take a particularly negative attitude. And those who do have now somewhat changed their tactics. They challenge the findings of the Stern Review in terms of economics rather than the fact that change is taking place. And even those who accept that change is taking place, but say it's all quite normal, find it very difficult to contest the fact that change is accelerating.

Current views

How do you define sustainability?

It's a much abused word. The one that was used all the time was sustainable development. And of course that opens up the question, what do you mean by development? Which is itself another big booby trap. I used to run the British Overseas Aid Programme

Sustainability is a much abused word. The one that was used all the time was sustainable development. And of course that opens up the question, what do you mean by development? Which is itself another big booby trap.

and it's quite difficult to know what you mean by it. I was always against the idea that everyone should follow a kind of blueprint of the sort that the Western industrial nations laid down because every country has different resources and different aims.

People feel they have to follow a Western track. One of the biggest problems of today is just that. So sustainable development was always a phrase I disliked and the definition that I always use both for that and sustainability – though I can't claim authorship – is 'treating the earth as if we intended to stay'.

Do you find that businesses are becoming more receptive to this message?

Well, I've had lots of discussions with business and industry. Their attitude has changed radically recently. Before, business leaders were not unaware of the issues, but many didn't want to hear about them. They were, nonetheless, conscious of the fact that they were running risks and that this required more thought than they had given it so far. I always think there's a nice distinction between those companies who regard issues of the environment as something that involves all the members of the executive branch of the company, and those who appoint a director in charge of the environment who is usually very junior and usually ignored.

I was a non-executive director of a number of companies, IBM among others. Again, we used to discuss these issues and how companies should take account of them. Some were taken up one way and some another, but as the evidence has mounted more and more companies have moved it up the agenda. It's quite interesting what happened with GE. I'm sure you know about GE and its chairman/CEO, Jeff Immelt.

Yes, and Ecomagination.

I'd advised GE some months before Jeff came up with Ecomagination. He was one of those rare people who could suddenly see we had to take a big jump forward. So Ecomagination was just that.

But in recent years I've addressed many industries, whether it be agriculture, the paper industry or IT, and I find that everyone is aware this is now a major dimension.

The problem is that they still report to their shareholders, who may demand short-term results. So how do they win investors over?

Today the jargon phrase is 'risks and opportunities'. Climate change constitutes a risk, yes, but does it also constitute an opportunity? Yes, again. In which case you have to get down to work and you find that, on the whole, larger companies are more aware of that than smaller companies, which just feel more threatened. Larger companies don't just see the opportunities; they've also put people aside to try to develop those opportunities.

Does the person who heads the company make a difference to their attitude to this issue?

Well, companies are like governments. They are run by individuals. It matters a lot to have someone who believes in all this rather than someone who is interested only in the short term, or who, like the former Senator Jesse Helms in the United States, thought the whole thing was cooked up by academics looking for research grants.

Interestingly, I find that the business community is partly divided by generations on this. Many of the older CEOs still live in a world that no longer really exists. But there is a younger generation of executives who are much more aware of some of these longer-term issues than those at the top. When I addressed a meeting of chief executives, for example, it was very interesting to see that some of them had got the message very well, loud and clear, but others just didn't want to hear it. At a meeting of the World Insurance Forum at Dubai in 2008 – an industry whose people are trained to look ahead and try to assess future risks – there were still some who didn't want to hear the news and others who were very ready to embrace it.

In terms of the triumvirate of business, government and consumers, where do you think the impetus to change comes from?

There are three ways in which change takes place. The first is when you've got leadership from above and, in the case of Margaret Thatcher on climate change, you can see what she did. Although she is perhaps the most conspicuous example, there are others who have shown a measure of leadership. Then there is public pressure which arises from non-governmental organisations and increasing public awareness from the work of bodies such as the Intergovernmental Panel on Climate Change.

The third is what I call benign catastrophes, which is when something goes visibly wrong and where you can safely attribute cause and effect. That acts as a great stimulus. Within the last two years I think everyone has realised that change has taken place quite rapidly and that people have to adjust their daily lives, their business and reconsider their way of looking at the world in ways they didn't think of before.

But how do you deal with consumer scepticism about 'greenwashing'?

Previous debates about changes that have taken place in public mood show that it is sometimes quite a long process which accelerates. It took a long time, for example, for people to give up smoking or to avoid drink driving. But then you cross a threshold, a tipping point, and it all happens much more quickly.

And are we at that threshold?

I think we're aware of that threshold on climate. I'm not sure we are on some of the other related issues.

Such as?

You can't isolate climate change as a major threat to society without taking into account human population increase. This is a hugely important problem which people have not been so willing to talk about for 20 years or more. You've got resource depletion, waste disposal and something that I gave a talk about recently: the destruction of biodiversity and the need for conservation, which people find very hard to interpret or understand. It's much easier to talk about or participate in a radio or television programme on climate change. It's relatively simple. But talking about the need for conservation is trickier.

Do governments have the ability to see these 'tipping points'?

The trouble is, as a concept it's rather loose because you frequently don't know you've been over a tipping point until it has passed. It's a useful way of explaining a problem, but you can't say to a government, we're just approaching a tipping point. Because they'll say, well, how can you prove it, until the tipping point has been passed?

And supposing, for example, that the world warms up in the next 10 years and this leads to changes that cause it to cool down again? How can you show that the threat is from global warming? In fact, it seems likely that if you get certain alterations of ocean currents around the world you might delay the further acceleration of global warming.

Global warming has taken place many times before in history. The last big time was round 125 000 years ago when it warmed up more than it is today. But we then lived in a very different world, with few humans, no civilisation, no huge population increase that now makes it so difficult for us to cope.

Global warming has taken place many times before in history. The last big time was round 125 000 years ago when it warmed up more than it is today. But we then lived in a very different world, with few humans, no civilisation, no huge population increase that now makes it so difficult for us to cope.

Does technology have any answers?

My usual experience of technology is that by solving one problem you create another. But there are certain technological solutions to specific issues. You then, however, have to factor in not only the direct effects of the technology, but also its long-term effects, which are sometimes very hard to assess. Suppose you decide to put all your options into generating energy by nuclear power: what's the penalty for burying high-level waste which won't diminish its toxicity for a million years?

That's a typical example of something that has to be taken into account, yet often isn't. There are possible answers. I was always very interested in the idea of a technology that would reduce the volume of high-level waste. But, 10 years ago, people wouldn't invest in it when I thought they should.

So is that changing? Do you see people investing in technologies that might offer some solutions?

That links in to what I was saying about looking for opportunities rather than risks. For example, there are certain biofuels that will do a good deal of harm, or at least won't do any good and would diminish world food supplies, but there are others which might have enormous benefits. That technology could provide a lot of answers.

I'm in favour of biotechnology. For example, if you can produce plants that resist salinisation that would deal with another huge problem: in areas we've been irrigating, like the valleys of the River Indus, the valleys of the River Ganges, and indeed in China, the salt content of the soil has actually increased. So if you can find ways of coping with the salinisation problem you'd be solving a lot of other problems.

Technology might be good in other areas, too. Take acidification of the ocean, which affects the entire marine ecosystem. Can you consider ways by which you reduce it? And then there's the forest question. It's important that, if you prompt people to look after forests and preserve the natural environment, you make it in their interests to do so.

You have much experience of China. How is it dealing with environmental issues?

It's essential to remember that China is, and always has been, extremely vulnerable to environmental problems. Not just hits from asteroids coming from space – although there was a big one at the end of the fifteenth century – but rather to shortages of water, earthquakes and extreme events of all kinds. So Chinese civilisation is dotted with threats, as it were, from nature.

This is why one of the underlying Chinese aims, repeated by successive governments, including the present one, is the search for what they call harmony. Harmony is the balance between human prosperity and environmental protection. Indeed, the present government of China has spoken of what it calls the three transformations. The first treats environmental protection and economic growth on the same basis. The second brings those two together. And the third applies the result throughout all activities of Chinese society, whether it be trade, universities or anything else.

For that reason the Chinese are very conscious of the threats they face. They are sometimes wrongly presented as being the enemies of a global agreement. In fact, I think that few countries would be more helped than China by global agreement because they fear what's going to happen there if the carbon emissions are not limited.

The Chinese currently emit more carbon than anyone, including the United States, but their per capita emissions are much, much less, possibly just over one-fifth of the American equivalent. And China's population is 1.3 to 1.4 billion at the moment. They're very keen to increase their wealth and they're torn between the desire to protect their environment and the desire to advance their living standards. Like all countries they face a lot of contradictions. Also, the point that is frequently missed about China is that the relationship within the government is often fraught. Firstly, different government departments, agencies and provinces feel differently about big problems. Secondly, the relationship between the centre and the parts is also often fraught because what happens in the centre government isn't what local provinces might wish. The third point is that even a provincial government has big problems with local communities. They, too, feel differently. So the picture of China as a monolithic culture in which the man at the top says, do this, is completely false.

I was a founder member of a body called the China Council for International Cooperation on Environment and Development. Every year we met in Beijing or elsewhere in China and we had access to the Chinese leadership. I've seen the changes that have taken place over the last 15 years in terms of an awareness of environmental problems which was, of course, accentuated by the prospect of the Olympic Games in 2008. That's a lesson that perhaps the British government might take into account for 2012.

Can we talk about the economics of all this?

We live in a world of fairly crazy economics because we don't take account of what are true costs and externalities. You know the famous saying: markets are marvellous at fixing prices, but incapable of recognising costs. It's important that government sets the ground rules within which the market can operate. And that means subsidising some things, but not others. In other words, you want to give incentives and bring in disincentives. So governments have a huge role in the business of persuading public opinion to do whatever should be.

We live in a world of fairly crazy economics because we don't take account of what are true costs and externalities. You know the famous saying: markets are marvellous at fixing prices, but incapable of recognising costs. It's important that government sets the ground rules within which the market can operate.

But these are some very big issues that haven't been properly thought through. Just building wind power isn't going to solve the problem. Tidal power has got enormous possibilities. Solar power has, too. There are also some new and interesting ideas, for example, about generating new power sources for Western Europe by covering parts of the Sahara Desert with solar panels.

We know perfectly well that the UK is not going to be able to make itself independent. In fact, no one can think it really feasible. As long as we have some oil and gas under the North Sea we can nourish that illusion for a bit, but only in the short term. But it's not just energy, it's everything. Indeed, I think one of the most interesting developments of the last few years has been the realisation that national sovereignty, as previously cherished, is very much diminishing. Indeed, you could argue that we only have degrees of sovereignty over certain things.

What is going to make the world address this issue on a global basis?

You need some really startling change and people will then be forced into it. We're currently confronted not so much by climate change as by climate destabilisation. All over the world rather unlikely events are happening. In Western Europe we're relatively privileged, but if you look at what's going on in Africa, at the Sahara area generally, at parts of South East Asia, at what's happening in China, you realise that in a way it's fairly unpredictable but also more extreme. So when these various changes take place it won't just be a simple movement of people going northwards to cope with climate change. It's a question of extreme events taking place, such as ocean currents shifting, and that makes it very, very difficult to assess what's going to happen.

Living as we do in the northern hemisphere, where the winds move mostly from west to east, and on the edge of a major ocean – we're relatively privileged. But if you look at Asia, at China, they are much more vulnerable to extreme continental conditions. Chinese history is full of examples of that.

Are you optimistic about the future?

I have optimism of the intellect but pessimism of the will. In other words, one can be optimistic about the human ability to judge these issues and to draw up reports and understand what's going on. But what we lack at the moment is political will to do anything about it – and that's partly because the message hasn't been fully communicated.

Getting more personal

What do you think it is about you as a person that made you decide it was so important to disseminate this message?

That's rather hard to answer. I do think though that, if you've been involved in policy problems as well as intellectual problems and sense that a whole lot of looming dangers are not properly understood, then you have a moral obligation to convey these things – preferably in language that everyone can understand.

Was science an important part of your upbringing?

I always had science in the background, but I wasn't a scientist myself. At 13 I was told by my school that I had to choose between studying science, history or English. I chose history and English because these were things I felt I already knew about, whereas science was rather alarming. Well, that's why we have terrible problems when we try to make people choose things far too early in life.

But there are lots of scientists in my family and I was brought up with them so I was always aware of scientific considerations. For example, in the pre-war years a cousin, Julian Huxley, was the secretary of the London Zoo and he made me a Fellow of it for a year, as a present, when I was about eight.

It was wonderful. On Sunday mornings I played with the chimps and I even brought a lion cub home in a taxi late one afternoon. Have you ever played with a lion cub? They have strong paws! I don't think a zoo would let you do that today, would they? But I had many animals, too. I used to keep guinea pigs, rabbits, stick insects – even tortoises. I was a mother's nightmare.

Also, there are people in the family like Freeman Dyson, the astrophysicist at Princeton, who is a cousin, and Andrew Huxley, who won the Nobel Prize in 1963 for physiology and medicine. And, looking further back, there was Mary Anning. She was the first fossil woman – a palaeontologist – who lived between 1798 and 1847, and discovered the early plesiosaur and ich-thyosaur fossils. My grandmother was an Anning, so Mary was my many-times removed great aunt.

But it all kicked off with Darwin, and his relationship with T.H. Huxley, my great, great grandfather. So it's in the blood and in the air.

Do you have what you would describe as a campaigning nature?

Maybe a campaigning instinct. I became aware of these issues, particu-larly in relation to climate change, early on. And if you see people ignor-ing something that will play a big part in their lives you try to interest them in it. It then becomes less of an amusing personal eccentricity, into something that has real importance. And my own contacts with the political world and policy-making generally made me realise that. When I was Permanent Secretary of the Overseas Development Administration, I discovered that when British money was given overseas to improve standards locally and 'develop' that country, no environmental assessment was commissioned. So one of the first things I did was to make environmental impact assessments mandatory.

I became aware of these issues, particularly in relation to climate change, early on. And if you see people ignoring something that will play a big part in their lives you try to interest them in it. It then becomes less of an amusing personal eccentricity, into something that has real importance. And my own contacts with the political world and policy-making generally made me realise that.

Do you enjoy your reputation as someone who speaks his mind?

I rather enjoy, when people ask me something, challenging the conven-tional wisdom, but not in an offensive way. I just like to say things that people perhaps might not like to hear in order to challenge their underlying assumptions and possibly persuade them to think a bit differently about things – but without provoking them.

And what are you proudest of in terms of your work?

Well, I don't claim credit for the fact that the world is now aware of these issues in a way it never was before, because a lot of people have done that. I suppose I can modestly claim credit for being one of the pioneers in building the bridge between science, environment and globalisation on the one side, and public understanding and policy-making on the other. That's why I still run a think tank in Oxford devoted just to that, called the Policy Foresight Programme with the James Martin 21st Century School. But nowadays, just reading the scientific journals, as I do every week, you realise how much all these issues have now become commonplace. But they certainly weren't 30 years ago.

Index

Index compiled by Annette Musker

The Twenty-seventh Lancers took six hours to cover the eight leagues which separated Nancy from N——. The regiment was delayed by the artillery. Colonel Malher received three couriers, and each time he had the horses of the ordnance changed, dismounting the lancers who seemed to have the strongest horses for hauling the heavy gun carriages.

When they had proceeded about half way, M. Fléron, the prefect, caught up with the regiment, arriving at a fast trot. To speak to the colonel, he was obliged to pass along the whole length of the column from its tail to its head, and had the pleasure of being hooted by all the lancers. He wore a sword which, because of his tiny stature, seemed enormous. The muffled jeering swelled into a burst of laughter which he tried to escape by spurring his horse to a gallop. The laughter redoubled with the usual cries of: "He *will* fall! He *won't* fall! He *will* fall! He *won't* fall!"

But the prefect soon had his revenge. Hardly had they started through the dirty, narrow streets of N—— than the lancers were hooted by all the women and children crowding the windows of the poorer quarters and by some of the weavers themselves who, from time to time, appeared at the corners of the narrowest little alleys. They could hear the shops being hastily closed on all sides.

Finally the regiment came out onto the city's chief business thoroughfare; shops were all shut up, not a head in any of the windows, a death-like silence. They reached an irregular and very long square, ornamented with five or six stunted mulberry trees, and with a foul stream, full of all the filth of the town, running down its entire length. And, as it also served as a sewer for several tanneries, the water was blue.

The garments hanging in the windows to dry were so miserable, so tattered and filthy, they made one shudder. The windowpanes were tiny and dirty and in many of the windows the glass had been replaced by old paper covered with

Colonel Malher went from one end of the barracks to the other shouting to the officers so that all the lancers could hear:

"What we have to do is to give them such a lesson they'll never forget it. No mercy for the b——! There are crosses to be won."

Riding past Madame de Chasteller's windows Lucien looked up searchingly, but there was no sign of life behind the closely drawn curtains of embroidered muslin. Lucien could not blame Madame de Chasteller: the least sign might be noticed and talked about by the officers of the regiment.

"Madame d'Hocquincourt," he thought, "would certainly have been at her window. But then, would I ever love Madame d'Hocquincourt?"

If Madame de Chasteller had been at her window, Lucien would have found this mark of attention adorable. As a matter of fact, the ladies of Nancy were occupying all the windows along the Rue de la Pompe and the next street, through which the regiment had to pass on its way out of the city.

The Seventh Company, to which Lucien belonged, rode directly in front of the artillery consisting of half a battery with linstocks lighted. The wheels of the ordnance gun carriages and caissons shook the frame houses of Nancy and gave the ladies a pleasurable thrill of fear. Lucien bowed to Madame d'Hocquincourt, Madame de Puylaurens, Madame de Serpierre and Madame de Marcilly.

"I should like to know whom they hate most," thought Lucien, "Louis-Philippe or the mill-workers. . . . Why couldn't Madame de Chasteller have shared the curiosity of all these ladies and so given me that tiny proof of interest? Well, here I am, off to slaughter weavers, as M. de Vassigny so elegantly puts it. If the affair is hot enough, the colonel will be made a *commandeur* of the *Legion d'Honneur,* and as my reward, I shall have won remorse."